# JOE LOUIS
## *vs.*
# BILLY CONN

# JOE LOUIS
## *vs.*
# BILLY CONN

## BOXING'S UNFORGETTABLE SUMMER OF 1941

**ED GRUVER**

**FOREWORD BY TIM CONN**

GUILFORD, CONNECTICUT

An imprint of Globe Pequot, the trade division of
The Rowman & Littlefield Publishing Group, Inc.
4501 Forbes Blvd., Ste. 200
Lanham, MD 20706
www.rowman.com

Distributed by NATIONAL BOOK NETWORK

British Library Cataloguing in Publication Information available

**Library of Congress Cataloging-in-Publication Data available**

ISBN 978-1-4930-6664-3 (hardcover : alk. paper)
ISBN 978-1-4930-6842-5 (electronic)

♾™ The paper used in this publication meets the minimum requirements of American National
Standard for Information Sciences—Permanence of Paper for Printed Library Materials, ANSI/
NISO Z39.48-1992.

# CONTENTS

# FOREWORD

# "WIN OR LOSE FIGHTING"

Tim Conn

In January 1935 an up-and-coming Joe Louis arrived in Pittsburgh to fight fellow heavyweight Hans Birkie at Duquesne Gardens. Louis, soon to earn a reputation as one of the best boxers in the country and the nickname "The Brown Bomber," would knock out Birkie in 10 rounds and in just two years would be the new heavyweight champion of the world.

In Louis's corner that night was an obscure, 147-pound local boxer in charge of the rosin box. He had but five pro bouts under his belt and at night's end received from Louis $20—a healthy sum at that time for working in the corner. Who could imagine that the young fighter working in Louis's corner that wintry night in Pittsburgh would, in less than six years, encounter Louis again? This time he would be trying to take the Bomber's title in a battle that is still remembered as one of the greatest fights in ring history.

That young fighter was my father, and his name is Billy Conn. His climb to the top of the fistic ladder was not an easy one. It began when his father, a steam fitter for Westinghouse, would take him to a local boxing gym to get a few lessons to learn how to defend himself. The gym was run by Johnny Ray, a former top-ranked lightweight who fought the best of his era. He would school my dad in the fundamentals of the sport. At the age of 16, without any amateur experience, Dad would be on the road fighting more experienced fighters. There were few soft touches. Dad would lose 6 of his first 13 bouts, but he was learning. Under Johnny Ray's guidance, my father would compete in 4 different weight divisions, registering victories over 11 present or former champions. At 21 years of age, he was the light heavyweight champion and at 23, he was well prepared to contend for Louis's heavyweight crown at the Polo Grounds in New York on June 18, 1941.

It is universally accepted that my dad was ahead on points late in the match. From the 8th round on he had taken the fight to Louis. Dad felt he had hurt Louis in the 12th round. Johnny Ray encouraged my father to lay back, box, and not go for the knockout that was my dad's stated intention. But Dad's instincts were that he was a fighter, and he was going to win or lose fighting. I can't fault him for that decision and, even when asked later in life about his strategy, my father always responded that he would do it the same way again if given the chance.

After the fight ended, Dad walked from the Polo Grounds back to the Waldorf Hotel where my mother, Mary Louise, was staying with her aunt. They weren't married yet but were planning to elope. Dad walked through Harlem on his way to the Waldorf and African Americans cheered him along the way. When he got to Mom's room and knocked, he had tears in his eyes and was pretty badly cut up and bruised. He said, "I did the best I could do" and fell into her arms.

My dad took the defeat hard but felt confident that if the return match with Louis was held in 1942, as originally planned, the result would have been different. Unfortunately, World War II intervened. Both Joe and my father were called to duty and the rematch was postponed for four years.

Dad was a true Pittsburgher. He loved the scrappy industrial city with its ethnic neighborhoods and strong work ethic. He often said that while he was frequently ready to leave Pittsburgh, he couldn't wait to get back home. His circle of friends wasn't limited to just the Irish Americans with whom he had grown up. Over the course of his fighting career and afterward, he befriended many prominent Pittsburghers, including members of the Thomas M. Jones family of Jones & Laughlin Steel, one of the largest steel manufacturers in the country at the time. Katie Jones and her three sons were very close to our family. Dad was the sponsor for Mike Jones at his confirmation in the church. I remember

"Aunt Katie" coming over to our house to help my mother rearrange the furniture! Dad also befriended Richard King Mellon, the head of Mellon Bank, and Herb May, the head of Union Switch and Signal. Herb was a close family friend who married Marjorie Merriweather Post in 1958. He often stopped by our house in Squirrel Hill to visit with Mom and Dad. Dad told me that R. K. Mellon and Herb May bet $100,000 each on him winning the fight in 1941. Their friendship never waned.

I am glad that the story of this famous fight is finally being told in the format of a full-length book. It deserves no less. While my father achieved fame and notoriety from boxing, he never wanted my brothers or myself to follow in his footsteps. He wanted us to get a good education. Boxing was the path he chose, and he wanted us to find our own way in the world.

# A MATCH OF WILL AND SKILL

Billy Conn, the Hollywood-handsome Irishman, grinned broadly at a reporter's question regarding his physical fitness.

"I feel good," Conn told a national radio audience. "Really swell."

The cocky kid from Pittsburgh, Pennsylvania, was in the basement of the New York State Athletic Commission office awaiting the arrival of heavyweight champion Joe Louis for their noon weigh-in on the morning of June 18, 1941. The former light heavyweight champion of the world, Conn had surrendered his title to campaign among the heavyweights and challenge Louis for his coveted crown.

"He was a wonderful 175-pound champion," says boxing historian William Detloff, "who made three defenses against good competition before realizing his quickness and skill could make an awful lot of heavyweights look silly and at the same time, line his pockets green."

Fleet of feet, hands, and mind, Conn outfought and outthought seven straight heavyweights—"They're easier to hit than smaller guys," he said with a winning smile—and at 10:00 p.m. that night would look to handle the fearsome Louis in their 15-round title fight in New York's famed Polo Grounds ballpark.

As noon approached, Louis was running late. Conn, meanwhile, was running out of patience. Turning to General John J. Phelan, chairman of the New York Boxing Commission, Conn asked, "Where's that Louis?" Billy, his manager Johnny Ray, trainer Freddie Fierro, and the remainder of Conn's team had arrived at the Athletic Commission office at 11:45 a.m., 15 minutes before the scheduled time.

"I was told to be here at noon," Conn told Phelan. "I was 15 minutes early."

Phelan suggested they wait for Louis; there were more than 200 writers and photographers on hand for the traditional prefight posing for pictures and interviews. Surely the Detroit "Brown Bomber" would arrive soon.

Conn smirked. The brash "Pittsburgh Kid" would recall thinking, "Louis, he's just another guy." Billy had his Irish up, but it wasn't reflected when Dr. William Walker took the Kid's vitals; Conn's pulse was 64, his blood pressure 128/70.

"Billy's pulse was perfectly normal, he wasn't the least bit nervous," Fierro recalled in a 1956 article in *Boxing and Wrestling* magazine. "This was a big switch because all of Joe's previous opponents were scared to death and usually died at the weigh-in."

Previous opponents of Louis quivered in fear at the prospect of facing a man considered by many the hardest hitter in heavyweight history. Reports of the Brown Bomber's punching power from men who faced him led to Louis being feared and revered.

Jimmy Braddock, the celebrated "Cinderella Man" who surrendered his title to Louis in 1937 after being knocked cold in the eighth round, told reporters, "Nobody hits like Louis. When he hit me with that left-right combination I could've stayed down on the canvas for three weeks." It took Braddock's handlers a full two minutes to revive their fallen champion.

In 1935 Louis left Kingfish Levinsky on the canvas pleading with the referee, "Don't let him hit me again!" A Louis punch pushed Paulino Uzcudun's gold teeth through his mouthpiece. In '38 the champion's power paralyzed Max Schmeling, the German, screaming in pain. In '39 the Brown Bomber butchered "Two Ton" Tony Galento, leaving the beer barrel–shaped brawler soaked in blood and looking, as one ringside reporter put it, "like a stuck pig." Galento's wife wept when she saw what Louis's slashing blows had done to her husband.

Scary stories didn't frighten Conn. The Kid laughed off horror tales. Some observers likened it to whistling past a graveyard at the witching hour and wondered what the Bomber's blows would do to Sweet William's matinee-idol features. But fast-talking Billy wasn't awed by Joe's violent power. This son of the Steel City was silver-tongued and self-assured.

"I'm in great shape," the Kid told reporters. "I'll give him more fight than he ever got before.

"And," Conn added defiantly, "I'll beat him."

Reporters took note of the Kid's curly dark hair, deep-set blue eyes, and creamy white skin, and they feared for him. What many didn't realize was that Conn was fighting for more than money, more than fame. His beloved mother, Margaret—Maggie, he called her—was suffering from terminal uterine cancer. Billy had hurried from his Pompton Lakes, New Jersey, training camp more than once to attend Maggie's bedside in Pittsburgh. At the end of his last visit, the Kid leaned forward and kissed his mother on the forehead.

"Maggie, I gotta go now, but the next time you see me I'll be the heavyweight champion of the world."

When Conn said that he had a lot to fight for, he was thinking of his mother.

At the weigh-in, Billy stripped down to his dark purple trunks—purple being the color of kings and Conn being intent on adding Louis's crown to his laurels—and stepped on the scales. Promoter Mike Jacobs was shocked. Conn's weight of 169 was 11 pounds lighter than what he scaled just three weeks earlier in his eighth-round technical knockout of heavyweight Buddy Knox. Knowing the odds were stacked in Louis's favor at 17–5 and 8–5 by knockout, and fearing fans would consider Conn too slight to stand up to the Bomber's rib-bending blows, the promoter promptly announced the challenger's "official" weight as 174.

Tim Conn, Billy's oldest son, recalls his father telling him that "Uncle Mike," as Jacobs was affectionately called by boxers he promoted, believed Billy's actual weight would have negatively impacted attendance at the Polo Grounds that night.

"Dad always told me he weighed 169 for the first Louis fight," Tim remembers. "Mike Jacobs said Dad weighed 174, otherwise not as many people would come to see the fight and that would hurt the gate."

His exam complete, Conn dressed. Louis was still nowhere to be seen. Anger clouded Conn's countenance. "I'm not going to wait for him," Billy brazenly declared. Johnny Ray—in Conn's native Pittsburgh tongue, Johnny was pronounced "Jawnny"—agreed with his young warrior.

"Louis ain't gonna make no chump out of us," Ray stated. "We were here at 12 o'clock. We weighed, and we're leaving!"

At that moment, an air of excitement filled the building. Word spread like sunrise that Louis had arrived, his entourage of co-managers Julian Black and John Roxborough, trainer Jack "Chappie" Blackburn, and assistant trainer Mannie Seamon striding in step with him. Louis and Conn passed each other in the office; yet even though champion and challenger were so close to one another they nearly brushed shoulders, no words were spoken.

While his handlers explained that the champion had been delayed by New York traffic, Louis shed clothing down to his black boxing trunks. Wearing little more than his familiar deadpan expression, the most feared fighter on the planet stepped forward to be weighed. The Bomber watched calmly as the scale moved back and forth. Some said it stopped at 202, very close to the fighting weight he maintained for years. Yet there were allegations that Uncle Mike, wary of the weight difference between Louis and Conn, intervened again, announcing Louis's weight as 199½ to make the official disparity 25½ pounds rather than a more alarming 33 pounds.

Alarmed by the difference in weight, Jacobs reportedly murmured at the weigh-in, "This is homicide."

Yet Louis said years later that he dieted and drank as little water as possible to get his fighting weight below 200 for the first time in years.

On the 1970s sports program *The Way It Was*, the Bomber explained to host Curt Gowdy his decision to fight Conn at a lighter weight.

"Hype Igoe, who was a sportswriter for the Hearst papers, told me three or four days before the fight that Conn would weigh less than 170 pounds," Louis recalled. "I used to weigh 202, that was my fighting weight. I said, 'I can't let the people say that Billy Conn weighs 170 pounds and Joe Louis 202.' So, I trained an extra day to get down to 199½."

Louis, like Conn, was a striking-looking man with a near-perfect build. Joe's long, smooth muscles glistened beneath coffee-colored skin, and he had a broad, freckled face and dark almond-shaped eyes. Addressing his radio audience, Louis announced he was ready for combat. "I'm in very good shape."

Privately, Joe bristled at Billy's belief that the Bomber was no longer the ferocious fighter he had been from 1935 to 1939, when he churned his way through the heavyweight ranks, former champions falling like cut timber before his buzzsaw attack. Max Baer was blasted out in four rounds, the first knockout he suffered in his long career; Jack Sharkey was felled in three rounds; Primo Carnera in six; Braddock, then the champion, in eight; and Schmeling in less than a round.

Conn told scribes Louis was now "slow-moving." Louis snapped a response as forceful as his ramrod-like left jab. "That Conn boy talks too much."

Among the hundreds of writers, photographers, and interested observers on hand for the weigh-in was Don Dunphy, a young sportscaster who had auditioned for the right to join Bill Corum on the national radio broadcast. Dunphy would in time become known as the "Voice of Boxing" but in the summer of 1941 he was three months shy of his 33rd birthday and trying to break into big-time broadcasting. He hadn't seen Conn at the weigh-in, but he did see Louis and decided to approach the champion and wish him luck. Realizing this was a big night for Dunphy as well, Louis said, "I want to wish you luck, too, Don."

"As always, Joe was thoughtful," Dunphy would remember. "That made me feel good."

Fans could feel something special in the air that day. Some 6,000 Conn supporters from the Steel City boarded specially chartered trains bound for the Big Apple. The trains reflected the fans' patronage of Irish Billy Conn, sparks flying from the steel wheels of the *Shamrock* and the *Ham and Cabbage*, both chartered by Pittsburgh restaurateur Owney McManus. In a case of delicious irony, a chartered train also bore the name *Brown Bomber*.

The Conn contingent converged on New York's concrete jungle several days prior to fight night. The 'Burghers were a rough and raucous bunch; they dressed like it was St. Patrick's Day, wearing leprechaun hats, dangling clay pipes from their lips, and carrying paper shamrocks. Spilling out from the Edison Hotel, they filled New York City streets and saloons, bending elbows to down pints of beer and shots of whiskey, bragging in their Pittsburgh accent about hometown boy Billy "Cawn" and providing a colorful counterbalance to the large Louis following known for making its presence felt throughout New York's five boroughs on fight nights.

Celebrations in Black communities following Louis's victories were so wild they were said by writer Ben Davis Jr. to combine "a dozen Harlem Christmases, a score of New Year's Eves, and a bushel of July 4ths." In 1938 an estimated 500,000 people poured into New York City streets following Louis's electric first-round KO of Schmeling in Yankee Stadium, a bout so laden with overtones of international politics its radio audience included US president Franklin D. Roosevelt and Nazi führer Adolf Hitler.

Delirious fans streamed into the Savoy Ballroom to hear jazz trumpeter Dizzy Gillespie; those on Seventh Avenue could see Stepin Fetchit, the first millionaire Black actor, in his luxury Duesenberg. Joyous celebrants banged on tin pots and trashcan lids, immobilized traffic from 116th to 145th Streets, and unfurled homemade banners proclaiming "The Black Race Is Supreme Tonight."

"Somehow in those precious years blacks felt that, putting it frankly, every time Louis beat up a white man, it was a vindication of their self-worth," Jerry Moore, who would grow up to be a reverend at the Nineteenth Street Baptist Church in Washington, DC, told Joe Louis Barrow Jr. for the latter's book *Joe Louis: 50 Years an American Hero*. "Best of all, he could do it legally."

Race remained a big part of boxing in 1941; Louis was just the second Black man to hold sport's most celebrated title. Jack Johnson, the first Black heavyweight champion, had ironically drawn his own "color line" to avoid fighting outstanding Black contenders Sam Langford, Joe Jeanette, and Sam McVey. Johnson claimed that a title fight between two Black men wouldn't draw as big a gate as a fight with "Great White Hope" contenders Jim Jeffries, "Fireman" Jim Flynn, Frank Moran, and even middleweight king Stanley Ketchel. Johnson did fight one Black contender, "Battling" Jim Johnson, in the first heavyweight title bout featuring two Black fighters, but Jack's color line frustrated the Black contenders of his era.

"Jack forgot about his old friends after he became champion," Jeanette said, "and drew the color line against his own people."

A decade later Jack Dempsey's promoter Tex Rickard, vilified for sending the popular but aging Jeffries to slaughter against Johnson at Reno, Nevada, in 1910, drew a color line of his own to avoid another mixed-race match. Rickard refused to match his Manassa Mauler with highly ranked contender Harry Wills in what promised to be a Roaring Twenties super bout on the scale of Dempsey's million-dollar gates with Georges Carpentier and Gene Tunney. It wasn't until 1937 that a Black man was again allowed to challenge for the championship, making the Louis-Braddock bout the first mixed-race heavyweight title fight since Johnson lost to Jess Willard 22 years earlier.

By 1941 boxing promoters were routinely seeking out racial bouts in their matchmaking, knowing that fights between Blacks and Whites, Irish and Italians, or Jews and Germans were moneymakers. When Joe Louis, Black champion in White America, climbed the ring steps to face Irish Billy Conn, he would be seeking to defend his title for a record 18th time. All but one of Joe's previous 17 title defenses had been against white fighters. The lone exception was Louis's first-round KO of highly regarded former light heavyweight champion John Henry Lewis at Madison Square Garden on January 25, 1939, an historically significant bout in that it marked just the second time two Black men fought for the title. Joe gave his friend the title fight to provide him one final big payday prior to John Henry's forced retirement due to deteriorating sight in his left eye.

Reverend Moore recalled that in the summer of 1941 talk of a "Great White Hope" had again emerged. "If Billy Conn could do his thing on Joe Louis, it would reestablish the supremacy of the white man," Moore told Joe Louis Barrow Jr. "This was unspoken, but you could feel it everywhere."

At the time of the Louis-Conn fight, Moore was living in Minden, Louisiana, a small town 29 miles east of Shreveport. Racial discrimination in the South was so rank, Moore remembered, one could cut it with a knife and serve it up on a platter. This racism was directed toward Louis, even though Joe had represented American democracy in his international fights against Carnera and Schmeling.

"My father was a national hero, but only up to a point," Joe Louis Barrow Jr. says now. "He was still a Black man."

Sports fans had much to occupy themselves with in the summer of 1941. On June 2, New York Yankees legend Lou Gehrig died at age 37 of amyotrophic lateral sclerosis, a disease that now bears the baseball immortal's name. Five days later, Craig Wood won the US Open amid sweltering heat at Colonial Country Club in Fort Worth, Texas. That same day Whirlaway, spurred on by jockey Eddie Arcaro, thundered down the stretch to victory in the Belmont Stakes to capture the US Triple Crown.

In American League ballparks, superstars Joe DiMaggio of the Yankees and Ted Williams of the Boston Red Sox were producing daily headlines with their diamond gems. DiMaggio was engaged in a consecutive-game hit streak that began May 15; Williams was in a grim, summer-long pursuit to become the first man since St. Louis Cardinals star Rogers Hornsby to hit .400 for an entire season.

On June 18, as Conn and Louis were weighing in, DiMaggio and the Yankees were preparing to host the Chicago White Sox in an afternoon game in the Bronx. With his hit streak at 30, DiMaggio drew an intentional walk off Sox southpaw Thornton Lee in the first inning and ground into a double play in the third. His streak in jeopardy, the Yankee Clipper singled past future Hall of Fame shortstop Luke Appling in the fifth. It was his lone hit of the day in a 3–2 loss before 11,918 fans at Yankee Stadium.

That same afternoon in Boston's Fenway Park, Williams was handled by Detroit Tigers starter Schoolboy Rowe, a rube right-hander who once interrupted his interview on Rudy Vallee's nationally broadcast radio show to ask his fiancée, "How'm I doin' Edna, honey?" Williams went 0-for-3 and Detroit's 5–2 win disappointed a crowd of 5,400, who saw the Splendid Splinter's batting average dip slightly to .417.

Like the gods of ancient Greece, DiMaggio was immortalized that summer in song, Alan Courtney and the appropriately named Ben Homer penning a popular tune. Performed by the legendary Les Brown Orchestra and sung by Betty Bonney, "Joltin' Joe DiMaggio" was released on radio airwaves to celebrate his startling accomplishment.

While DiMaggio and Williams made news across the United States, ominous headlines were being produced around the world. In Europe, heavily armed troops of Hitler's Third Reich massed along an 1,800-mile front facing communist Russia, preparing for an offensive codenamed Operation Barbarossa. The führer boasted, "When Barbarossa begins, the world will hold its breath."

For several hours on June 18, world news would be eclipsed by the event unfolding in New York. Big fights, particularly those in boxing's glamour division, have a history of seizing the public's imagination. Sullivan-Corbett, Johnson-Jeffries, and Dempsey-Carpentier transcended sports; now came Louis-Conn, the latest "Fight of the Century." These were two champions fighting for a title only one could claim.

Louis had turned 27 a month earlier; Conn was 23. Joe's gloved fists had pounded out 25 straight wins and he was seeking his 50th victory against just one defeat; slick-boxing Billy had won 19 straight. Louis hadn't lost a fight in five years; Conn was unbeaten for the past three years.

Something was going to give this night. Dempsey, who had been in a similar circumstance to Louis 20 summers earlier when he faced Carpentier, previewed the coming confrontation in *Liberty* magazine and wrote that Conn had the skill and science to outpoint Louis over 15 rounds and take his title. Conn could beat Louis, Dempsey opined, but only if the Kid kept his cool and refrained from rushing into a slugging match with the Bomber. Ultimately, Dempsey didn't think Conn could avoid such a scenario. Billy, he wrote, "has too much 'Irish' in him."

The nation's sporting press joined Dempsey in feeding the beast that was Uncle Mike's publicity machine. Most favored Louis. Damon Runyon was the most prominent sportswriter who picked Conn. Renowned writer Grantland Rice previewed the bout by noting that Conn had never faced as powerful a puncher as the hammer-fisted Louis, and that Joe had never encountered a boxer the equal of the stylish, swashbuckling Billy. Historically, Louis was the lineal descendent of sluggers Sullivan, Jeffries, and Dempsey; Conn claimed kinship with the crafty Corbett, Johnson, and Tunney.

The collision of contrasting styles, the classic confrontation of boxer versus puncher, a legendary big man against a legendary little man, quickened the pulse of the public. Ticket sales were brisk; 54,487 seats were sold in less than three weeks. Fierro noted at the weigh-in that 5,000 fans filled the streets just to get a look at Louis and Conn. On fight night, more than 500 sportswriters from around the world would file into the Polo Grounds. Louis versus Conn succeeded in transcending sports; it was an event.

America's rich and famous converged upon the horseshoe-shaped ballpark. Representing the sports world was DiMaggio; Bob Feller, the Cleveland Indians ace who was fresh from firing a complete-game victory over the Philadelphia Athletics in Shibe Park that afternoon;

welterweight champ Fritzie Zivic and former ring kings Dempsey, Braddock, and Tony Canzoneri.

Bob Hope, Al Jolson, Olivia de Havilland, Barbara Stanwyck, Robert Taylor, and Burgess Meredith, who would go on to play the fictional Rocky Balboa's grizzled trainer Mickey in the film franchise, represented Hollywood. The entertainers joined J. Edgar Hoover in the ringside section that reached from the ring apron to several rows back. Steelers owner Art Rooney, a close friend of Conn, was part of a Pittsburgh contingent that included several politicos. General George C. Marshall, ranking officer of the US Army, was among the more notable attendees at ringside.

Settling in behind the Mutual Radio microphone, Dunphy looked to his left and saw James Farley, FDR's postmaster-general; the broadcaster then turned to his right and noticed 1920 presidential candidate James Cox. Interest in the much-ballyhooed bout was such that former bantamweight champion Pete Herman, who was blind, made the trip from New Orleans to New York just so he could "witness" the big fight.

Nat Fleischer, editor of *The Ring* magazine, thought Louis versus Conn proved once again the tremendous impact a big fight has on the public. "Even in one of the crucial periods in our American history," he wrote, "interest in the sport is still so great that throughout the entire war-torn world, untold millions listened avidly to the broadcast and one of the largest crowds in many years, 54,487 people, paid the staggering sum of $451,743 to watch the contest."

Fleischer felt a flattering sidelight to the fight showed itself in the unprecedented number of celebrities and world figures who attended. "The ringside at every important bout is always well sprinkled with famous people," he wrote, "but the turnout of notables for the Louis-Conn show was record breaking. All fields of life were represented by their outstanding figures."

With clocks ticking toward 10:00 p.m. Eastern Standard Time, millions of fans tuned their dials to the Mutual Radio Network. TV being still in its infancy, the broadcast would claim a rating of 56.4, the highest of any Mutual Radio program to that time.

"In those days, the most powerful individual in the world was the heavyweight boxing champion of the world," Joe Louis Barrow Jr. said. "When the heavyweight championship was fought, millions upon millions of people listened simultaneously by their radios all across the world."

Radio connected people to places and events; no longer was it necessary to travel long distances to experience an event. This was vitally important to Black communities, since their members were still subject to segregation laws. Broadcasts allowed them to access events they were restricted from viewing in person.

In Pittsburgh's Forbes Field, the Pirates' front office was honoring their native son by interrupting the Bucs' rare nighttime hosting of the New York Giants to air the broadcast of the bout over the public address system. The announcement drew a crowd of 24,738—a stark contrast to the previous day's paltry attendance of just 1,586—for the 9:15 p.m. first pitch. The spike in attendance was proof that in the summer of 1941 Billy Conn owned the town; he *was* Pittsburgh.

Not far from Forbes Field, on the porch of 5435 Fifth Avenue in Pittsburgh, seven young colleens clad in light summer blouses and dresses, their dark hair tumbling to their shoulders, huddled together to listen to the broadcast. They were members of the Conn clan—family and friends who gathered to hear Billy's battle with the great Louis. Seated on the far right of the front row of women was Mary Jane Conn, the Kid's sister. She was the boss of the Conn kids; even tough guy Billy acknowledged to amused sportswriters that he took orders from her. Dressed in a knee-length white skirt and matching white blouse, Mary Jane would spend the next hour clapping her hands in celebration one moment and covering her face in anguish the next.

The radio the Conn women formed a half-circle around was one of three in their home carrying the broadcast. Maggie lay upstairs; her cancer had left her in such a weakened state that she was under doctor's orders not to listen to the radio. She would instead spend the night praying for her son in this, the fight of his life. One of Billy's aunts, anxious and fraught with nerves, would flee the room and the crackling commentary at the opening bell. Davey Herr, Billy's six-year-old cousin, sat pensively near a table stacked with phonograph records.

The year 1941 may have been the most memorable in the history of American sport, and Louis and Conn were its boys of summer. As the world held its breath at events unfolding with gathering speed around the globe, fans would hold their breath at the action that was taking place on a patch of white canvas illuminated by bright lights. The drama would prove too much for some.

"The fight was so damn dramatic it killed people," wrote Randy Roberts, a Louis biographer. Andrew Burke was one of three people in Philadelphia who died from heart failure while listening to a fight featuring a seemingly unbeatable champion locked in a desperate struggle against a challenger brimming with "Conn-fidence." En route to being hurried to the hospital, Burke exclaimed, "It was a great fight!" before expiring.

In Buffalo, Delia Griffin suffered a heart attack listening to Louis and Conn wage their ring war; a fire department squad working frantically for two hours to save her life. Upon being revived, Griffin's first words were, "Who won the fight, Louis or Conn?"

One of the greatest fights in history was fought that sultry summer night. Writing in the *New York Times*, James P. Dawson would proclaim it "a battle that was thrilling and highly spectacular."

Joe Louis Barrow Jr. calls it "my father's toughest fight." It began with a roar from the excited crowd at the first bell and Dunphy's descriptive call of the opening seconds:

"They advance to the center of the ring. Conn, as expected, is dancing around. Louis is trying to crowd him into a corner. . . ."

Back and forth two legends battled: the pugnacious Conn and indomitable Louis matching their will and skill. As the hour grew late and clocks ticked toward midnight in New York City, the classic fight crescendoed toward its climax. The ending would come with such suddenness and surprise it sent shock waves across America and still spurs debate to this day.

"Such a great story," Detloff says. "It's almost too romantic to be true."

Indeed. Decades after the final bell sounded, what took place in the Polo Grounds that night was still being called by editors of *The Ring* the greatest fight in boxing history.

# CHAPTER ONE

# DETROIT BROWN BOMBER

Joe Louis would rather have been playing baseball.

An ardent fan of his hometown Detroit Tigers, Louis pored over Major League Baseball box scores printed in the morning newspapers and was a frequent visitor to Navin Field, the Tigers' home turf. In 1935, photographers pointed their box cameras and snapped photos of Louis posing playfully with Tigers manager Mickey Cochrane and sharing a light moment with a fellow Detroit slugger, "Hammerin'" Hank Greenberg.

The year 1935 had been an awesome one for the brawler and the ballers. Louis emerged as a top contender for heavyweight honors with impressive knockouts of former champions Max Baer and Primo Carnera; Greenberg earned American League Most Valuable Player honors and the Tigers roared to their second straight pennant and avenged their World Series loss to the St. Louis Cardinals' riotous "Gashouse Gang" the year before by beating the Chicago Cubs in six games.

Born May 13, 1914, in rural Chambers County, Alabama, to tenant farmer Munroe Barrow and his wife Lillie, a laundress, Louis's infatuation with baseball began during his childhood days when his family resettled in Detroit's Black Bottom neighborhood. Young Joe would head to Navin Field to watch the Tigers take on American League teams or to Mack Park to see the city's Negro National League squad, the Detroit Stars.

Louis would occasionally shag flyballs for the Stars, but it was the Tigers whom he favored. If the two Detroit teams were playing home games at the same time, Joe would go to Navin Field. Attending major-league and Negro League games, Louis saw many of the game's greatest players—Greenberg, Babe Ruth, Lou Gehrig, Lefty Grove, and Jimmie Foxx in the American League; Satchel Paige, Josh Gibson, and "Cool Papa" Bell in the Negro National League.

As Louis began his ascent in professional boxing, his love of baseball continued unabated. The summer of 1935 saw him organize a softball team that carried his ring moniker, the Brown Bombers. When he wasn't training for a fight, Louis would don his uniform for a Bombers game at Mack Park or join the team on tour.

Powerfully built and with great hand and eye coordination honed through long hours of training in the gym, Louis was a slugger who could drive the ball a long way; in the field he usually played first base, though photos also show him squatting with a catcher's mitt behind home plate. At a time when Louis could have been earning extra money boxing in exhibitions, no small thing during the Great Depression, he was helping his struggling buddies gain much-needed cash to survive hard times. Louis gave the gate receipts from Bombers games to his friends, never taking any money for himself.

Gus Greenlee, a speakeasy owner who reputedly ran gambling and bootlegging operations and owned boxers as well as the renowned Pittsburgh Crawfords baseball team, sought to sell Louis in January 1936 on financially backing a Negro National League team based in Detroit. Louis liked the idea, but his co-manager, John Roxborough, convinced the boxer that as he had already lost a substantial amount of money supporting his Brown Bombers softball team, it would be financially unwise to underwrite another such venture.

Louis maintained a lifelong love for the American pastime, forming friendships with Ruth, Paige, Joe DiMaggio, and Jackie Robinson. DiMaggio and Ruth visited Louis at his training camp in Pompton Lakes, New Jersey; Ruth would tell his fellow Sultan of Swat he should have played baseball, it was easier on the chin. Sparring with Tiger Hairston, Louis turned to Ruth at ringside and yelled, "Watch me hit a home run." Joe then wheeled around and knocked Hairston flat. The Babe smiled at the Bomber and exclaimed, "Done!" Louis would have some of his most famous fights in The House That Ruth Built, Yankee Stadium.

"If it hadn't been for boxing," Louis would say, "I would have loved to have been a baseball player." If Lillie had her way, her seventh of eight children would not have been a ballplayer or boxer but a violinist. When Joe was just two years old his father Munroe was confined to the Searcy State Hospital for the Colored Insane. Not long after that, Lillie was told her husband had died; he was, in fact, alive and would live for another 20 years, knowing nothing of his son's eventual fame.

Believing she was widowed, Lillie married Pat Brooks, a widower with five children. Joe would call Pat "the father I really knew." He was a good stepfather who worked hard and provided for a blended family of 16 children. Joe and his siblings worked in the cotton fields to help support their family. In 1926 Pat and Lillie, having tired of scratching a meager living from the land and turning their earnings over to the landowner, followed the example of so many other struggling families and headed north.

Louis thrilled at the train ride, at leaving behind the red clay of Alabama for the concrete streets of Detroit. Yet while the South was segregated during Louis's childhood, Joe said he never experienced racism until he reached the Midwest. Joe and his family moved in with relatives in their gray wooden house on Macomb Street on Detroit's east side. Pat got a job as a street cleaner and Joe's older brothers found work in the factory of the Ford Motor Company.

Dressed in knickers, sweater, and a shirt, Joe enrolled in Duffield Elementary School. He was 12 years old but, ill equipped for his new school, was placed in third grade. School bored him; he spent much of his time staring out windows and wishing he was playing baseball. His teachers liked him, Joe being quiet and respectful. Because he was bigger and stronger than his classmates, Joe was chosen to carry the US flag on assembly days. On such occasions Lillie made certain her son had a starched white shirt and blue tie to wear. Louis later remembered assembly days as the only thing about school he liked.

When his stepfather and older brothers joined millions of unemployed workers in the Great Depression, the family suffered. "First time in my life I remember being hungry," Louis recalled in his autobiography. The situation was so desperate Joe didn't have shoes to wear to school. He couldn't keep pace and struggled to get past the sixth grade. His younger sister, Vunice, passed him in grade. Recognizing that Joe might be better with his hands than his head, a Duffield teacher, Miss Vada, helped him transfer to Bronson, an all-boys vocational school. Louis liked working with his hands; he enjoyed making cabinets, shelves, and tables that he could take home to his family and spare them the expense of buying furniture.

As the Depression worsened, Joe's family had to go on a soup line to eat. Lillie waited in long relief lines to get money from the government. They would borrow more than $400, Joe eventually paying back every penny when he turned pro in 1934.

With his family on relief Joe began working odd jobs. He and friend Freddie Guinyard, whom he had met at the Calvary Baptist Church, secured a job on an ice wagon. The two made quite a team, Freddie wearing a sailor hat with a silk ribbon hanging down and Louis pulling on a skull cap because, as he said, nobody was gonna put Freddie's funny hat on him.

Dressed in their knickers, Joe and Freddie rode a horse-drawn ice wagon. Theirs was an important job; as not every home had a refrigerator or freezer, people were dependent on ice to keep their food from spoiling. Joe and Freddie wrapped the ice in thick brown burlap to prevent it from melting. At each stop, Freddie remained with the horse while Joe carried 60 pounds of ice up several flights of stairs. Joe didn't mind the heavy lifting. He knew that Freddie, tough as he was, was too small to lug ice any distance. Joe hustled to earn extra money. Saturdays saw him scrubbing floors for a quarter; he also hauled coal in addition to ice, delivered groceries, and worked in the vegetable section of the Eastern Market.

Looking to help her son find a profession, Lillie heard about a music teacher on Warren and Woodward Streets and started giving Joe 50 cents a week to take violin lessons. Joe hated the violin; the small instrument felt funny in his huge hands. Neighborhood toughs mocked him when they saw him carrying the violin. One person who didn't laugh was Thurston McKinney, the Detroit Golden Gloves welterweight champion. McKinney persuaded Louis to accompany him to Brewster's Recreation Center.

Entering the professional gym, Joe looked at the ring, the punching bag, pulleys, and exercise equipment and liked what he saw. He used his music money to rent a locker and stuffed his violin inside. McKinney loaned him boxing trunks and old tennis shoes, and Louis began working out on the punching bag.

"That's how it began," he remembered in his autobiography.

Sparring with McKinney, Louis took a battering until he caught the champ on the chin with a thunderclap right hand. McKinney's knees buckled and his eyes got glassy. He was on his way to the canvas when Joe caught him and held him up. McKinney shook his head to clear the cobwebs. "Man, throw that violin away!"

The punch Joe threw left him with a feeling he had never experienced before. "It was like power pumping through me," he said later. "That was the first time I knew what I really wanted to be."

Concerned his mother would discover how he was spending the money she scraped together, Joe hid the fact he was training to be a boxer until his music teacher told his mother about the missed violin lessons. When Lillie asked Joe for his lesson punch card, he said nothing; he had already torn it up and thrown it away. The teacher told Lillie that Joe didn't have the talent to be a musician and she was wasting her money on lessons. She and Pat weren't thrilled about Joe's desire to pursue pugilism as a career, but they allowed him to keep training.

When he wasn't in Bronson Vocational School or working, Joe was in the gym. Realizing there was nothing he could do as well as he could fight, Joe quit school at age 17 to spend more time training. He fought in street fights to protect his siblings and his reputation as a hard puncher soon preceded him; thugs thought better of it when they came face to face with Joe. He developed a fan following among the kids in his neighborhood. One thin child carried his gym bag for him to Brewster's. The boy's name was Walker Smith; he later became known as Sugar Ray Robinson.

Louis's labors left him too tired to train properly. He was up early, worked till 5:00 p.m., gulped dinner, and hustled to the gym. His step-father tried to talk Joe into getting a steady job and forget about fight-ing for a living. Lillie, however, took a different approach and urged Joe to box if that made him happy. "If you want to be a fighter," she told him, "be one."

It wasn't until Joe spoke of the merchandise checks ranging from $7 to $25 that he could earn boxing that his stepfather relented. Trained by Atler Ellis, who ran Brewster's, and middleweight Holman Williams, Joe in 1932 was matched in his first amateur fight with Johnny Miler, a member of the US Olympic boxing team.

To keep his parents from seeing his name in the sports section of the newspaper, Joe dropped his Barrow surname and entered the ring as Joe Louis. Undertrained and overmatched, Louis was knocked down by Miler seven times in the first two rounds. When he returned home that night Lillie cried when she saw her son's battered face. Embarrassed by his per-formance, Louis quit the ring to follow his stepfather's advice to focus on finding a steady job. Within a few days full-time work was found in the Ford factory at River Rouge. He earned $25 a week pushing truck bodies to a conveyor belt; his back hurt so much after work he sometimes couldn't straighten up. "It wasn't my idea of fun," Louis recalled. But with his step-father out of work, Joe had to continue in his job. Eventually he decided that if he was going to hurt that much he might as well return to the ring.

Back in the gym following a two-month absence, Joe continued his training with Ellis and Williams. Realizing that Louis had a powerful right hand but that he was not using his left enough, Ellis tied Joe's right hand to a ring post and got McKinney in the ring with him. McKinney proceeded to pound his one-armed opponent—"beat the hell out of me," Louis remembered—but the point was made. Louis learned the importance of using his left hand and in time his jab became one of the most feared weapons in boxing history.

When Louis climbed the ring steps for his fight with Otis Thomas at the Forest Athletic Club in Detroit, he wasn't thinking about Thomas. He was thinking about his lone previous amateur bout and the beating he took from Miler. "Not this time," Joe thought. Tearing into Thomas with a left hook and right hand to the jaw, Louis scored a first-round knockout, his first KO. Feeling as if he was on top of the world, Joe knocked out his next 13 opponents, earning a $25 merchandise check for each victory.

Buoyed by his success Louis took his amateur career to the next level and entered the Golden Gloves. He lost decisions to heavyweight Clinton Bridges in Chicago and to Max Marek, a star of the Notre Dame football team, in the National Amateur Championship in Boston. Despite the defeats, Joe's world was expanding. Being away from home and fighting in Chicago, Boston, Kansas City, Florida, and Toronto provided life lessons for the 19-year-old.

Louis won 50 of 54 amateur fights and scored 43 knockouts. His impressive performances attracted the attention of John Roxborough. The real estate agent and reputed racketeer was known for helping poor kids escape the Detroit ghettos; he sent several through college. Louis's new trainer, George Slayton, brought Roxborough to Joe's dressing room and the dapper civic leader made an immediate impression on Louis. "This man had real class," Louis thought. Roxborough was stylish and wealthy. He wore a gray silk suit that Louis knew had to be tailor-made. Roxborough presented himself as a gentleman, and he and Joe clicked personality-wise. Roxborough invited Louis to stop by his real estate office, which Joe would learn was a front for a gambling operation.

Roxborough brought Louis into his home for dinners and provided him with money, clothes, and new boxing equipment. On June 27, 1934 [some sources report it as being June 12], a well-fed, well-trained Louis knocked out Joe Bauer in less than two minutes of the opening round in Detroit's Ford Field. It was the last amateur fight Louis ever fought. "I think you're ready, Joe," Roxborough said. "Time to turn professional."

The following day Roxborough told Louis he wanted to send him to Chicago to live and train. He also informed Joe that Julian Black, a long-time business associate and like Roxborough a reputed numbers man, would be co-manager and help fund Louis's career. Julian had a stable of Black fighters in Chicago and he and Roxborough told Louis they could help him in ways a white manager couldn't. Louis would look back years later and remember that conversation and realize that Roxborough was talking about Black Power before it was popular to do so.

Julian Black was at the Chicago train station to meet Louis and when Joe arrived, he saw a fine-looking man who stood a shade under 6 feet, had a stocky build, light-brown complexion, straight hair, and a slight limp. Black was a tough guy, Joe thought, but friendly. Black told Louis his first professional fight would be in a month. He was making a big investment in him, the numbers man told the boxer, and he expected Joe to make a big investment in himself. Black informed Louis he was dropping the other fighters he was working with to con-centrate on him.

Two days after arriving in Chicago Louis was in Trafton's Gym on West Randolph Street when he was introduced to his new trainer, for-mer fighter Jack Blackburn. The ex–lightweight contender was wiry and bald. Louis studied Blackburn and thought the man strong and mean-looking, Joe noting the scar that ran down the left side of Blackburn's face from his ear to his mouth.

Blackburn was tough and talked rough; he had spent five years in prison on a murder rap. He had trained two world champions—both white—and was skeptical that any Black fighter would get an oppor-tunity to win the heavyweight title. He knew Jack Johnson personally, knew the controversy the first Black heavyweight champion had created decades earlier by whipping "Great White Hopes" with smiling ease and dating white women.

"If you really ain't gonna be another Jack Johnson," Blackburn told Louis, "you got some hope. White man hasn't forgotten that fool with his white women, acting like he owned the world."

Roxborough and Black distanced Louis from Johnson as much as possible, instructing him to never mock or taunt an opponent, to refrain from smiling after beating a white fighter, and to never date white women.

While Roxborough and Black polished Louis's social skills, Blackburn honed his boxer's ring strategy. "You got to listen to everything I tell you," Blackburn said. "You got to jump when I say jump; sleep when I say sleep. Other than that, you're wasting my time."

Louis promised there would be no time wasted. Blackburn issued a tight smile. "OK, Chappie," he said. Louis smiled back. "OK, Chappie." From that point on, the two would call each other "Chappie" as they forged one of the great trainer-boxer relationships in history. Blackburn became for Louis a father, teacher, and friend. Joe thought so much of Chappie that he named his first child, Jacque, after Jack.

Blackburn put Louis on a rigorous training schedule, up at 6:00 a.m. to run six miles and then into the gym. For the first week the two worked together, Blackburn did not allow Louis to enter the ring. Instead, he had Joe hit the heavy bag repeatedly. Morning, noon, and night Blackburn held the heavy bag while Louis pounded away.

When Blackburn finally let Louis spar, he saw Joe's faults immediately. Louis was off-balance; he was swinging with his arms and not putting his body behind his blows. Blackburn showed his protégé how to plant his feet properly when he punched to get full power. He told Louis that fans didn't go to see dancers and clinchers; they wanted a guy to go for the opponent's guts. Blackburn built up Louis's confidence by telling him he had the power to knock out anybody if he planted his body in the right position.

During rubdowns Blackburn reminded Chappie the deck was stacked against him because he was a Black boxer taking on white opponents. He warned Louis that he could not win on points; Joe would have to go for knockouts to ensure victory.

"Negro fighters," Blackburn stated, "do not go to town winning decisions. Let your right fist be the referee."

The old trainer spoke from experience. In his prime years Black fighters were usually permitted in the ring with whites only to make the latter look good. Promoters allowed Blacks to put on a good show against whites but were warned not to be *too* good. Black fighters faced handicaps when meeting whites; Blackburn once had to wear size 10 ring shoes—he was a size 8—to hinder his footwork. Before boxing white fighters Blackburn made sure he was paid in advance; promoters had a habit of skipping out before the bout was over to avoid paying.

Blackburn taught Louis balance afoot and blurring combinations, each punch connected to the one that preceded it and the one that followed. He instructed Joe to cut off the ring against an opponent, to move forward behind a pole-like straight left jab that jolted a man's head back with shocking force and accuracy, to parry punches with an open right glove which closed quickly into a clenched fist when Joe was in striking range.

"(Louis) had a great teacher," champion and ring historian Mike Tyson stated. "He had a great trainer, who was also a great fighter, prepare him for his life as a fighter."

On July 4, 1934, Louis, Blackburn, Roxborough, and Black headed to Bacon Casino, located on 47th Street on Chicago's South Side, for Joe's professional debut against Jack Kracken. It would be a main event; Louis's amateur record and reputation meant he never had to be relegated to preliminaries. Louis was accustomed to fighting three-round Golden Gloves bouts; going longer worried him. Blackburn calmed his concerns. If you can go three rounds, you can go six, Blackburn reasoned. When Louis entered the ring, his concerns grew. Kracken didn't look like the amateurs Joe was used to boxing. Kracken was older, and while he was lighter than Louis, weighing 175 to Joe's 181, he appeared unconcerned about facing a first-time pro.

Before the first bell Blackburn leaned toward Louis. "Remember everything I taught you. Get in there and knock that guy out as fast as you can!"

When the fight started Louis approached the top heavyweight in Chicago and went straight for his body. Feeling Louis's power Kracken lowered his arms to protect his midsection. Joe switched his attack and landed a left to the chin. Kracken crashed to the canvas and was stopped out less than two minutes into the fight. Louis's purse for his first pro fight came to $59. Pretty good money, he thought, for a couple minutes' work.

Before the calendar flipped to 1935 Louis fought 11 more times, each bout taking place in Chicago or Detroit and all but two ending with his opponent being stopped. Louis's rapid rise continued into the following year with 11 straight victories, 9 by stoppage. His fight sites expanded from the Midwest to both coasts and points in between. "I really stormed the country," Louis said. On June 25, 1935, Louis made his New York City debut, fighting former heavyweight kingpin Primo Carnera in Yankee Stadium.

Making his first trip to the city he had heard so much of, Louis was thrilled to take in the sights; he visited Central Park, Seventh Avenue, Harlem, and the Cotton Club. He also visited the office of promoter Mike Jacobs, who was signing Louis to an exclusive contract.

Jacobs had organized the Twentieth Century Sporting Club and was competing with promoters who monopolized the mecca of boxing—Madison Square Garden. Taking on entrenched power is a tall task; fortunately for Jacobs he had powerful friends. Nat Fleischer, a respected boxing writer and owner of *The Ring* magazine, also known as the "Bible of Boxing," and sportswriters of William Randolph Hearst publications were powerful allies of "Uncle Mike."

Louis's bout with Carnera created tremendous interest at home and abroad. It was the first of several Louis fights that produced international intrigue. Carnera, a former champion, was as much a personal favorite of Italian fascist leader Benito Mussolini as German heavyweight Max Schmeling was of Nazi führer Adolf Hitler.

Just as Hitler saw Schmeling as the symbol of Aryan supremacy, Mussolini viewed the huge Carnera as a sign that Italy was reclaiming the glory of ancient Rome. Primo stood 6-foot-6 and weighed 260 pounds; a man-mountain, his monikers were the "Ambling Alp" and "Vast Venetian." Primo was the heaviest of all champions to that point, outweighing even Jess Willard, the Pottawatomie Giant who scaled 242. At 6-foot-7 Willard was an inch taller, but Carnera was more muscular.

Carnera captured the crown in June 1933 with a six-round knock-out of Jack Sharkey. Because Primo was said to have ties to organized crime, some speculated the fight was fixed, and that Sharkey had taken a dive. No conclusive evidence was discovered, and the result went into the official record books as one of 72 KOs Carnera claimed among his 89 victories. Originally a circus strongman, Primo could punch; he owns more knockout victories than any champion in heavyweight history. Called "The Monster" by *Time* magazine because of his gigantism, Carnera stopped Ernie Schaaf in the 13th round with heavy punches on February 10, 1933. Schaaf went into a coma and was taken to the hospital. He passed away four days following the fight. An autopsy showed that Schaaf was suffering from a swelling of the brain, likely incurred in part by a brutal battering administered by Max Baer on August 31, 1932.

Mussolini's threats that summer to invade Ethiopia caused political turmoil to surround the Louis-Carnera bout. Racial tensions were roused in New York City and Jacobs added fuel to the fire by selling Louis to fight fans as an ambassador of his race. Sportswriters similarly played up the race angle, describing Louis in alliterative terms as the "Dark Destroyer," "Mahogany Mauler," "Chocolate Chopper," "Saffra Sandman," "Sepia Socker," "coffee-colored KO king," and most famously, "Brown Bomber." The latter nickname stuck and remained with Louis for the rest of his ring career. Less racist were monikers that focused on Joe's background— "Alabama Assassin," "Detroit Destroyer," and "Michigan Mauler."

With talk of war between Italy and Ethiopia escalating, racial friction between Blacks and Italians grew as fight night neared. Black groups showed up at Joe's first training camp in Pompton Lakes and told him he was representing Ethiopia in this battle with an Italian fighter. Louis acknowledged it was a heavy burden to bear for a man just 20 years old.

The importance of the Louis-Carnera bout caused unease and uncertainty; realizing the potential danger, the Hearst people met with Jacobs and considered canceling the bout. Roxborough talked them out of it, and 62,000 tickets were sold for a fight that had taken on immense racial and political overtones. Louis trained diligently; he punctuated his work by punching a speed bag so hard it flew several rows into the audience. "That's what you're gonna do to Carnera!" observers shouted excitedly. Louis's training was further enlivened by his meeting Jack Johnson, dating Lena Horne, listening to the big band music of Cab Calloway and Duke Ellington, and visiting nightspots like the Memo Club on Seventh Avenue with Bill "Bojangles" Robinson. Joe also found time to buy his mother a new house, which he presented to her on Easter Sunday.

Despite the friction between Blackburn and Johnson, Louis liked the ex-champ; he found Johnson to be impressive looking and a good talker. Johnson spoke with Louis about situations he was going to run into as a Black fighter and warned the up-and-coming contender to always keep his head.

The weigh-in at the State Office Building nearly resulted in a riot. For the fighters to enter the building, New York's Finest had to clear a path through a surging crowd eager to get a glimpse of the two fighters. Seeing Carnera up close startled Louis. "A huge hunk of man," Joe thought. At a time when the average height of a male adult was 5'5" in Italy and 5'7" in the United States, Carnera was a giant. Primo weighed in at 260½; Louis 196. The 64-pound difference in weight, and 4 inches' difference in height, didn't leave Louis intimidated. "Bigger target to punch," he reasoned.

What did leave Louis awestruck was the sight of 60,000 fans in Yankee Stadium, the largest New York City fight crowd since 1927 when the Jack Dempsey–Jack Sharkey bout drew 82,000. Climbing into the ring, Louis thought for a moment of the situation he was in. He was Joe Louis Barrow, hailing from a little farm in Alabama, and tens of thousands of fans had made their way to the famous Yankee Stadium to see him fight.

Called to the center of the ring, Louis and Carnera were given their final instructions by referee Arthur Donovan. The father of future

Baltimore Colts defensive tackle and Pro Football Hall of Famer Artie "Fatso" Donovan, Arthur would officiate so many of Louis's bouts—20—that he became known as "Joe Louis's referee." From 1933 to 1946 Donovan was one of boxing's top referees. He grew up around boxing; his family was known as the "Fighting Donovans." His father Mike fought in the Civil War and in not so civil bare knuckles brawls. He was a middleweight champion and boxing instructor, teaching Teddy Roosevelt the Manly Art of Self-Defense.

When Donovan's father retired as a boxing instructor, Arthur took over the position and held it 50 years. Urged to become a referee in 1933 by New York State Athletic Commissioner James Farley, Arthur agreed. He became a fan favorite and was stopped often by autograph seekers. Donovan was also a favorite of the New York State Athletic Commission, being called on to work 14 title fights. He was inducted into the Boxing Hall of Fame in 1993.

Awaiting the opening bell, Blackburn reminded Louis of their strategy. "Work on Carnera's body till he drops his guard," Blackburn shouted above the din, "and then go to the head."

Louis drove home hard punches in the first round; Carnera was content to move and push out a ponderous left. "He had a pretty decent jab," Joe recalled. Louis was less impressed with the Italian's right hand, which he saw as awkward. Primo's plan, the Bomber thought, was to scare him with his size.

Fans expecting Carnera to push Louis around were surprised to see Joe maneuvering Primo with ease. In Round Five the two clinched and Louis moved the bigger man. Carnera's eyes widened; the Ambling Alp was amazed by the strength of his smaller opponent. "Oh, oh," the goliath gasped. "I should be doing this to you."

Louis found it difficult for a time to get under Carnera's guard, but between rounds Blackburn preached patience; the openings would come. When the bell rang for Round Six, Blackburn shouted, "Go get him!" A hard right hand from the Bomber brought blood spurting from Carnera's mouth. Another right put Primo on the canvas. Carnera went down, journalist John Kiernan observed, "like a great chimney that had been dynamited."

Carnera arose but returned to the ring floor following another hard right cross. His face dripped with blood; his lower teeth had been driven through his upper lip by the Bomber's blows. Louis pounded Primo's body, reddening his ribs; the Vast Venetian proved as big a target as Joe expected. The giant was spitting blood when a right-left combination cratered Carnera for a third and final time. Donovan stepped in and stopped the carnage, causing a ringside reporter to label the referee's decision "an act of humanitarianism."

His record now 20-0 with 17 KOs, Louis told reporters, "I thought I'd get him, but I wasn't sure when his big arms would drop and I'd get to his chin."

The victory increased Louis's fame as well as his fortune. His payday was $60,000, an astronomical increase from the less than $60 he earned for his first pro fight just a year earlier. The fact that he had made it big in New York City—"Boxing Capital of the World," he called it—erased questions about his ability to draw a crowd.

With Louis now a national hero for striking a symbolic blow for democracy and against fascism overseas, newspapers went wild with stories about the phenom. Black people approached him to shake his hand or kiss him. Where they had once congratulated him on his fighting abilities, they now showered him with higher praise. "Joe, you're our savior!" Some implored him to "Show them whites!" Others chanted "Brown Bomber!"

Fans included women of every variety—chorus girls, dancers, singers, and movie starlets, white as well as Black. Despite the strict orders of Roxborough and Black, Louis dated white women, albeit discreetly. Skater Sonja Henie and singer Lena Horne were among the rich and famous females Louis kept company with; Julian Black said women went after the fighter "like Grant storming Richmond." But as Joe approached his next big fight—a September 24 bout with another former heavyweight boss, Max Baer—his sights were set on marrying girlfriend Marva Trotter and settling down.

Louis knew Baer was no pushover, and as much as Joe wanted this fight, Max wanted it just as much. Both men believed a victory would put them in line for a shot at Jim Braddock's title. The celebrated "Cinderella Man" had shocked the sports world by beating Baer in one of boxing's biggest upsets. Louis saw Baer as a glamour boy; it was not for nothing he had the moniker "Madcap Maxie." Still, Baer hungered for redemption and a chance to regain his crown.

Called the "Livermore Larruper"—Baer was born in Nebraska, but he and his family moved to Livermore, California, when he was 17—Max earned a reputation as a heavy-handed slugger. Like Carnera, Baer had killed an opponent, Frankie Campbell, in August 1930. On June 14, 1934, Baer became champion by knocking down Carnera 11 times before Donovan stopped the fight in Round 11.

Living the high life, Max lost his title to Braddock one day shy of a year later. Just three months later Baer was meeting Louis because the Cinderella Man resisted an immediate rematch. Braddock knew bread lines and hard times and wanted to hang on to his newly won title. For Max to get a shot at reclaiming his crown, he would have to beat Louis. It was not a scenario that Baer relished. He had seen the Brown Bomber fight and knew Joe's style would be a problem.

Making matters worse, Max had hurt his hands in his loss to Braddock. His right hand, which housed his power punch, was broken; his left wrist had a floating bone chip. Baer's manager Ancil Hoffman tried to talk Max into postponing the bout until his hands healed. The two men flew to Johns Hopkins University Hospital in Maryland. William Healy, an orthopedic surgeon, examined Baer and advised an operation on his right hand before he fought again.

Realizing a postponement could cost him another crack at Braddock, Baer began training at Speculator, New York. Newly married, Baer wrote his wife Mary, "I hope to God my hand heals before the fight."

Mary was a positive influence on Max, helping him shed his playboy lifestyle and become a family man. The couple would have three children—Max Jr., James, and Maude. Max Jr. grew up to star as backwoods bumpkin Jethro Bodine in the 1960s TV series *The Beverly Hillbillies*. Years later Max Jr. excoriated director Ron Howard for the negative portrayal of Max Sr. in the film *Cinderella Man*.

Along with having Hoffman in his corner against Louis, Baer would also have Dempsey, his ring idol. Jack believed boxing's future rested on Baer's broad shoulders. "He's the biggest, strongest man fighting today, and he hits with terrible power."

Told that Dempsey would be in Baer's corner, Louis asked, tongue in cheek, that the rules did state that, "Dempsey can't hit me, right?"

At the weigh-in, flashbulbs popped as Baer smiled at Louis. Joe maintained his stoic demeanor. Baer weighed 210½, Louis 199¼. In his dressing room in packed Yankee Stadium—the paid attendance was 84,841 and 11,000 passes had been issued—Baer told Dempsey his right hand was hurting. He knew he couldn't beat Louis with damaged hands, could he call off the fight? Impossible, Dempsey replied. There are 95,000 fans in the stadium waiting for this fight to happen. Fight Louis in that ring, Dempsey growled, or fight him, Dempsey, in the dressing room.

Hoffman came into the room with Max Stern of the New Jersey Boxing Commission. Stern opened his doctor's bag and pulled out a large syringe and a small bottle of clear liquid—Novocain. He inserted several shots into Baer's right hand to numb the aching pain. Baer's best chance was to try to take out Louis early before the painkillers wore off. Unfortunately for Baer, a rain delay postponed the start of the bout for 45 minutes. By the time Baer climbed through the ropes, his right hand was again aching.

The Louis camp had another advantage. Mike Cantwell, a former trainer for Baer, had a falling out with Max and sent a letter to Roxborough detailing his former employee's fight plan. Louis was the betting favorite, Baer the sentimental one. Both men had their moments in the first two rounds, the Larruper landing looping rights and the Bomber countering with combinations. At the end of Round Two, Dempsey told Baer that Louis hadn't landed a punch. "Then you better keep an eye on the referee," Baer replied in true Madcap Maxie form, "'cause he's beating the hell out of me!"

In the third round Louis's left jab snapped Baer's head back repeatedly. Joe landed an overhand right that put Baer on the floor for the first time in his career. Ever the showman, Madcap Maxie thrust his right glove in the night air while seated on the canvas.

Baer pulled himself up and was dropped again, this time by three rapid-fire left hooks to the jaw but was saved by the bell. Round Four saw Louis deliver a right hand–left hook combination that sent Baer to the canvas a third time; he took Donovan's 10-count on his right knee, his head bowed. The ex-champ left the ring to a chorus of catcalls from fans who believed he could have continued to fight.

"I could have struggled up once more," Baer acknowledged, "but when I get executed people are going to have to pay more than $25 a seat to watch it."

For the rest of his life Louis would call his fight against Max Baer the best of his career. He never had greater hand speed than he did that night, and his conditioning was such that he felt in his words, "I could have fought for two or three days straight."

Informed that a timekeeping error caused Round Four to run longer than the regulation three minutes and was 3:09, meaning Baer should have been saved by the bell as he had been in Round Three, Max shrugged. "What's the difference? I was beaten and beaten in grand fashion."

In his dressing room Louis, having married Marva hours before, surprised no one when he told the press, "I wanted this to be a quick fight."

When Louis's remark was relayed to Baer, Max replied, "I define fear as standing across the ring from Joe Louis and knowing he wants to go home early."

Baer's fear of Louis disturbed a prominent personality sitting ringside. Ernest Hemingway, writing for *Esquire* magazine, called the fight "the most disgusting public spectacle, outside of a hanging, that your correspondent has ever witnessed. What made it disgusting was fear."

One man unafraid of the Detroit Brown Bomber was another former heavyweight champion named Max, surname Schmeling. Nicknamed the "Black Uhlan of the Rhine"—in his native tongue "Der schwarze Ulan vom Rhein"—the dark-featured German was considered by most to represent little more than a speed bump on Louis's fast track to the title. Schmeling, however, was a skilled defensive fighter and solid counterpuncher with a right hand that proved instrumental in providing 41 punch-outs among his 57 career victories.

Schmeling's interest in boxing was heightened when, as a 16-year-old in 1921 Germany, his father took him to the theater to view the film of that summer's Dempsey-Carpentier fight. Though Max idolized the Manassa Mauler, he favored a ring style more cautious and calculating. Still, Schmeling proved proficient enough to impress Dempsey when the two met during Jack's triumphant tour of Europe in 1925. The champion sparred two rounds with Schmeling and praised the aspiring contender's abilities.

Schmeling's ring career was marked by controversy. In 1930 he was awarded the heavyweight title vacated by Gene Tunney when a low blow by Sharkey in the fourth round left Max writhing on the canvas in Yankee Stadium. Schmeling remains the only heavyweight to win the title on a foul. Schmeling and Sharkey rematched two summers later in New York, this time in the Madison Square Garden Bowl, and when Jack was awarded a disputed 15-round split decision, Schmeling's manager Joe Jacobs uttered the famous quote, "We wuz robbed!"

In June 1933 Schmeling met Baer in Yankee Stadium at a time when the Nazi Party was rising to power in Germany. While Schmeling was cast as a symbol of Nazism, Baer wore satin trunks with the Star of David emblazoned on the front left panel, his grandfather being Jewish. Schmeling and Baer both gave Max-imum effort, but it was Baer who battered his way to a brutal 10th-round technical knockout.

Signed to fight Louis on June 19, 1936, in Yankee Stadium, Schmeling studied the Bomber's fight films. "I see something," Max told skeptical sportswriters. What Schmeling saw was Louis's tendency to lower his left hand following his jab. The flaw played to Schmeling's strength as a counterpuncher with power in his right hand.

When Schmeling arrived in New York for the fight, the sports pages of the nation's newspapers were filled with stories of the 30-year-old ex-champ being washed up and worse, a Nazi sympathizer and puppet of Hitler. For the second time in a year, Louis found himself in a fight that was bigger than sports. Because of their respective races and nations they represented, the Louis-Schmeling bout became an event of international importance, like the Louis-Carnera fight in 1935.

Louis and Schmeling had met once before, Max showing up in Pompton Lakes to watch Joe train for Max Baer. The two contenders sized each other up. "I'll take him," Louis thought. Louis's confidence was peaking. He had closed out 1935 with a punishing knockout of Paulino Uzcudun in Madison Square Garden. Louis split the Spaniard's face with a left and right that sent Uzcudun reeling into the ropes, Paulino's gold teeth sprinkling onto the canvas.

The Bomber bought into stories that Schmeling was a has-been. Over the first two months of his career Louis had been fighting regularly. He crammed 27 fights into 25 months, at times fighting two, and sometimes three times a month. The steady schedule had Louis finely honed. Perhaps recognizing this, Joe Jacobs, Schmeling's wily manager, insisted that a clause be inserted into their fight contract that neither boxer would have an interim bout prior to their June meeting. Louis had last fought on January 17, 1936, and the subsequent six-month layoff left him with more time to pursue an old passion—women—and a new passion in golf. He also went to Hollywood to star in a motion picture titled *The Spirit of Youth*. "I was going to be a damn movie star," he recalled in his autobiography.

The layoff hurt Louis more than the experienced Schmeling. Too much partying and soft living had the Bomber struggling to melt unwanted pounds. The day of the fight dawned gloomy. Skies were cloudy and threatening rain; lightning flashed from time to time. A 10–1 underdog, Schmeling weighed 192 to Louis's 198. The two men mumbled hellos to one another.

Joe Louis Barrow Jr. notes that many Americans were pulling for Schmeling, even though he hailed from Hitler's Germany.

"People in this country were rooting for Schmeling in that first fight with my father," Joe Jr. says, "because they couldn't accept the fact that a Black man could defeat a white man, no matter where he was from."

In Round Four, Schmeling's due diligence in dissecting the Detroit sensation's style delivered dividends. An overhand right caught Louis on the left cheekbone. Joe did a half-stagger backward and Max followed with a two-fisted barrage. Two more hard rights to the head put Louis on the seat of his satin trunks; it was the first knockdown of his pro career. The Bomber bounced up at the count of "two," but damage had been done. "I could've sworn my damn jaw was broken," he remembered. By his own account, Louis never fully recovered from that fourth round.

Blackburn recognized Schmeling's fight plan, but it was too late to correct his fighter's flaw. The best he could do was to tell Chappie, "Keep your guard up!" Joe did but as the bell rang to end Round Five, he was smashed in the jaw by an unexpected punch that some argued was after the bell and thus a foul. Louis staggered back to his corner, his ears ringing. He fought the rest of the fight in a fog and took so many Schmeling rights to his face his features swelled and became distorted.

Joe's mother, who was in Yankee Stadium, began praying. "My God," she cried, "don't let him kill my child!" Guinyard hurried Joe's hysterical mother out of the stadium.

In the 12th round, Schmeling pounded home one final right hand that spun the dazed and disfigured Louis to a kneeling position facing the ropes. For a moment Joe hung onto the middle strand with both gloves to keep from falling flat on the canvas. He let go, fell on his side, shook his head in one last attempt to clear the cobwebs, then rolled over on his stomach. As Donovan tolled "10!" Louis laid face down, his bruised face buried in his arms. Schmeling, a sportsman, rushed to lift the beaten Louis off the canvas.

Louis was so concussed he didn't remember being helped to his dressing room by stunned attendants and policemen. Joe looked in a mirror and was shocked at what he saw. His forehead was swollen, he had a grapefruit-sized lump on his left cheek, and his lips were bloodied.

The Bomber's fans took the loss hard. There were riots in Chicago's "Little Harlem"; people stoned streetcars. In New York a girl tried to commit suicide by drinking poison in a drugstore and had to be hurried to the nearest hospital. Unable to believe their hero had been beaten, fans concocted conspiracy theories. Louis had been drugged, they said; Schmeling had iron pieces in his gloves. The frenzied theories made Louis realize how important he was to so many people.

"I was the only hero they had," he said, "and heroes aren't supposed to lose."

Louis had little time to dwell on his defeat. Almost immediately he was signed to fight yet another former champ, the fourth in two years, Sharkey. Known as "The Boston Gob"—he was born in Binghamton, New York, but moved to Massachusetts as a young man—Sharkey had worn the championship belt for one year and like Louis was on the comeback trail.

In 1927 Sharkey fought Dempsey to determine the top contender to Tunney's title. Like Baer and Schmeling, Sharkey idolized Dempsey. For the first six rounds he had his hero beat—"I thought he was going to knock me out," the Mauler admitted—but when Sharkey left his chin unprotected to turn and complain to the referee about what he thought were blows below the belt, Dempsey worked his left glove free and exploded a short hook on the Gob's exposed chin. Sharkey collapsed and was counted out, and Dempsey went on to battle Tunney in a rematch that resulted in the infamous "Long Count."

Sharkey increased interest in the fight with Louis by stating that he could beat any Black fighter. "I have always had the Indian sign on Negro boxers. Remember what I did to George Godfrey and Harry Wills?"

Returning to the same Yankee Stadium ring where he had been counted out almost two months to the day earlier, Louis was reminded by Blackburn that Sharkey would employ the same strategy as Schmeling. Joe nodded. He was more nervous and worried for this fight than any other; Louis knew his career was riding on the outcome. He couldn't afford two straight losses.

At the first gong, the Gob threw his entire game at the Bomber—arm feints, body feints, sneaky right hands. Louis fought more aggressively than he had against Schmeling but took care not to get hit with the same counter rights Max had used so successfully. In the second round a Louis right knocked Sharkey's feet out from under him. The knockdown gave the Bomber back his confidence; he sent Sharkey down on his purple trunks for a count of nine.

Grimacing through a mouthful of blood, the gritty Gob kept getting up. The ex-champ was crafty; he rolled with Louis's punches and sought to confuse and frustrate Joe with timely clinches. Not to be deterred Louis drove Sharkey face first through the ropes for an eight-count. The Bomber connected again, a three-punch combination that felled the tough Irishman for a fourth time. This time, Sharkey didn't beat Donovan's count. "Louis convinced me that I have no business in trying to continue," Sharkey said.

As the only man to have fought Louis and Dempsey, Sharkey was asked who the harder puncher was. "Dempsey hit me the hardest because Dempsey hit me $211,000 worth," he remarked, noting the difference in paydays, "while Louis only hit me $36,000 worth."

International politics prevented Schmeling from fighting Braddock. Jacobs feared that if Max won, he would take the title back to Nazi Germany where it could remain indefinitely. After months of high-stakes negotiations between the Braddock-Schmeling and Braddock-Louis camps, Louis on February 19, 1937, signed to become the first Black man to fight for the title in two decades. Clinching the deal was a clause—unprecedented in boxing history—that gave Braddock a percentage of Louis's future ring earnings.

The fight was set for June 22, 1937, at Soldier Field in Chicago but switched to Chicago's Comiskey Park to save on rental fees. Blackburn took no chances with this historic opportunity. He told Louis at the start of training what was wrong with his style.

"You have a weakness for a right hand," Blackburn began. "You always jab with your left and drop it, leaving yourself wide open for right-hand punches by your opponents. You have to change your pattern. You're always shuffling in, jabbing with a left and crossing with a right. That makes you too predictable."

Blackburn would show Joe how to step back, weave, and counterpunch.

"You son of a bitch," Blackburn snarled. "You made it to here and I'm going to see you make it all the way. When I finish with you, you're gonna be a fighting machine!"

Louis looked ferocious at the weigh-in; he sported a 10-day stubble that got the Cinderella Man's attention.

"Hey, Joe, you need a shave." Turning to reporters, the champ stated, "I'm in shape, Joe's in shape. There'll be a hell of a fight tonight."

Bettors made Louis a 2–1 favorite, but Braddock remained a crowd favorite, a man whose incredible story inspired sportswriter Damon Runyon to state, "In all the history of the boxing game you find no human-interest story to compare with the life narrative of James J. Braddock." The life stories of Braddock and Louis have become the subjects of feature films.

Braddock entered the ring first, and when Louis climbed through the ropes the Cinderella Man walked across the ring and shook the Bomber's hand. Before the bell, the Irish Catholic Braddock made the Sign of the Cross. Louis, a Baptist, said a silent prayer. As Louis advanced, he heard Blackburn yelling from the corner. "Don't get careless! Keep your hands up!"

Braddock brought the big crowd to its feet in the first round when he dropped Louis with a short counter right. Joe recalled wondering when he hit the deck, "What the hell am I doing here?" It was just the second fight in which he had been knocked down as a professional, but unlike the Schmeling bout, Joe's head was clear. The Bomber bounced up at "two" and jolted James J. with a left hook and right cross just before the bell.

Louis believed he could take Braddock out, but Blackburn cautioned him. "Wait, take it easy. He's game and he knows a lot. Keep sticking and countering, don't get in too close. Let him do the crowding. He'll come apart in five or six rounds. I'll tell you when."

Braddock brought the fight to Louis again in Round Two but was stung by right hands near round's end. By Round Four Joe could feel the 32-year-old champion slowing down. Blackburn urged Louis on. "Pour it on him a little now. Be careful, and don't shoot all you've got, but let him have a little."

Louis's punches were taking effect. Braddock's eyes were swollen, and he was cut on his forehead. In the sixth, Louis landed a right that split the Cinderella Man's lip. When the bell sounded for Round Eight, Louis could see the champ was finished. Above the crowd Joe heard Jimmy's manager Joe Gould screaming, "Keep your hands up!"

The Bomber blasted Braddock with a left to the body and right to the chin that corkscrewed the Cinderella Man to the canvas. *DOA*, Louis thought as he headed toward a neutral corner, referencing a term he learned in Detroit gyms during his amateur days, DOA an acronym for "Dead on his ass."

The *Chicago Tribune*'s Arch Ward, who four years earlier had dreamed up the hugely successful Major League Baseball All-Star Game—the inaugural of which was held in the same Comiskey Park—described the end of one era and start of another:

"Braddock's knees sagged. He did not stagger back as he might have from a less deadly wallop. He started to sink slowly but certainly."

Face down on the ring floor, Braddock barely moved as referee Tommy Thomas counted out the fallen king at 1:10. Louis looked across the heads of 50,000 fans in the crowd and felt "in a complete daze." The former cotton picker was now heavyweight champion of the world.

The new champion's dressing room was crowded with reporters, governors from across the country, mayors from several big cities, high society types, movie stars, and baseball players. Blackburn grabbed Louis's right glove, the one that had won his fighter—a Black man—the title.

"I'm gonna take this glove," Blackburn said. "I earned it."

Amid the commotion, Louis told reporters, "Bring on Schmeling."

Fans, sportsmen, and politicians on both sides of the Atlantic echoed the Bomber's demands. Joe defended his title three times before signing for the long-awaited rematch. Both men would get what they wanted. For Louis, that meant redemption. For Schmeling, it was another shot at the title. For millions of fans around the world, it meant the much-anticipated fight was finally a reality.

In the interim since their first fight, Louis had visited US president Franklin Roosevelt in Washington, DC, and Schmeling had gone to Berlin and posed for photos with Hitler. Everyone from the Democrat in the White House to the dictator in the Reichstag had a stake in Louis-Schmeling II.

Blackburn instructed sparring partners to fire right hands at Louis's head. Bundists began hanging around Joe's training camp at Pompton Lakes. They watched him work out and laughed at "America's African Auxiliary," as Nazi propaganda minister Josef Goebbels mockingly called Louis. The Bundists strutted around Joe's training grounds with Swastikas on their sleeves. The Bomber boiled. *Jackasses*, Louis thought. Joe knew the political picture, knew the Nazis had trumpeted Schmeling's victory over him in 1936 as proof of Aryan supremacy. Word reached Louis that Schmeling's trainer, Max Machon, was parading around in a Nazi uniform.

At the White House, FDR squeezed the Bomber's bicep. "Joe, we're depending on these muscles for America." Louis nodded. The president's words thrilled the champion. *The whole country*, he thought, *is depending on me.*

Louis was no longer the savior of Black people alone, but of all America. People of every age, in the United States and Europe and around the world, saw Louis-Schmeling as good versus evil, a force of light versus a force of darkness. If Louis could beat the Aryan Superman, then Hitler's Germany was not a master race after all.

"The irony of that second fight is that my father represented freedom and democracy and Schmeling represented fascism, but Max wasn't a fascist," Joe Louis Barrow Jr. says.

Hours before the fight Louis told friend Freddie Wilson he was scared. Wilson was surprised. Joe scared?

"Yeah," Louis replied. "Scared I might kill Schmeling tonight."

Blackburn told Louis to keep his cool. "It's going to be alright." Louis knew it and knew something else as well. "Three rounds, Chappie," he told Blackburn. "If I don't have Schmeling knocked out ... I'm through."

The Brown Bomber was planning a *blitzkrieg*, a lightning war, of his own. He had no intention of pacing himself this night. Louis would go all out at the opening bell in a seek-and-destroy mission. If it wasn't mission accomplished by the end of Round Three, Joe figured the enormous energy expended in his daring plan would leave him exhausted. If that happened, the champion would be finished.

At 10:00 p.m. in New York, a Yankee Stadium crowd of 72,000 and a worldwide radio audience estimated at 70 million, the largest in history, turned their attention to this enormous event. It was close to 3:00 a.m. in Germany but Hitler, Goebbels, and much of the Fatherland was tuned to the broadcast. Heading to the ring Louis felt like a racehorse at the starting gate. Here was America's real Man O' War. Sweat poured from every pore in Louis's body.

Donovan brought the principals together at center ring for prefight instructions. Returning to their corners, Schmeling stood impassively; Louis couldn't stop moving. "I was rarin' to go," Joe remembered.

The bell rang and the champion leapt from his corner. Two left hooks snapped the challenger's head back. Joe followed with a right to the jaw and danced away from Max's meal ticket, the counter right. Super confident, Louis drove Schmeling into the ropes with right hands. NBC Radio broadcaster Clem McCarthy, in a gravelly voice described as a "whiskey tenor," informed listeners Louis was landing "more blows in this one round then he landed in five rounds of the other fight."

A great roar shook Yankee Stadium. A sledgehammer right to the jaw sent Schmeling staggering backward like a drunken man. Louis saw Schmeling's legs shake. Max's face, McCarthy noted, "is already marked." Time for the kill, Louis thought. The Bomber moved in, measured Max, and fired half a dozen devastating punches to head and body. In staccato tones McCarthy reported that Louis "brought over a hard one to the jaw and again a right to the body, a left hook, a right to the head, a left to the head, a right!"

The last was a piston-like right to the body. Schmeling turned his torso to avoid the punishment and took the blow in his lower back. He screamed in agony, a tortured cry that ringsiders could vividly recall years later. Schmeling's knees sagged; his face was resting on the top rope, his dazed eyes looking out toward the crowd. Donovan stepped in and gave Schmeling a "one" count. Max grabbed the top rope to stop from falling. He turned sideways, his eyes blinking, his face contorted in pain.

"Schmeling," McCarthy yelled into his mic, "looked to his corner in helplessness."

The Bomber's body blow paralyzed Schmeling. Unable to move his legs to get away from danger or raise his arms to defend himself, Schmeling was in no-man's-land. Rocked by a perfectly placed right cross to the jaw, Max pitched forward to the floor.

McCarthy: "Schmeling is down!"

Max rolled over and got up but was still unable to avoid Joe. Louis rushed forward and landed a series of rapid rights and lefts. Down went Schmeling again, this time for a "two" count. The German radio broadcast suddenly fell silent; it was said later that Goebbels ordered it cut. When Louis heard that the German broadcast had been stopped, he smiled. They didn't want their people to know, the Bomber said, that a Black man from America was beating the hell out of an Aryan superman.

A rib-crunching right hand, followed by a left to the shoulder that straightened Schmeling up for the clincher—a right hand to the side of the head—returned Max to the canvas. Machon threw a white towel into the ring signaling surrender; an angry Donovan tossed it out. Fearing for their fighter's very life, Schmeling's handlers hurried into the ring.

McCarthy: "The men are in the ring . . . The fight is over!"

The *New York Times* reported that the count was "five" but noted, "Donovan could have counted off a century and Max would not have regained his feet. The German was thoroughly 'out.'"

The long-awaited rematch lasted just 2:04. A year after winning the title, Louis finally felt like a true champion. He had his revenge and damn, he thought, it was sweet. On that night Louis was arguably the greatest fighter in ring history. Boxing historian Tommy Dix has studied film of Louis-Schmeling II and doesn't believe any heavyweight ever could have defeated the Louis who destroyed Schmeling.

"That man that night was unbelievable," said Dix. "If anybody was an assassin, it was Joe Louis that night."

"The second Schmeling fight was one of the three great fights of my father's career," states Joe Louis Barrow Jr., who cites the titular win over Braddock and the first fight with Billy Conn as the other two great fights.

While fans filled the streets to celebrate, Schmeling was taken to Polytechnic Hospital. The beaten challenger suffered fractures of the vertebrae and badly bruised back muscles. Released from the hospital Schmeling returned to Germany on a stretcher. Five months after the fight, on the night of November 9, Schmeling, never a Nazi, sheltered Jewish people in his hotel suite in Berlin on *Kristallnacht.*

Louis's sensational victory vaulted him into the status of conquering hero; whites as well as Blacks were drawn to him "Louis was the first black athlete white kids would imitate," boxing historian Douglas Cavanaugh says. "He was a hero long before Jackie Robinson."

Says William Detloff, "Louis was popular. He had remarkable appeal."

His rival defeated; Louis looked for new worlds to conquer. His next big fight came a year later against "Two Ton" Tony Galento. A brawler from Orange, New Jersey, the 5-foot-9, 235-pound Galento got his nickname after telling his manager he was nearly late for a fight because, "I had two tons of ice to deliver on my way here."

Galento was one of the more colorful personalities in ring history. He trained on beer, spaghetti and meatballs, and to promote his bouts, would fight a kangaroo or wrestle an octopus; he once boxed a 550-pound bear. Showman though he was, Galento owned a left hook that he boasted in his North Jersey lingo could "moider" opponents. Matched with Louis, Galento crowed that he would "moider da bum." The Bomber brushed off Two Ton's braggadocio. "People like a different kind of person," Louis reasoned, "and Tony was it."

Rocky Marciano, a rugged character in the ring, once called Galento "the roughest, toughest street fighter in the fight game." Entertainer Jackie Gleason found that to be true when he was doing stand-up comedy at the Miami Club in Newark, New Jersey. The club was nicknamed the "Bucket of Blood" for its rugged clientele, and the self-proclaimed "Great One" was being heckled one night by a short, balding man in the front row. Gleason invited the heckler to step outside onto Clinton Avenue, and as soon as they hit the street, Gleason said, "Now you're going ..."

The next thing Gleason recalled he was on the floor of the cellar of the Bucket of Blood. Regaining consciousness, he asked the doctor attending him, "Who was that guy?"

"Tony Galento."

Gleason was shocked. "Did you know it was Tony Galento?"

"Sure!"

"Why didn't you tell me?"

Galento's street tactics worked not only against Gleason but also against Louis. Two Ton attacked the Bomber like it was the kind of brawl he engaged in years later while playing an enforcer for fictional mob boss Johnny Friendly years later in the film *On the Waterfront*. Tony's feared left hook staggered Joe. "Everything glazed over," Louis remembered. After the round Blackburn steadied his champion. "He's strong but a bluff. Box him!"

In Round Two Louis lifted Galento off the canvas with a blistering right hand to the side of the head followed by a left hook to the jaw. Tony emerged for Round Three bleeding from his eyes, nose, and mouth and with gobs of salve over both eyes. Louis knew he had Galento beaten, but his confidence betrayed him. To his credit Tony came out firing and a counter left hook put Louis down for the first time since the Braddock fight. The Bomber quickly arose and the two banged one another with a bevy of blows. In Round Four Joe tagged Tony with a crushing right to the jaw that ripped Galento's mouth and backed him into the ropes. Louis followed with a series of devastating punches, capped by two over-hand rights and a left hook that sent Galento stumbling blindly into the ropes, where he collapsed. Louis later praised Galento for his ability to take a punch.

"I must have thrown a hundred hard punches to his head before he finally fell to his knees," Louis said later.

Galento sank to the floor and Donovan halted the massacre. It reportedly took Galento's cornermen, Whitey Bimstein and Joe Jacobs, five minutes to revive their fighter. Louis would defend his title five times over the next 18 months. Like everyone else, he cast a wary eye at world events. No one knew what would happen next. But as the calendar flipped to 1941 the heavyweight champion of the world knew one thing.

"This," Louis thought, "is going to be one hell of a year."

# CHAPTER TWO

# PITTSBURGH KID

"Let's give credit where credit is due, and credit certainly goes to Billy Conn for one of the greatest exhibitions of slugging, of boxing, of footwork that we've seen in Madison Square Garden."

NBC Radio announcer Bill Stern's commentary on the light heavyweight champion during his 15-round decision over Gus Lesnevich on November 17, 1939, perfectly captured what many boxing experts believed about the Pittsburgh Kid. Sam Taub, Stern's broadcast partner, told his radio audience that Conn is "a great champion who put up a remarkable exhibition of boxing skill and hard punching. Truly a man who may go on some day to become our heavyweight king."

Taub wasn't the only one who believed Billy the Kid was the boy who would be king. Conn believed it too. He knew the time was coming when he would face Joe Louis for the Brown Bomber's title. It's what Conn dreamed of when he gave up his hard-earned championship belt after defeating Lesnevich a second time over 15 rounds on June 5, 1940, and began taking on heavyweights.

By his own account Billy had been waiting for this chance since he was a kid growing up in the East Liberty section of Pittsburgh. William David Conn was born in the Steel City to first-generation Irish immigrants William Conn Sr. and Margaret "Maggie" McFarland on October 8, 1917; a true son of the Emerald Isle, Billy's grandfather, Joseph R. Conn, hailed from a small town in county Tyrone, Northern Ireland, according to Tim Conn. Billy's mother Margaret was born in County Antrim, also located in Northern Ireland.

Billy was the oldest of the Conn children, their father working 40 years as a steamfitter for Westinghouse Electric Company. "His father took him when he was a kid to the mills and said, 'This is where you'll work the rest of your life,'" Tim Conn says. "Scared my father to death."

Scared him right into Johnny Ray's run-down East Liberty gym, the Kid first wandering in on a hot summer's day in 1928. Ray remembered Billy as one of the "little hero-worshipping kids" who went into his place every afternoon to watch fighters train. Ray told *Sports Illustrated* that the first time he saw the kid who would become his most famous protégé, Billy's head was only as big as Johnny's small fist. Billy had a baby face, and the curly-haired, dimpled look of the altar boy that he was.

A lithe 100-pounder with sparrow-wing shoulder blades, the Kid was chased out of the gym and pushed around by bigger boys. Pushes turned to punches, which suited Billy fine. "I never did anything in my life but fight," he said once. "I liked to fight."

Billy would say he started fighting in the alleys and had to work his way up to the streets. "It was a long time," he stated, "before I got to the street from the alley."

When he wasn't fighting neighborhood toughs, Billy was battling with his kid brother, Jackie. The Conns were a fighting clan. Billy Sr. was nearly 50 years old when he was fined for street fighting in the summer of 1941. His son told New York sportswriters, "My old man is a fighting mick." Give his father a day or two in Gotham, Billy said, and he'd find some guys to slug it out with. The lure of the street was passed on to his sons. Billy and Jackie brawled in back alleys, and it was said by wizened New York writer Jimmy Cannon that if boxing rings were made of cobblestones rather than canvas, Jackie would be a world champion.

The Conns stood straight and tall, young Billy demonstrating as much when he was told by Ray, "Look out boy, you're blocking the way to the dressing room. The fighters can't get past you!"

"Let me get in the ring with them and they won't get past me, either!"

"Okay, punk," replied Ray. "Let's see if you're as good as you talk. Put on these gloves and get in there with Angelo."

Angelo was 20 pounds heavier than Billy and sneered as the dirty-faced Kid pulled on the oversized sparring gloves. Yet it was Conn who was the aggressor, his bony arms windmilling in a style similar to his ring idol, fellow Pittsburgh native Harry Greb.

"I think maybe you got it, son," Ray said, throwing an arm around the Kid's shoulders. "We'll see. Come back every day after school. We'll teach you how to box."

He asked the Kid his name.

"Billy . . . Billy Conn."

Johnny Ray knew the Conn family; he and Billy Sr. spent many an afternoon bending elbows at an East Liberty bar. Knowing his boy Billy was a regular in Johnny's gym, Bill Sr. struck a deal with Ray.

"I'll give you a buck a week if you let him in the gym," the elder Conn stated, "and teach him a few things about boxing."

A buck a week in those Depression days could buy a couple of meals—or four drinks—depending on one's preference. Johnny took "Pop," as he called Bill Sr., up on his deal. Billy became an accepted visitor at Ray's gym, no longer subject to being chased out by bigger boys. Five days later Billy went off to a corner and when he thought no one was watching, began shadowboxing.

"So help me, as soon as he put up those little fists and made his first move," Ray recalled once, "I fell in love with him. From that day on, Conn, Ray and Company went into business."

Ray knew boxing. "He was a good fighter," says Tim Conn, "a stable mate of Harry Greb. Johnny was with Greb all the time."

Greb was idolized by 'Burghers, the Conn family among them. When Billy's mother Maggie was dying in the summer of 1941, it was important for her to know she would be buried as close to Greb as possible in Pittsburgh's Calvary Cemetery.

Greb earned renown as the "Pittsburgh Windmill" for his nonstop punching and relentless style. Light heavyweight champion from 1922 to 1923, Greb fought in 299 official bouts according to the International Boxing Hall of Fame, as well as several unofficial punch-ups in the street. Among his many victories is a 15-round decision over Gene Tunney, the only loss the future heavyweight champ ever endured. Greb died suddenly in 1926 at age 32 from heart failure while undergoing an operation to repair damage to his broken nose and respiratory tract.

"Harry Greb was my dad's boxing idol," Tim Conn says. Yet Billy remained his own man; despite his admiration for Greb, Billy never tried to copy Harry. It's unlikely anyone could.

"Greb was a freak of nature," Tim Conn states. "He just swarmed all over you in the ring."

Ray shared some of Greb's leathery toughness; Johnny was never stopped in 138 bouts, according to a search by Luckett Davis of Pittsburgh newspapers. Ray won 68 bouts by decision, 15 by knockout, and was a skilled and elusive boxer, traits he would pass on to his protégés, most famously Billy.

"Johnny was great in the beginning," Tim Conn states. "He was drunk a lot; my father called him 'Moonie,' which was short for 'Moonshine.' But my father would say, 'Johnny knew more drunk than most guys who are sober.'

"He taught my father when he was young the right things to do, like keep his hands up high. Johnny would tell my father, 'See that telephone pole over there? What's the quickest way to get there? Go straight at it. Same thing with throwing punches. Throw them straight, don't throw roundhouse punches.'

"Johnny was a great boxer; I don't think he was ever knocked down. [Pittsburgh middleweight] Al Quail was a pretty good fighter. He told me, 'I boxed your dad 1,200 rounds in the gym. Your dad made Johnny Ray; Johnny Ray didn't make your dad.'"

Billy Sr. gave his boys boxing gloves one Christmas, and Maggie made a pair of boxing trunks as green as the grass in Ireland. Billy was less interested in his studies; at Sacred Heart Grammar School, he and several other boys were confronted by a nun. "Why don't some of you big boys get out of here and go to a trade school? All you do is keep the smaller children out!"

Leaving school in the eighth grade, Billy began boxing in earnest. As he grew and gained weight, he would graduate from welterweight to middleweight and to light heavyweight. Since he only had interest in fighting for money, Billy never boxed as an amateur. Instead, he sparred with seasoned pros in Ray's gym.

"I worked there three years," Conn recalled in a 1988 article in the *Pittsburgh Post-Gazette*, "and got lots of practice against some real good talent who worked out there."

The Steel City where Conn came of age in the 1930s had been hard hit by the Depression. Tough times led hungry young men desperate to make a buck into boxing gyms in and around Pittsburgh. The city became a destination for Henry Armstrong, John Henry Lewis, Al Gainer, and Holman Williams, the latter being one of Joe Louis's mentors. Master trainers such as Johnny Ray, Jack Blackburn, and Ray Arcel all taught boxing in Steel City gyms and fight clubs.

Douglas Cavanaugh, who authored the book *Pittsburgh Boxing: A Pictorial History*, says the Depression proved beneficial for competitive sports like boxing. "It did so by becoming the great catalyst and motivator for young men who wanted to break free from the dismal economic circumstances and make something better for themselves and their families."

Billy worked with Johnny in their gym, learning Ray's shell defense ("Hands high, chin low") and setting his sights on the pros. "Why fight for tin watches," Ray reasoned, "when you can be making good money for the same work?"

Ray had Billy, whom he took to calling "Junior," work with pros who visited East Liberty. Among the visitors was middleweight great Mickey Walker, a tough guy known as the "Toy Bulldog."

"Get in there with a guy like Mickey Walker," Ray told Billy, "and you'll come out a real fighter."

The Kid shrugged and climbed into the ring with the famous former champ. Conn surprised Walker with his speedy hands and feet. Three hard rounds later, Walker told Ray, "The lad's got what it takes."

The Walker sparring session marked the first time Conn earned money in the ring, Mickey giving him $10. Ray grabbed half of the money and from that point on he and Billy split their purses 50-50.

Walker wasn't the only famous champ the Kid would dazzle in a sparring session. Visiting Oakdale, California, on September 12, 1934, the teenaged Conn boxed three rounds with then heavyweight champion Max Baer.

"This is not only an honor," Ray told Billy, "it'll get in all the papers and it'll save us a year on the road."

At 6-4, 220 pounds, Baer dwarfed the skinny Conn. The champ toyed with the Kid in a fatherly way for the first few moments of the session, but that changed when Billy bloodied the big man's nose with a lightning left. Wiping away the blood, Baer was done clowning with Conn. Yet for the following three rounds the heavyweight champion of the world could barely land a meaningful punch on the teenage sensation. Onlookers were stunned and broke into spontaneous applause at the final bell.

"My only advice to you, son," Baer told Conn, "is don't grow up! At least, not until after I retire!"

Said Ray, "That big bum couldn't lay a glove on my Junior."

Billy was 15 when Johnny told Billy Sr., "Your kid is a hell of a fighter. In my book he's ready to make money. I'm asking for your okay." The elder Conn nodded, and Junior and Johnny said so long to East Liberty. The Kid was just 16 years old when he had his first professional fight, losing a four-round decision to the more experienced Dick Woodward in West Virginia on June 28, 1934. For his troubles Billy's purse was $2.50.

Conn's first pro victory came in his next outing less than a month later on July 20 when he knocked out Johnny Lewis in three rounds in Valley Bell Park in Charleston, West Virginia. Conn won his following two fights—including his hometown debut that saw him defeat Paddy Gray—before losing to Pete Leone. Billy would suffer seven defeats in his first 15 bouts before hitting his stride.

Billy and Johnny hitchhiked, rode the rails, fast-talked conductors into free rides, and took fights where they could. If Billy lost a bout, he and Johnny wound up on the short end of the purse and stayed in a cheap motel. When Billy won, they spent their earnings on first-class accommodations.

Conn would tell author Peter Heller in 1971 that he didn't know how to fight at the start of his career, that he was learning on the go. "It was like going to school," Conn said, "learning how to box."

It was a School of Hard Knocks and the Pittsburgh Kid, as Conn came to be called, took his lumps and learned his lessons. Conn's motivation was clear. He wanted to be the best; "I didn't want to be a bum."

Writer Mila Sanina opined that no athlete captured the Pittsburgh ethos more fully than Billy Conn. The Pittsburgh Kid, writes Sanina, was "a tough and spirited underdog."

When Billy and Johnny returned to Pittsburgh, the Kid told his manager, "In no time, we'll own this town."

It was during Conn's first months as a fighter that he met the man with whom he would make sports history. On January 11, 1935, promising young heavyweight Joe Louis arrived in Pittsburgh's Duquesne Gardens for a 10-round bout with veteran Hans Birkie. Louis was 20 years old, Conn 17. Billy helped work Joe's corner, handling the spit bucket for the Brown Bomber. A 10th-round stoppage improved Louis's record to 14-0.

Following a loss in August 1935 to Teddy Movan, Billy beat George Liggins the following month to begin a 28-bout unbeaten streak that stretched into late summer 1937. Writer Monte Cox notes that most of the defeats Conn suffered early in his career can be attributed to the fact that he started fighting professionally when he was very young, having turned pro at such a tender age. Because he had never boxed in the amateur ranks, Billy's defeats early in his career came against older, stronger, and more experienced professionals.

Says Tim Conn, "The whole idea is to make money. Johnny would tell my father, 'These amateurs aren't any better than you are. You aren't going to learn anything from them.'

"Johnny wanted my father to fight better fighters so he sort of threw him to the wolves, fighting more experienced fighters. They were all good fighters, ranked fighters. My father learned from them."

Billy learned so well that many, including Louis and Madison Square Garden matchmaker Harry Markson, called Conn the best light heavyweight they ever saw.

"Markson said the only problem he ever saw with my father was that he was lazy when he wasn't fighting ranked fighters," Tim Conn says. "My father rose to the competition. Willie Pep told me, 'Your dad was the best light heavyweight I ever saw.'"

As he matured physically and polished his skills, Billy endured just three defeats over the following six years; each of those came via decisions to world champions. By the time he was 20, the Kid had defeated five world champions along with a future champ and fellow Hall of Famer in Fritzie Zivic.

A Pittsburgh native like Conn, Zivic met Billy on December 28, 1936, at Duquesne Gardens. The contract for the fight stipulated that Conn couldn't weigh more than 160 and Zivic not less than 150. At the weigh-in, Conn was heavier than 160, Zivic lighter than 150. Because both men had a $1,000 forfeit in their contract, Conn had to quickly shed weight and Zivic had to promptly put on pounds.

Billy called Fritzie "real tough, real experienced." In just his third year as a pro, Conn compared the education he got fighting Zivic for 10 rounds to going to college for five years. He told Heller that while Zivic would do everything but kick you, the minute Billy retaliated Fritzie would holler and scream. Zivic put what Conn recalled as "an awful face" on his handsome countenance: "busted me all up," said Billy, who thought Zivic the dirtiest fighter he ever encountered.

Zivic believed his roughhouse tactics had been enough to earn him the decision. "The referee gave it to me, and the papers gave it to me," Zivic told Heller. The ringside judges awarded the split decision to Conn, giving him his 18th victory of that year alone. Zivic considered Conn at that time to be a good boxer but weak puncher. "Couldn't knock your hat off," said Fritzie.

Conn beat world champs Babe Risko and Vince Dundee and ran his win streak to 24 before losing on points over 10 rounds to Young

Corbett III in August 1937. Billy evened the score three months later with a 10-round unanimous decision over Corbett. He lost his next outing the following month to Solly Krieger but won a return match in November 1938.

Conn knew that facing experienced pros like Zivic, Krieger, and murderous-punching Oscar Rankins taught him how to fight. Rankins's blows rivaled a mule's kick; Conn called him the hardest puncher he ever faced. Knocked down by Rankins in the second round of their May 1937 bout, Billy fought back and won a 10-round split decision, but as late as the next day had no recollection of the fight's outcome.

"The Oscar Rankins fight, my dad thought he was knocked out," Tim Conn says. "He apologized for it. Dad didn't know until the next day when he read the newspapers that he won. Joe Louis told my dad, 'Your manager must not have liked you to let you fight Rankins. My people wouldn't let me fight him.'"

Krieger was another fighter Conn learned from. Billy said he was out of shape for his fight with Krieger in December 1937 and Solly fixed him up, "banged me all over the place." Following the loss by decision, Conn vowed to never again be out of condition for a fight.

Six wins in seven fights in 1938, including a 12-round unanimous decision over Krieger in their rematch, earned Conn the coveted call to New York by boxing promoter Mike Jacobs. It had taken five years, but Billy was finally going to fight in a featured main event in famed Madison Square Garden. His opponent would be middleweight champion Fred Apostoli. Fate had lent a hand in the Kid's destiny; Ceferino Garcia, who was scheduled to meet Apostoli, injured his right hand and arm during training.

Jacobs heard about the Pittsburgh Kid who fought with fire and flash. Uncle Mike's talent scouts told him, "This boy is headed straight for the title."

"Which title?"

"*Any* title. Depends on how big he grows."

"Book him!" Uncle Mike growled.

It was at this time that Freddie Fierro first met the Kid he would help train to become one of the greatest boxers ever. Fierro was working in the Pioneer Gym in New York and received a message that someone wanted to see him. Fierro saw two men standing in the doorway. Freddie recognized Johnny immediately. "Jolly little guy, with a shoved in face and a mop of sandy hair which always hung into his eyes."

Ray turned to the young man standing next to him.

"Freddie, this is the Billy Conn I told you about."

The Kid shoved out his hand. "Hiya Fat."

Fierro flashed a furious look at the pugnacious Conn. "Don't mind him," Ray said. "He's always sounding off."

Ray added that he had just two weeks to get Billy ready for the Apostoli fight and wanted Fierro to help train the Kid.

"Conn," Fierro said, "be here at 9 [a.m.] tomorrow."

Billy turned to leave. "So long, Fat."

Fierro blew up. "What's this Fat business?"

"I don't know. You just look fat to me, that's all."

Like Ray before him, Fierro grew fond of the Kid. "To watch him in the ring you'd think he'd been turned out in a factory, he was that perfect," Fierro told writer Hal Hennesey. "Poetry in motion, you might say."

Billy was a student of his business. Fierro recalled Conn working like a coalminer, spending hours each day exercising, running for miles, sparring, and practicing his punches. Billy read every book he could find on boxing and kept a suitcase full of clippings on the fight game. He underlined key passages in blue pencil, studied fight films of the great champions, and picked the brains of veteran fighters like Tony Canzoneri and Abe Attell. "A perfectionist," Fierro called Conn.

Fierro would learn that training Conn wasn't just a job; it was a complicated experience. No one made Billy a great fighter, Fierro thought. The Kid was born with a chip on his shoulders and clenched fists. Freddie's job was to control Conn, keep him in check, smother Billy's burning temper. Over the next 10 years Fierro would become the Kid's Father Confessor, close friend, and trainer.

Fierro said Billy boasted and bragged but sincerely believed he could beat any fighter in the world. Because Billy's personality was like talcum powder—"it rubbed off on people," Fierro said—the Kid's confidence was shared by those closest to him.

On the night of January 6, 1939, Conn climbed through the ropes for the first of two memorable bouts with Apostoli, the man he called his toughest opponent ever. The match marked not only Conn's Madison Square Garden debut but also his first fight in New York.

A classmate of Joe DiMaggio—they grew up in the same North Beach neighborhood in San Francisco—Apostoli was a lifelong friend of the "Yankee Clipper." Fred was called the "Boxing Bell Hop" because as a teen he had worked in a hotel. Conn called Apostoli something else—"a great fighter." Billy found in fighting Apostoli that he couldn't make a mistake because Freddie could box and punch. Jacobs thought so highly of Apostoli he tried to match him with Louis.

"How much *can* you weigh?" Uncle Mike asked.

Realizing that a proposed fight with Louis was prompting the promoter's question, Apostoli balked. "Are you crazy?" Apostoli asked.

That Apostoli was a skilled fighter was evident in his features. "There wasn't a mark on him," Conn observed.

Nor was there an ounce of fear in Billy. Fighting in the Mecca of Boxing before the biggest crowd of his career to that point didn't frighten Conn; the Pittsburgh Kid would make this Garden his Eden. On their walk from their hotel to MSG, Conn casually threw an arm around the shaking shoulders of Johnny Ray.

"Now, Jawnny," Billy said. "Stop worrying. Nothing can happen to me tonight. You know there's nobody in the world can beat me. And New York doesn't scare me a bit."

Ray was amazed. It was Billy, he stated in the May 1941 issue of *Collier's* magazine, who should have been the nervous one. After all, Billy was but a kid, barely 21 years old. Not only would Conn be facing a fine, smart fighter in Apostoli, he would be doing so in front of a big New York crowd.

Apostoli won the middleweight title in September 1937 with a 10th-round technical knockout of Marcel Thil. Although the New York Boxing Commission withheld its recognition, Apostoli's eighth-round TKO of Young Corbett III on November 18, 1938, dispelled all doubts and earned him recognition as world champion.

Two months later the middleweight champion, sporting a 34-2 record, took on Conn. A prefight publicity photo depicts the height difference between the two men, the 6-foot-1½ Conn towering over Apostoli, whose official height was listed at 5'9½" but was reported to be closer to 5'7".

Boxing writers picked Apostoli to beat Conn. Since Billy had outgrown the middleweight division, Apostoli's title was at stake. Because it was a non-title bout, the fight was scheduled for 10 rounds rather than the 15 rounds customary for championship contests. The New York crowd cheered Apostoli and jeered Conn. "They'll be laughing out of the other sides of their mouths in an hour," the Kid told Ray and Fierro.

What took place was one of the great fights of 1939 and one of the more memorable bouts of that era. Sportscaster Bill Stern said later he didn't believe any fighter ever made a more auspicious debut in Madison Square Garden than Conn.

Fierro would never forget the night Conn was unveiled in New York. Freddie heard the "oohs" and "aahs" from the Garden crowd as Conn and his corner men strutted toward the ring. "What a handsome sight he was," Fierro said of Conn, "curly hair bouncing as he walked; laughing and waving and flashing a perfect set of white teeth; bright green robe with his name written in across the back in white letters; not a mark on his face and those funny dimples around his cheeks. The men in the place hated him on sight but the ladies loved him."

The Associated Press reported the bout being "as wild and wooly a 10-round punch party as MSG's fistic arena has seen in years. . . . From start to finish the blistering action had the crowd roaring as the two clouters tore at each other." The Garden crowd of 10,918 thrilled at the sight of the rugged body-puncher trying to work his way inside the defenses of the dancing master.

Beginning in Rounds Two and Three, Conn's looping left hand kept the smaller Apostoli from getting in close. The AP reported that Apostoli, a crouching tiger, was the more aggressive fighter and effective puncher. At the end of Round Five he landed a right hand that cut Conn's cheek and staggered him. The Kid recovered and his flashy left hand consistently "piled up valuable points," according to the AP. Sports cartoonist Jack Sords said Conn's boxing skill reminded him of Tunney.

At fight's end, Conn's jarring combinations earned him a unanimous decision. Referee Billy Cavanaugh scored it 5–2–3, judges Bill Healy and George LeCron 5–4–1 and 6–4, respectively. The unofficial AP scorecard saw Conn the winner by the slimmest of margins, 5–4–1.

"He did a job on Apostoli," Fierro said.

The rematch was held just over a month later, February 10. Frenzied fight fans, recalling the 10-round war, packed Madison Square Garden for a sequel that was scheduled for 15. Sitting ringside was the radio team of Stern and Taub. Stern began his color analysis of the main event noting that the appearance of Conn, "the happy-go-lucky smiling Irish lad," brought a tremendous roar from his fans. Above the noise, ring announcer Harry Balogh bellowed the introductions of the two principals.

The first round accentuated the height difference between Conn and Apostoli. Taub told his listeners Apostoli was moving forward out of a crouch—"his left shoulder high, his head low"—while Conn stood straight and tall. Yet their difference in height was dwarfed by their difference in nationalities; their ring war became an Irish versus Italian feud escalated by a series of racial slurs.

Conn claimed that Apostoli started roughing him up on the inside. Billy stepped back and warned Apostoli. "Listen, you dago bastard, keep your thumb out of my eye!"

Apostoli fired back, "You Irish son of a bitch. Quit beefin' and fight!"

Because the ring microphone was lowered, the crowd of 18,988 that included trainloads of Billy's fans from Pittsburgh, many of them wearing shamrock green papier-mâché hats, heard every racial insult. They roared as one of the wildest Garden parties in years got into full swing. "We had a hell of a fight," Conn told *Sports Illustrated* in 1966.

The fireworks started in the first round when a flashbulb from a ringside photographer's camera exploded and sent shattered glass flying into the ring. A pattern was established early. Conn would dance and move, inviting the crouching Apostoli to advance and then pop him with an educated left jab and solid right. When Apostoli got in close, he cut loose with hard lefts and rights to Billy's ribs.

"They really traded some wicked punches," Stern said between Rounds One and Two.

The nonstop action continued in Round Two, rousing the rabid fans in the Garden. "The crowd is going haywire!" Taub exclaimed. Billy was animated as well, complaining to the referee that Apostoli was fouling him in close. As he refused at times to wear a mouthpiece—the Pittsburgh Kid loved to insult opponents—Conn's complaints could be heard loud and clear.

Conn cursed Apostoli and Fred responded. "Stop talking, you Irish son of a bitch, and come on and fight!"

"I'm coming!" an enraged Conn snapped.

The bitter rivalry excited spectators. Stern noted the "complete reversal" in Conn's fight plan. Five weeks before, Billy had been content to box his way to a victory by decision. The rematch saw the Kid going all out for a knockout.

The torrid pace continued round after round, resulting in a fight described by reporters as a "bloodbath." Cheered on by their Irish and Italian fan bases, Conn and Apostoli fought furiously. Billy unleashed a barrage of blinding left jabs, quick right crosses, and hard left hooks in attempts to slow Apostoli's relentless body attack. The two men mauled along the ropes and in the corners; Conn would call this fight his toughest ever. In the middle rounds Taub described the action as "a couple of railroad trains" colliding with one another.

Low punches and backhand blows mixed with sizzling hooks to the head and right hands ripped to the ribs. "Dynamite in both hands," Taub declared of the fierce, two-fisted action. Amid the sound and fury, Conn remained as Taub said, "mighty cool."

Taub: "He's one of the coolest fellows we've seen in the ring in many years . . . Just like an iceberg."

In Round 12, Conn caught Apostoli with a right to the chin and left to the body. Apostoli staggered and sought to survive by bobbing and weaving. Conn's offense electrified the crowd and excited Taub.

Taub: "A beautiful boxer is Conn, and a good puncher!"

Late in the fight another pattern emerged that saw Conn dominate the first half of the round before Apostoli bullied Billy in the final 90 seconds. Drenched in perspiration, cut and bloodied, Conn and Apostoli flailed away with rights and lefts as their fight rushed to its conclusion. Stern noted at the end of Round 13 that this bout meant a great deal to both fighters.

Stern: "For Apostoli it means the vindication of his class, for which he is the titleholder. For Conn it means that he can go into the light heavyweight class convinced he is the master of anything the middle-weight class can offer."

The 15th round proved a fitting ending to an enduring effort by both men. "A pair of tigers!" Taub stated at the height of the nonstop action in the final round. At the bell Conn and Apostoli shook gloved hands as the Garden lights were turned on and a shower of torn paper was let loose by exuberant fans in the balconies.

Conn was awarded a close but unanimous decision, winning 9–6 in rounds on two judges' cards and 8–7 on the third. Interviewed in the ring, a happy but exhausted Conn told fans it was "one of the greatest fights I was ever in with the greatest fighter I think there is today." Years later Conn would say of Apostoli, "He could really fight!"

Billy's bloodied face was wrapped in yards of bandages that left Conn looking like Boris Karloff's lead character in the 1932 horror movie, *The*

*Mummy.* A photographer snapped a picture of Conn that remains famous in boxing circles.

"Those (Apostoli) fights were so hard-fought," Tim Conn says. "I don't think there was a clinch in the whole fight. My dad always said Apostoli gave him his hardest fights. His favorite photo was of himself in the hospital after the second fight with his face all wrapped in bandages; he had a lot of cuts. A caption in the newspaper said, 'If this is the winner, what does the loser look like?' Apostoli didn't have a mark on him! I think my dad was an underdog in both fights. He always said what a great fighter Apostoli was."

Following the Apostoli rematch Billy was called on the carpet of boxing commissioner General John Phelan. The general wasn't happy with the rough language used in the ring.

Billy threw on the charm. "Why, general, you know I'm an old altar boy," the Kid said with a syrupy smile. "It was that dago doing all the talking."

Conn was no choir boy, and he didn't pretend to be. Like Kid McCoy and Greb before him, Conn cursed opponents. He caroused with young women eager to spend time with Sweet William. Ray worried about Conn's stamina but discovered that in Billy's case, time spent with women seemed to make the Kid stronger.

The Conn-Apostoli bouts were non-title fights, but the frenzy with which they were fought, and the fierce loyalties of the large crowds, reflected the tumultuous times. In his climb through the professional ranks, Billy battled the best young fighters of various ethnic backgrounds. He had two rugged wars with Apostoli, three fights with Jewish Solly Krieger, three with Polish Teddy Yarosz, and notable bouts with Black boxers Oscar Rankins and Roscoe Manning.

The ethnic mix reflected the melting pot that was Pittsburgh, a smoky city whose fire and heat prompted its being called "Hell with the lid off." Factories and furnaces produced a special breed of fighters. 'Burgher Buck Crouse would proudly state, "Boys fight to win in our town." That included boys of every ethnicity and race, as Monongahela middleweight "Bulldog" Harris pointed out. "If a fellow's got it, he gets a chance in the ring," he said. "Boxing and music give everybody a chance."

Douglas Cavanaugh notes that nearly every sector of the Steel City had a fighter representing its population. There were Northside Irishmen, Southside Poles, Blacks in the Upper Hill district, and Jews in the Lower Hill.

"On almost any night of the week one could find a fight card featuring pugilists of all races and ethnicities, all hungry for the promise of quick fame and fortune that only boxing could bring," says Cavanaugh. "The fighters themselves were loved by the people because they were *of* the people, many working side by side at their day jobs with the fans that came to root for them."

Cavanaugh adds that Pittsburgh matchmakers, managers, and promoters understood that neighborhood and ethnic pride translated into ticket sales; to generate revenue, bouts were often promoted as ethnic or race contests.

"The racial angle was played up and it was good box office," he says. "Black fighters flooded to Pittsburgh because there wasn't a 'color line.'"

Conn was only 19 when he fought fellow Steel City son Yarosz, who was 27 and an ex-world champion with more than 100 fights to his credit. The Kid lost one fight to Yarosz but took two sensational split decision upset victories from Teddy, who was one of the more skilled fighters in middleweight history. Billy also avenged losses to champions Corbett III and Krieger. Conn then stopped hard-hitting Ray Actis in Round Eight.

Conn's triumphs in these highly publicized ethnic encounters earned him national notoriety. William Detloff, editor of *Ringside Seat* magazine, believes Billy's best fights came at middleweight and not at light heavyweight.

"For all of his accomplishments at 175 and above, Conn's best work came at middleweight," Detloff says.

Douglas Cavanaugh agrees. "Conn was more accomplished as a middleweight. He was in his prime."

Conn's impressive victories put him in line for a light heavyweight championship bout with Melio Bettina. The fight was set for July 13, 1939 in Madison Square Garden, Billy's fourth straight bout in the arena but his first as a light heavyweight. The winner would get the chance to fight Louis for the heavyweight championship.

Ray and Fierro wondered if Melio might be too tough for Billy. The Kid was winning on the strength of his skill, self-confidence, and electric left hand. To beat Bettina Billy would need more; he would need a right-hand power punch.

Fierro called Conn's right hand "a blank cartridge." To get more leverage and power into his right cross and right uppercut, Conn spent hours in front of the heavy bag trying different ways to hold his hands and position his legs. He soon began stunning sparring partners with right-hand punches and stopped one sparring partner cold with a right hand under the heart.

Bettina, a burly southpaw, presented a pair of problems for Conn. Billy would have to deal with Bettina's unorthodox style—southpaws lead with their right hand—and with his unorthodox manager, Jimmy Grippo. Part hypnotist, part magician, and some said, a practitioner of the dark arts, Grippo would put the *malocchio*—Italian for "evil eye"—on opponents.

After Bettina beat "Tiger" Jack Fox on a ninth-round TKO at MSG for the light heavyweight title vacated by John Henry Lewis, Fox griped that he lost because Grippo had put a curse on him. Bettina scoffed at such claims. A man whose moniker was Melio the Mighty hardly needed magic to be successful. A future World Boxing Hall of Fame inductee, Bettina beat Apostoli and Krieger and took the measure of middleweights, light heavyweights, and heavyweights. In 1941 he was scheduled to meet Louis for the title, but the fight fell through. It was said that Louis disliked fighting southpaws, particularly one who could punch like Melio the Mighty.

Bettina's nephew Vinny told writer Michael Turton of the *Highlands Current* that he met Louis in Joe's retirement years and the Bomber told him it wasn't "smart business to fight your uncle in those days."

June 1936 saw Bettina play a small part in international politics. US president Franklin Roosevelt and James Forrestal, America's first secretary of defense, the latter a resident of Beacon as was Bettina, posed for pictures with the fighter. The photos were Roosevelt's response to Adolf Hitler, who celebrated Max Schmeling's victory over Louis that month by sending flowers to the fighter's wife along with a message of congratulations to "our greatest German boxer."

By the time he met Fox for the title in February 1939, Bettina was 43-6-2: an impressive ring record but one that was dwarfed by Tiger Jack's 99-15-10 mark. This being a time before television, many Beacon residents braved a snowstorm and boarded excursion trains to MSG. Those remaining in Beacon tuned their radio dials to the broadcast. If Bettina was nervous about fighting for the title, he didn't show it. Because boxer's purses were based on attendance, the only thing that frightened Melio the Mighty upon entering the ring was seeing empty seats. Because of the inclement weather, Bettina's victory over Fox earned him a purse of just $750.

If Fox fell victim to Grippo's curse, Conn didn't. He had gotten his Irish up moments before the bout, his brother Jackie stumbling into the Garden dressing room that Billy was pacing in like a caged lion. Jackie had fought on the undercard to Billy's main event and lost to Mutt Wormer. Jackie was bleeding and sporting a black eye; he was also tearing up. The sight enraged Billy.

"Get the hell outta here!" Billy shouted. "From now on there's gonna be just one fighter in this family, understand? *Me!* I'm going up there now and when I come back I'm gonna be champion. And if you're still here I'm gonna finish what Mutt Wormer started!"

Wearing a large outline of a shamrock on the left leg of his green trunks, Conn strode to the ring and showed why he was the glamour boy of boxing, why he was called "Sweet William."

Fierro would never forget the look on Conn's face as he sat in his corner waiting to be introduced to the crowd. About a hundred men and women began parading around the ring with signs reading, "Good Luck Melio" and "Beacon, New York's World Champion, Melio Bettina."

Looking at Fierro, Conn snapped, "Beacon ain't gonna have a champion an hour from now."

Stepping inside of Bettina's right-hand leads and slipping other punches with side-to-side movement, slick-boxing Billy would appear to be dancing away from Melio only to stop and fire several left jabs and uppercuts at the crouching champion. Bettina forced the action with right-hand leads to the head and left hooks to the body; Conn countered with quick combinations and fast footwork.

By Round 10 Conn was clearly outboxing Bettina. Melio mauled Billy along the ropes and outmuscled him in clinches, but Conn fought his way free and returned the action to center ring, where he could box and move. The fight was close heading into the final two rounds, and Bettina appeared to have floored Conn in the 14th with a left to the body; the referee, however, ruled it a slip. Conn continued to tattoo the right side of Bettina's face with left jabs; Melio, meanwhile, mounted ferocious assaults on Billy's body.

When the bell sounded at the end of Round 15, Balogh strode to center ring, grabbed the lowered microphone and announced, "The winner and new world light heavyweight champion, Billy Conn!" The decision was unanimous, Conn winning by scores of 8–7, 9–6, and 10–5. Still, it was disputed, the *New York Times* and others believing Bettina had won.

Following the fight, Jacobs approached Johnny. "Ray, maybe in a year or two, if you can get some meat on his bones, Billy will get a chance at the big boy."

Realizing the "big boy" was Joe Louis, Ray was taken aback. In his high-pitched voice he shrieked, "You think I wanna get my Junior killed?"

Conn had succeeded in chasing down his dream; he was king of the light heavyweights. The Pittsburgh Kid was on top of the world, professionally and personally. Billy had fallen for Mary Louise Smith, later described by son Michael Conn as "a real Pittsburgher." Doug Cavanaugh said she emanated life from "every pore of her being. She was lively, effervescent, friendly and beaming good cheer."

Mary Louise's energy and beauty captivated Billy, and "the boxer and the blonde" as they were called in a 1985 *Sports Illustrated* article written by Frank Deford, became forever linked.

A lifelong resident of Squirrel Hill, Mary Louise was the daughter of Nora and James "Greenfield Jimmy" Smith, a fiery former major-league ballplayer. He was a member of the Cincinnati Reds' 1919 World Series squad that faced the favored Chicago White Sox in the series that led to the infamous "Black Sox" scandal.

One of six children born to Scottish and Irish immigrants, Smith's father James emigrated from Edinburgh, his mother Katherine from Wales by way of Ireland. James was a blacksmith in Pittsburgh's J&L Steel Mill, and he and Katherine raised their family in the Greenfield section of the city. Jimmy grew to be 5-foot-10 and 160 pounds, and at age 18 the slick-fielding shortstop was signed by his hometown Pittsburgh Pirates as a possible replacement for aging great Honus Wagner.

Smith proved to be as much agitator as athlete. A bench jockey supreme, Smith's .219 lifetime batting average led to his being characterized as good mouth, no hit. His heckling earned him the nickname "Serpent Tongue," and prior to Game Three of the 1919 World Series Greenfield Jimmy goaded White Sox star second baseman Eddie Collins with pregame verbal barbs. Smith said later he was designated as part of Cincinnati's strategy to get under the skin of the peaceful Collins.

Wrote the *New York Tribune* in its coverage of the incident, "Jimmy Smith, who has a hard head and a wonderful flow of language of a sort, undertook to disturb the equanimity of the second baseman."

Greenfield Jimmy succeeded in getting to Collins. One newspaper report stated that Smith, coaching at third base, "uttered some joshing utterance. Collins snapped a retort and Smith came back in kind. Their loud tones attracted the other players who came hopping over." Smith so incensed Collins that Eddie spit at him. Umpires separated the two men.

Smith's annoying ways followed him for the rest of his baseball career and beyond. Returning home to Pittsburgh, he sold bootleg booze and opened an upscale restaurant called The Bachelor's Club after Prohibition was repealed in the early days of FDR's presidency.

Mary Louise was 15 years old and attending Our Lady of Mercy Academy when she met Billy, who was 20 at the time. The petite blonde with the megawatt smile would win a Miss Ocean City, New Jersey, beauty contest. Family and friends thought her a beautiful person inside and out. She was a warm, engaging girl whose life revolved around her loved ones and summers in Ocean City, New Jersey. Billy had taken a chauffeur-driven Cadillac to Greenfield Jimmy's summer home in Ocean City; during his stay he offered to take Mary Louise to dinner in nearby Somers Point.

"My mom first met my dad in Ocean City," Tim Conn says. "Her dad was a big supporter of my dad early on. He asked him if he had ever seen the ocean. My dad said he had not, so he then invited him to his home in Ocean City."

Conn was smitten, the champion taken with the young lady's charms. Over dinner he told Mary Louise, "I'm going to marry you." She laughed and replied, "You're crazy." In time, Billy and Mary Louise would become what Michael Conn calls "a unique couple."

Too unique, however, for Greenfield Jimmy, who thought her too young for the worldly fighter. He liked Billy and believed the Kid possibly the best boxer he had ever seen. But Jimmy believed all fighters ended up punchy and told his daughter to stay away from Billy.

"On their first date in Sommers Point, my dad told her that someday he would marry her," Tim Conn says. "My mom told him he was crazy and was not really that interested in him. She was more interested in lifeguards and college guys from Villanova. Once her dad saw that my dad was interested in her, he forbid her from seeing him and told my dad to stay away."

Jimmy encouraged Mary Louise to take up a career; she acted in stage plays in school and played the lead role of Jo in Louisa May Alcott's *Little Women*. Jimmy tried to create distance between the couple by sending Mary Louise to Rosemont College near Philadelphia, but his overbearing manner backfired. Mary Louise rebelled against her father's demands; she had fallen for Sweet William. He called her "Matt" for the way her blonde hair matted when it got wet from their romping hand in hand through the Ocean City surf.

"They had a good relationship," Tim Conn says. "They had their fights and arguments but that's normal. She was always sticking up for him."

In his later years Billy would joke that their home had seen many fights between he and Mary Louise, but that she always won by decision.

For the longest time they were kept apart, by Greenfield Jimmy and by circumstances beyond their control. Mary Louise was away at college; Billy was battling his way toward his big fight with Louis. One month and a day after winning the title, Conn met heavyweight Gus Dorazio in a non-title fight in Philadelphia's Shibe Park.

Rough-hewn but determined, Dorazio was said to be an inspiration for a fellow Philadelphia fighter, the fictional Rocky Balboa. Like Sylvester Stallone's Rocky, Dorazio had ties to the Philly mob, largely as a leg-breaker and enforcer. Just as Rocky earned extra green working as Tony Gazzo's goon, Dorazio's underworld associates reportedly included Blinky Palermo and Frankie Carbo.

In 1946 Dorazio was sentenced to a year in prison for draft dodging during World War II. His wartime job as a welder was an alleged "no-show," resulting in an FBI investigation that led to his conviction. On January 27, 1949, Dorazio delivered a violent beating that led to the death of 33-year-old Albert Blomeyer at a Philadelphia brewery. Dorazio was working as an enforcer at the time and Blomeyer had been circulating petitions at the plant that were pro-labor. Blomeyer suffered a fractured skull and died and Dorazio returned to prison, this time on a second-degree murder conviction that got him three-and-a-half years behind bars in violent Eastern State Penitentiary.

For much of his ring career the craggy-faced fighter seemed to be straight out of central casting. Dorazio's mauling, brawling style resulted in several wins, but even in victory he suffered. His eyes became so damaged his mother would boil water on the night of his fights so she could soak his bruised face when he returned home.

Dorazio was born in Philadelphia on July 4, 1916, an Independence Day baby in the cradle of American liberty. Christened Justine Vincolota, Dorazio reached maturity during the Great Depression, when a quarter of Quaker City citizens were suffering joblessness. As a teen Dorazio scrapped on the streets of Philly's Little Italy; in his world, the City of Brotherly Love was more the City of Brotherly Shove.

Readying for Conn, the wisecracking Dorazio complained about the color of Billy's trunks. Gus's grievances raised the Irishman's ire and Billy responded with tough talk for his Italian foe. "Listen dago, all you're going to need is a catcher's mitt and a chest protector."

Billy backed up his barbs. Before a pro-Dorazio crowd, Billy beat the bigger man bloody for seven rounds, punishing his plodding opponent before stopping him in Round Eight. Dorazio displayed courage in defeat, drawing support from the 12,000 fans in the stadium. Gus protested the fight being stopped, but as writer Carlos Acevedo noted in the *Boxing Bulletin*, Dorazio had been beaten "like an old rug."

Having defeated Dorazio, Conn returned to the light heavyweight ranks to face Bettina in Pittsburgh's Forbes Field on September 25. Conn recalled the rematch as being easier than his first fight with Bettina. "I fixed him up pretty good in the second fight," he told Heller.

By Billy's own account the rematch didn't start out being less difficult. According to Conn, Bettina won the first six rounds. The tide turned in the seventh, and Billy believed he won every round the rest of the way. "The last couple of rounds I had him in trouble," Conn recalled. "I had him almost knocked out."

Johnny Ray told *Collier's* in May 1941 that 20 minutes after the rematch, Bettina was laying on a table in his dressing room, gasping. "So Conn can't hit?" Bettina grunted to reporters. "Don't let anybody kid you about him. He may not knock you out, but nobody knows how he hurts you."

Conn returned to Gotham in November 1939 to gain a 15-round decision over Lesnevich. Billy defended his title one more time when he had a rematch with Lesnevich in Detroit in June 1940.

The result was a repeat of their first fight, Conn claiming a 15-round decision over the sturdy New Jersey native. Lesnevich would eventually win the light heavyweight championship, claiming the title vacated by Conn in May 1941 via a 15-round decision over Anton Christoforidis. Lesnevich, like Louis, fought both Conn and Ezzard Charles. Both Lesnevich and Louis would state their belief that Conn was a better boxer than Charles, who is considered one of the greatest light heavyweights in history.

Eager for new challenges, Billy turned his attention to those he called "the big fellows." Traditionally, the heavyweight division is where the money is, and Conn knew it. Brash Billy decided he would try out the big boys.

"He only defended his light heavyweight title three times because there was no money in it," Tim Conn states. "He could have held that title forever. He was going to stay at heavyweight because there wasn't much competition or money in the light heavyweight division."

Archie Moore and Ezzard Charles, who would establish themselves as great light heavyweights by the late 1940s, were still relatively inexperienced middleweights when Conn was king.

First up was Bob Pastor, whose deft boxing skills succeeded in confounding Louis. To get Conn ready to fight a bigger man, Pastor weighing 181 pounds to Billy's 174, Johnny Ray had Billy box 10 to 12 rounds daily. Ray's preparation was such that he put Conn through several rounds the day before the bout.

Conn liked Pastor, but that didn't stop the Kid from hitting low in their September bout in New York. When Pastor complained, Conn hit him low again. Pastor complained and Conn sneered. "Now I'm really going to hit you (low), you crybaby!"

What the hell, Conn thought. He wasn't going to be an altar boy in the ring. Besides, what was anyone going to do about it?

Pastor had kept his feet against Louis in their first fight, but Conn battered him with a blistering body attack and dropped him three times. The first knockdown occurred at the end of Round Nine, the second in the 12th. Conn caught Pastor again in Round 13, "knocked his ass through the ropes," Billy recalled. Conn's left hook to the body resulted in Pastor being counted out by referee Bill Cavanaugh.

The *New York Herald Tribune* commented that fans had gone to see "a fencing match" between two master boxers but instead saw "a slugging affair." The *Tribune* stated that Conn crushed Pastor, "who didn't believe that Billy had anything except a left jab."

Fierro thought Conn did a beautiful job on Pastor, setting him up with left jabs and smacking him with hard right crosses. Following the fight Conn reminded everyone he had stopped Pastor in 13 rounds while it had taken Louis 21 rounds over two fights. "So they say I can't punch?" Billy asked.

Johnny Ray agreed. "Billy knocked him clean through the ropes, then flattened him. You don't do that with a love pat in your glove."

In quick succession, Conn beat Al McCoy on points in 10 rounds in October and Lee Savold, aka the "Battling Bartender" from Saint Paul, Minnesota, in 12 rounds in November. Conn's victory over Savold was notable, considering Lee's career. In 1942 he would record *The Ring* magazine's "Upset of the Year" when he knocked out Lou Nova in eight rounds.

Six years later on March 19, 1948, Savold registered the quickest KO in the history of Madison Square Garden's main events when he stopped Italian sensation Gino Buonvino in 54 seconds. Savold was a stand-in for Joe Baksi, who had injured his ankle and was unable to fight. Savold took the bout on just 48 hours' notice and pulled a stunning upset in record time. His mark was tied in 1981 by Gerry Cooney in his KO of Ken Norton but not topped until March 10, 2007, when Sultan Ibragimov stopped Javier Mora in 46 seconds.

A member of the Minnesota Boxing Hall of Fame, Savold's bio states that he "was not only a two-fisted dynamo, but also a smooth boxing heavyweight that could feint you out of your shoes while setting you up for his fatal blow."

Pinky George, Savold's chief second, promised Conn would take "a lot of punishment" from the man considered at the time the hardest-hitting heavyweight apart from Louis. If the Kid could handle Savold, fans would have what Pinky called "a pretty good line" on whether Billy could deal with the Bomber.

Savold dealt severe punishment to Conn, but Billy was outboxing Lee when the crowd began a rhythmic clapping in Round Eight demanding more action. Billy needed no such prompting and swapped blows with Savold. Lee landed three straight punches; the first landed on the top of Conn's head with such force Billy thought his skull had been fractured. Savold's second punch bloodied Billy's eye; the third broke his nose. Conn remembered it as the hardest single punch he ever took. "Damn near killed me," he said. Despite his dangerous power, Savold could not cope with Billy's boxing skills and was outpointed.

Savold had no business hitting him, Conn told *Sports Illustrated*. The reason he got caught, Billy said, was because he got careless.

Conn's performance was such that it won over not only the judges but Jacobs as well. Uncle Mike's critics claimed the promoter had a chunk of ice where his heart should have been. Never paying much attention to the action in the ring, he concentrated instead on the ticket windows in the streets. That all changed with Conn; Uncle Mike was fascinated by the Kid. Jacobs sat ringside at Conn fights and Fierro observed him flinging his fedora in the air and rooting as loudly as the fans in the $2 seats. "At-a-boy, Billy!" Jacobs exclaimed as Conn turned MSG into a Garden party.

Fierro understood Jacobs's favoritism toward Conn. Billy was a master boxer; he stabbed opponent's eyes out rather than bludgeon them. His left was a dream weapon, as perfect as any described in boxing manuals. The Kid's footwork was as elegant as Fred Astaire's; Sweet William was always bouncing up and down on his toes and avoiding opponent's punches with grace and style.

A father-son relationship developed between Uncle Mike and the Kid, Jacobs calling him "my boy." The promoter invited the boxer to spend weekends at his palatial home—"a rolling show place," Fierro called it—in Rumson, New Jersey. Billy also vacationed at Uncle Mike's Miami estate and used his duplex in Central Park West. Jacobs had Conn chauffeured around in his Cadillac, and bought Billy a flashy, cream-colored convertible. Sweet William was given expensive suits fitted by Uncle Mike's tailors and expensive ties. "Here, boy," Jacobs would say after hand-picking ties for Billy, "they go with your blue eyes."

Fierro thought it obvious that Jacobs was grooming Conn to succeed Louis. The calendar skipped to 1941 and Conn continued his rampage through the heavyweight ranks. The Kid was showing himself to be the successor to skilled stylists James J. Corbett and Tommy Loughran. Nat Fleischer complimented Billy for being in the "Corbett and Loughran School of cleverness."

One of Conn's strengths as a fighter was that he could read opponent's styles and develop a strategy to beat them. Typical of this had been the Kid's plan to deal with the much-respected middleweight Roscoe Manning in their 1936 fight.

"I knew Roscoe Manning liked fish," Conn said. "He wasn't going to hook me. I danced all night."

Conn's cleverness worked against the big boys as well. In February, Billy scored a fourth-round technical knockout of Ira Hughes; in March he knocked out Danny Hassett in five rounds. In April Billy recorded his third straight stoppage with an eight-round TKO of Gunnar Barlund; he followed it up in May with another victory inside the distance, an eighth-round TKO of Charles "Buddy" Knox.

"That's what winners do, they go for it," Douglas Cavanaugh says. "Conn's KO percentage spiked when he started fighting heavyweights."

The victories earned Conn the right to fight for the greatest title in sports. Relinquishing his light heavyweight laurels following his technical knockout of Knox, the Pittsburgh Kid now found himself face-to-face with the Detroit Brown Bomber.

Johnny Ray, who had recoiled two years earlier at Jacobs's suggestion of putting Junior in the ring against the "big boy" when Uncle Mike first mentioned it, now welcomed the opportunity.

"Junior," Ray boasted, "will win easy."

# CHAPTER THREE

# CHAPPIE AND JOHNNY

He was the son of a preacher man, a tortured soul given to red-eyed rage when under the influence of demon rum, given even to manslaughter.

But the balding, scar-faced Jack Blackburn was a talented trainer when it came to creating champions, and a shrewd strategist who crafted cunning fight plans. He knew all too well the problems Billy Conn could present Joe Louis.

"This fellow is mighty fast, Chappie," Blackburn warned Louis. "You've got to stalk him until you get him in a spot to nail him."

Sweet William was slick and quick and he knew how to trick. Chappie was aware of the difficulties a cutie like Conn could cause because Blackburn had been such a fighter.

Charles Henry Blackburn was born to a minister and his wife on May 20, 1883—some reports suggest 1882—in Versailles, Kentucky. Young Jack and his family moved to Terre Haute, Indiana, where he began boxing as a teen. It's been said that Jack was hired as a sparring partner for a day and did so well he nearly knocked out his more experienced opponent.

Blackburn was 18 years old when he made his pro debut, stopping Kid Miller in Indianapolis in eight rounds. Jack won his first three fights by knockout and quickly compiled an impressive ring record. Though he fought much of his career as a 135-pound lightweight and rarely weighed much more than the middleweight limit of 160 pounds, Blackburn boxed men much bigger than he, including light heavyweight champions Harry Greb and Philadelphia Jack O'Brien, and heavyweight contender Sam Langford. He sparred with future heavyweight king Jack Johnson, bloodying the big man's nose in the process.

Ray Arcel, who knew Blackburn and competed against him as a corner man and joined him as the first trainers inducted into the Boxing Hall of Fame, said it wasn't easy to be a Black boxer when Blackburn was in his prime. Promoters never bothered with scales; they just sent men into fight, regardless of the weight disparity.

In his prime, Blackburn stood 5-foot-10 and was string bean lean. In Conn, Blackburn could see his younger self. He, too, had been a boxer-puncher, his fast fists flashing a smart jab and powerful hook. Quick and clever, Blackburn confused opponents and kept them off balance by being alternately aggressive and cautious.

Blackburn faced legendary lightweight champion "Panama" Joe Gans three times, winning a decision on November 2, 1903. Taller than Langford but lighter by 45 pounds, Blackburn lost just once in six meetings with the heralded "Boston Strong Boy." Old-timers would get misty-eyed at the memories of Blackburn's 15-round draw with Langford; many thought it the greatest fight they had ever seen.

By 1908 Blackburn's reputation as a ring warrior was such that other Black fighters drew a "colored line" to avoid facing him. Writing in the *Freeman* newspaper, Charles D. Marshall said his wish was to see Blackburn face renowned middleweight champion Stanley Ketchel, whose fighting style earned him the moniker "Michigan Assassin."

"What I desire to see," Marshall wrote, "is a fight between Blackburn and Stanley Ketchel for I am of the opinion that this would be one of the greatest fights of all time."

Blackburn's proposed bout with Ketchel never happened. Moving east and continuing his career in Pittsburgh and Philadelphia, Jack was playing poker with his older brother Fred on the night of December 30, 1908. Both brothers were lightweight boxers at the time, though Jack was the better boxer of the two. Four days earlier, Johnson had beaten Tommy Burns in Sydney, Australia, to become the first Black heavyweight champion.

Blackburn, given to dark moods, drank heavily and became involved in two violent attacks. The first involved he and Fred the night before

New Year's Eve, the brothers becoming embroiled in a heated argument about Jack's common-law wife, Maud Pillian. Fred grabbed a razor blade and sliced a long line of blood on the left side of Jack's face. The scar remained with Blackburn the rest of his days, a constant reminder of that ugly dispute.

Two weeks later, on January 9, 1909, Blackburn spent the night drinking and at 3:00 a.m. arrived in a taxi at his Philadelphia home with friend Alonzo Polk. Their wives, Maud and Matilda, were in the home arguing; when Blackburn and Polk attempted to break up the verbal battle the situation worsened. Blackburn, known to have a hair-trigger temper, particularly when intoxicated, pulled a pistol and shot Polk in the stomach and neck. When Matilda tried to flee the scene, Blackburn turned the gun on her and shot her in the back.

Blackburn claimed self-defense, but the fact that Matilda's bullet wounds were in the back destroyed his alibi. It was reported at the time that while awaiting his trial Blackburn attempted suicide. Pleading guilty to Polk's murder, Blackburn was convicted of manslaughter and sentenced to 15 years in prison. Blackburn passed time by giving boxing lessons to the prison warden and his three sons. Four years and eight months into his sentence, he was released on good behavior.

Returning to the ring on April 4, 1914, Blackburn won a six-round decision over Tommy Howell. In his next bout on May 20, Jack surrendered four inches in height and 30 pounds in weight to Ed "Gunboat" Smith, a hard-hitting light heavyweight. The Gunboat was one of the Great White Hopes of the era. Five months before facing Blackburn, Smith won the White Heavyweight Championship with a 15th-round technical knockout of Arthur Pelkey. Crafty and strong, the much larger Smith and ring rusty Blackburn fought to a six-round decision. Some sources record the bout as a no-decision; others report it as a decision in Smith's favor.

One year later, Blackburn had one of his most famous fights when he climbed through the ropes in Pittsburgh's Duquesne Gardens on January 25, 1915, to face Greb. No film is known to exist of Blackburn or Greb in action in the ring, but a newspaper article from their fight illustrated the skills and strategies of both boxers.

"They call Mike Gibbons a ghost and they say that Johnny Kilbane is elusive, that Freddie Welsh fades away like a mist and that Jim Corbett was shifty," the article began, "but for dodging gloves that are coming with the profusion of a charge of 'Number Eights' from a 12-gauge shotgun, commend us to Jack Blackburn, the Eastern Pennsylvania negro, who opposed Harry Greb, the local middleweight, in the Duquesne Gardens last night."

The article stated that Greb launched "about a million—more or less—punches" at Blackburn, but that "an infinitesimally small proportion of them connected with those portions of Jack's anatomy on which blows must land to count."

True to his nature, Greb, who was 20 years old to Blackburn's 31 or 32 depending on which source is believed, was the more aggressive fighter. "He was after Blackburn all the time," the article noted, "working his arms like piston-rods from every possible angle, but Blackburn blocked, side-stepped, slipped, rode and ducked punches as easily and as calmly as we are led to believe that an aeroplane outmaneuvers a Zeppelin."

From the first bell to the final gong, Greb's relentless attack put Blackburn in the eye of a storm of gloves. Blackburn proved so elusive that, according to the ringside writer, "not one punch in 10 that Greb started ever connected. . . . He succeeded at times but couldn't inflict any considerable amount of punishment nor pile up a commanding lead."

The report stated that in the first round Blackburn slipped and was helped to one knee by a spent blow from Greb. Jack countered several times as Harry came in, but not enough to rob Greb of the advantage that his aggressiveness gave him.

Blackburn didn't have much trouble tagging Greb and directed most of his punches at Harry's middle. His blows failed to stop the Pittsburgh Windmill's spirited attack, but that Greb's pace was slowing indicated that Blackburn's jabs and hooks were having an effect. Greb won the third round as he solved the skilled defense put up by the savvy Blackburn and landed several rights and lefts. In the final minute of Round Three, Jack's body blows slowed Harry's rush. Greb responded with punches that brought blood from Blackburn's nose.

Round Four saw Greb escalate his attack. He succeeded in landing more blows and was firing both hands at Blackburn's jaw. Many missed their target, but several connected to even up for those Blackburn landed on Harry's head and body. The reporter rated the round even but awarded Blackburn Round Five. Continuing his attempt to slow Greb down by attacking his middle, Blackburn forced the fighting and scored often enough to earn the round.

Greb returned to the attack in Round Six. That his youthful, non-stop style was wearing down the aging Blackburn seemed evident by the report that Greb "did practically all the fighting. Blackburn was content to cover well and tie up Greb when he rushed in, occasionally countering. Blackburn played strictly a defensive game."

The fight went the full six rounds and depending on which ring record one believes the result was either a no-decision or a newspaper decision in favor of Greb. Newspaper decisions were awarded at the time by ringside reporters in lieu of official decisions by judges. The reporter covering the bout wrote, "Greb was on him all the time, and as Blackburn didn't start one-tenth the blows that Greb did, Greb must be accorded the decision."

Interestingly, Blackburn's protégé, Louis, would have the fight of his life against another 'Burgher who idolized Greb and was trained by Harry's stable mate, Johnny Ray.

Blackburn fought professionally until 1923. The International Boxing Hall of Fame lists his official ring record at 38-3-12 with 50 no-decision bouts. Blackburn claimed to have fought 385 bouts in a pro career that spanned three decades.

Blackburn retired as a fighter but remained in boxing, working as a trainer in Chicago gyms. He helped develop five future champions—welterweight Jackie Fields, lightweight Sammy Mandell, bantamweight

Bud Taylor, and heavyweights Joe Louis and "Jersey" Joe Walcott. But it was the years he spent working with Louis that earned Blackburn induction in the International Boxing Hall of Fame in New York.

After helping train Fields, Blackburn in 1926 coached the light-hitting Mandell to the lightweight title that had been denied Jack during his ring career. A product of Rockford, Illinois, Mandell's moniker was the "Rockford Sheik" because of his dark looks that reminded onlookers of Hollywood Latin lover Rudolph Valentino. His fast hands and speed afoot also earned him the nickname the "Rockford Flash."

In 1927 Blackburn guided Taylor, the "Blonde Terror of Terre Haute," to the bantamweight crown via a 15-round decision over the talented Tony Canzoneri. Blackburn was introduced to a young Louis in June 1934. Brought into the Brown Bomber's camp by Julian Black and John Roxborough, the hard-bitten Blackburn was skeptical of attempting to duplicate his title-winning training methods at the heavyweight level. A contemporary of the controversial Johnson, Blackburn was doubtful that a Black boxer, no matter how good, would get a crack at the crown.

"You know, the heavyweight division for a Negro is hardly likely," Blackburn told Louis. "The white man ain't too keen on it. You have to really be something to get anywhere."

In Louis, Blackburn saw a powerful but unpolished product. He watched Joe spar, saw the impressive punching power that had produced a sterling amateur record, Golden Gloves championships, and National AAU light heavyweight title. He also saw that Louis needed work. Joe was dancing around too much and not planting his feet when punching. Blackburn would teach Louis to back up his punches with timing and accuracy.

A year later on July 20, 1935, Blackburn looked back at his first days working with Louis and told the *Pittsburgh Courier*, "I trained him under the same methods I trained under when I was a fighter."

Louis said Blackburn "saw my faults right off." Joe was punching off balance, and Blackburn corrected this by showing him how to punch with his whole body and not just with his arms. Their first week together in training saw Blackburn hold the heavy bag and teach Louis how to throw punches. Ray Arcel observed that fighting men like Greb, Langford, and O'Brien taught Blackburn the importance of a good jab, and that's what Jack passed on to Joe—a jab that Arcel said could knock a man out. There were days when Blackburn had Louis jabbing the heavy bag for an hour following workouts. All Louis needs, Blackburn told Arcel, is that left jab.

When Blackburn allowed Louis to get in the ring, he taught him how to parry and elbow-block opponent's punches. He also taught Louis anatomy, and how to place his punches in the most vulnerable spots.

Blackburn convinced Louis to be economical in his attack. "One punch is better than a hundred punches," Jack said. He taught Joe how to finish a fight, a lesson Louis learned so well that Nat Fleischer called him the deadliest fighter ever.

"Don't get impatient," Blackburn would say. "Take your time but move right in. Don't throw your punches wild; shoot 'em in straight. Don't give him a chance to come back. Bide your time. Place your punches and knock your opponent out."

To illustrate his point about being a heavy hitter, Blackburn surprised Louis by swinging a brick at him. Joe ducked and Chappie caught him with a counterpunch.

"See what I'm trying to teach you?" the trainer asked. "Pretend you got bricks in your fists, your opponent is going to duck and then you hit him with the other hand."

Blackburn compared boxing to Joe's favorite sport. "Hitting in boxing, like hitting in baseball, has got to be done in combinations to be effective."

Blackburn was a sound strategist. As he would do with all of Louis's opponents, Blackburn thoroughly scouted Jack Kracken, Joe's first foe in the pros. He built his fight plan around a body attack, instructing Louis to fire hard lefts to Kracken's middle, then feint the same punch again. When Kracken dropped his guard to block the body blows, Blackburn told Louis to switch his attack to the head. Following Blackburn's strategy, Louis banged a left to Kracken's body, feinted another punch to the same area, and delivered a perfectly placed left hook to the jaw that finished the fight in the first round.

Louis's sixth pro fight saw him take a hard right hand from heavy-hitting Canadian Al Delaney in the second round. The punch broke one of Louis's molars, but Blackburn added insult to injury. "It's your own fault," he snapped. "You should have stepped inside." Blackburn told Louis to counter Delaney's hard punches by moving in and banging to the body with both hands. Delaney was hurt by a right to the heart in Round Three, knocked to the canvas in the fourth by a right to the head, and saved by the referee after Louis hammered away with both hands.

Louis faced another challenge in swarming Adolph Wiater. Blackburn's strategy was to teach Joe how to deal with a fighter who was forever moving forward. "When they charge into you like that, just step aside and catch his arm and spin him around," said Blackburn. "When you spin him, you force him off his course. He's off balance and unprotected, then sock him."

Against Art Sykes in October 1934, the Louis fight plan was to step back, find the range, and then cross a right hand to the jaw. The Brown Bomber did that and hit Sykes so hard he fell through the ropes and crashed his head against the platform outside the strands. The *Chicago Tribune* reported that Sykes "took referee Davey Miller's count without stirring, and it was several minutes before he was able to leave the ring."

Eddie Futch, who would help train heavyweight champions Joe Frazier and Larry Holmes, was a young welterweight at Brewster gym in Detroit when Blackburn was molding Louis's style. Futch said Blackburn not only taught Louis much but also took away from him what was unnecessary. Blackburn instructed Louis to shuffle forward behind his lethal left jab, and to cut off escape routes. Once Louis cornered his opponent or trapped him on the ropes, Futch would say, the fight was over.

Skilled boxer Lee Ramage was favored to deal the Detroit sensation his first defeat, and Ramage boasted beforehand that Louis could be had by a solid left lead. Blackburn's response was to work with Louis on slipping the left lead and countering with a left hook. A pair of Louis left hooks in Round Eight ended Ramage.

Against Hans Birkie, Louis was warned by Blackburn, "You're in with a very cute person this evening and you can learn a lot from him. Just bide your time and be careful. I'll tell you when to go to town." The tough German had never been knocked down and it wasn't until Round 10 that Blackburn told Louis, "Go to town this round." Five left hooks to Birkie's jaw left him defenseless and forced the referee to stop the carnage.

Facing former heavyweight champ Primo Carnera, Blackburn's strategy was succinct. "Go out and feint him." Louis wasted no time, feinting the giant out of position in the first round and ripping a right to the big man's mouth. "Carnera thought that Joe was going to shoot for his body," Blackburn said, "but Joe's right to da Preem's mouth in the first round handed the Italian one of the biggest surprises of his life."

Louis chopped Carnera down in six rounds. "The kid followed my advice perfectly," Blackburn boasted.

Carnera was the first ex-champ Louis faced, and Max Baer was next. Like Birkie, Baer had never been knocked down in his pro career. Blackburn devised a plan to, in his words, "beat Baer to the punch." Blackburn told Louis to wait for an opening and then use his speed and accuracy to get off first. Max was counted out in the fourth round.

Blackburn's strategies and Louis's willingness to follow instructions kept Joe unbeaten through the first two years of his career. It also left Louis cocky and overconfident in the summer of 1936 as he prepared to face a third former titleholder in Max Schmeling.

Blackburn warned Louis that Schmeling would throw counter rights and that Joe should keep his left hand up. "Keep jabbing him off balance so he can't get that right in, and for God's sake keep your left arm high," Blackburn said.

"Chappie warned me about Schmeling's right hand and that he would try to counter my left," Louis said. "I didn't listen."

Schmeling's right hand in Round Four sent Louis to the canvas for the first time in his career. He took countless right hands the rest of the way before being knocked out in the 12th.

"That was the first time I didn't listen to Chappie and it was the last time," Louis said later. "I never made that mistake again."

In June 1937 Louis became the first Black man in two decades to fight for the heavyweight title. A fired-up Blackburn vowed to turn Louis into "a fighting machine," and sharpened Joe's hand-eye coordination by having him catch flies out of the air—real flies, not baseballs as Louis would have preferred. Louis said later his reflexes were never sharper. "I became as fast as lightning because of those flies."

Blackburn knew Braddock was tough. He instructed Louis to stick and counter and wait for the older Cinderella Man to come apart in the middle rounds. It was sound strategy, and Louis rode it to an eighth-round knockout. Now champion, the Brown Bomber still had a score to settle. Blackburn's fight plan for one of the biggest sporting events in history—the June 1938 rematch with Schmeling in Yankee Stadium—was for Louis to pressure Schmeling from the start. That it was the exact opposite of the cautious, don't-crowd-him strategy that Blackburn had worked up for the Braddock fight is testimony to the flexible approach of both the trainer and his prized student.

Blackburn had seen in the first Louis-Schmeling fight that Max preferred to parry and counter, to wait out Louis and then attack. Blackburn was ready for the rematch, and he made sure Louis was ready as well.

In a tense training camp, Blackburn had sparring partners throw countless right-hand counters over Louis's left lead. Louis was taught to keep his left hand high after jabbing and to protect his jaw by tucking it behind a raised left shoulder. Blackburn further instructed Louis to crowd Schmeling at the opening bell to prevent him from getting set, a tactic which would put the Bomber in blasting range.

Blackburn's strategy and Louis's skill were too much for Schmeling, who survived just 124 seconds of the first round before the bout was stopped. Because of Blackburn's expert training techniques, Louis was recognized as a combination of many of the great champions of the past. Boxing writer Budd Schulberg, who penned the script for the film *On the Waterfront*, thought Louis could defend like Jack Johnson, punch like Jack Dempsey, and jab harder than Gene Tunney.

Langford was likewise impressed, and told the *Chicago Tribune*, "The Detroit Bomber is another Gans, whom I consider the greatest fighter of all time. . . . He (Louis) can hit, he is fast and is no slouch at employing ring craft. I am glad I am still able to see enough to watch the boy. He is the marvel of the age."

Even Blackburn, always reserved in his judgment and not given to rash statements, knew Chappie was something special.

"My boy Joe is not only a boxer but a puncher, too," he said. "When you get a combination like that, you maybe have a champion. He has balance after using his left or right, his judgment of distance is remarkable, and I believe he is the best-balanced fighter in the world today. If he misses with one hand, he is always in a position to punch with the other. He is the greatest puncher in the world barring nobody and is never out of position."

Blackburn continued to create winning strategies for his champion. He devised a plan to defeat awkward Arturo Godoy in a June 1940 rematch. Four months earlier Godoy had given Louis fits, Joe winning a disputed split decision in what he called "the worst fight of my life."

Blackburn and Louis went back to the gym and Jack's strategy for the return bout was to raise the Chilean from his exaggerated crouch with short uppercuts. Godoy was floored in the seventh round and twice more in the eighth before the fight was stopped. The effectiveness of Blackburn's plan is reflected in an Associated Press report that Godoy's face looked like "barbecued beef." Louis called it "the worst beating I ever gave a man."

The next big fight would be with Conn, and once again Blackburn and Louis went to work on strategy. Blackburn considered Conn a "cutie," Jack's term for boxers like Billy and Bob Pastor. He scouted Conn in person just as he had scouted Louis's previous opponents, attending

Billy's fights, and making mental notes. Louis, too, had seen Billy box firsthand, sitting ringside at a Conn sparring session at Grossinger's gym prior to the fight against Pastor. Asked what he saw in Conn, Louis said, "I saw he likes to fight."

Conn's quickness concerned Louis; Billy had fast hands and fast feet, fought in flurries, and threw punches in bunches. To counter Conn's quickness, Louis looked to enter the ring lighter than his usual 202 pounds. He would need to shed weight, Joe thought, to catch Conn, who was as elusive as a butterfly. Louis considered it solid strategy and was unconcerned about dropping a few pounds. After all, hadn't he weighed 198 when he battered Baer and he had never felt faster or stronger.

Still, the Baer fight had been six years before, and Louis had been fighting steadily at 200-plus pounds. The difference in weight wouldn't be great, but Blackburn didn't like Louis's idea. He figured a bigger, stronger Louis could inflict more damage once he cornered Conn or bulled Billy into the ropes. Blackburn didn't want Louis drying out to lose weight, a practice that could cause the champion to feel fatigued if the fight went past the middle rounds.

While Blackburn formulated a fight plan to solve the stylist, his counterpart Johnny Ray was setting traps for the slugger. Ray was a former fighter, a talented lightweight who fought bigger than his 5-foot-7 frame. He was born Harry Pitler, a son to Jewish parents from Pittsburgh's Hill District. Athleticism ran in the Pitler family; Harry's brother Jake was a second baseman for the hometown Pittsburgh Pirates and another brother was a quarterback for the University of Pittsburgh.

Harry was given his ring moniker Johnny Ray by manager Red Mason, and Ray's ring debut as a professional came as a featherweight at age 17 on January 13, 1913. He proved so skilled he was called the best featherweight prospect since Young Ziringer, a heady compliment in that era, and he eventually became the Steel City's top featherweight. Ray was never stopped in 138 bouts. His official record is open to question, but Luckett Davis researched Ray's career by poring through the pages of the *Pittsburgh Post* and the result is that Ray went 83-31 with 22 draws and two no-decisions. According to Luckett, Ray won 15 fights by knockout, 68 by decision, and lost 30 via decision and one by foul. The latter came in his sixth and final fight against rival Johnny Kirk, also a Pittsburgh product.

The roots of the Ray-Kirk rivalry ranged from ring style to ethnicity to territory. Ray was a boxer, Kirk a slugger. Ray was Jewish, Kirk Polish. One man hailed from the Hill District, the other from Southside. Their dispute began following their first meeting when Ray disagreed with sportswriters who believed Kirk won the fight. They had four more bouts, but neither man was able to demonstrate clear superiority over the other. The rivalry grew more heated after Ray and Mason had an angry dispute and the pair went their separate ways. An upset Mason sent Harry Greb to convince Kirk to sign Red as his manager.

The animosity between Ray and Kirk had Pittsburgh fans clamoring for a showdown. Fireworks began before the first bell, Kirk claiming that Ray attacked him at the weigh-in and scratched his face. Kirk entered the ring first and when Ray entered, he demanded the corner Kirk had already claimed.

Some 5,000 spectators showed up at Exposition Hall, and when the bell rang the two fighters hurled as many insults as punches. At the end of Round Two, Kirk was said to have given Ray a conciliatory tap on the shoulder. Believing it was a shot after the bell, Ray punched back, causing both corners to climb into the ring and igniting a riot. Kirk was kicked in the groin and carried to his dressing room.

Among the spectators who stormed the ring were Greb and another local fighter, Jackie Lightning. According to reports, Greb one-punched Lightning, knocking Ray's friend cold. Ray, Kirk, and Lightning were among those arrested.

Just as Ray had a volatile ethnic rivalry with the Polish Southsider Kirk, he had a similar one with Irish Northsider Patsy Brannigan. Additional highlights to Ray's career included battles with featherweight champ Johnny Kilbane and lightweight king Rocky Kansas, victories over the great Johnny Dundee and hard-hitting George "KO" Chaney, and making radio history by fighting in the first live sporting event to be broadcast. On April 11, 1921, KDKA-AM in Pittsburgh carried a bout between Ray and Dundee. Their lightweight fight was held at Motor Square Garden in Pittsburgh's East Liberty section and resulted in a 10-round draw. Florent Gibson, sports editor of the *Pittsburgh Post*, was behind the microphone providing commentary.

The broadcast attracted local attention since Ray and Dundee were popular Pittsburgh fighters. Dundee, born Guiseppe Corrara, was known as the "Little Bar of Iron." Ray retired from the ring in 1924 and became a fight manager. Like Blackburn, he had a soft spot for hard liquor and led to his moniker being "Moon," short for "Moonshine."

Times were lean. While Blackburn was training world champions, Ray was seeking ways to survive. "Things weren't any too hot," he told *Collier's* magazine in 1941. There were times when he'd have enough money to pay his rent and a little left over for a hamburger. And there were times when Ray would have what he called "the panic." It was then that he'd tell his landlord that his check was delayed or that his bill roll had slipped through a hole in his pocket.

But when young Billy Conn first wandered into his gym, Ray felt as if a "jackpot was laid right in my lap." Billy the Kid was something special and Johnny knew it. Ray remarked that his relationship with Conn was not the usual fighter-manager relationship. "I honestly love him as though he were my own kid," he said, "and I know he thinks the world of me."

Their father-son relationship often turned sour. Johnny labeled Billy a "dumb mick son of a bitch," and the Kid countered by calling Ray a "rummy Jew bastard." Douglas Cavanaugh describes Ray as "a loving but tough taskmaster," one who didn't hesitate to toss Billy into the ring with some of boxing's toughest talents.

"He had much confidence in his young tiger and knew full well what [Conn] was capable of," says Cavanaugh.

Ray's strategy to bring Billy along fast suited the Kid. There would be no amateur career for Conn; he and Ray were in it to make money and that meant fighting for pro purses. "All you fight for," Conn said later, "is money."

Nor would there be any building Billy's pro career slowly and fattening his record by beating inferior fighters. Beginning with Conn's pro debut in 1934, Ray arranged quality bouts, so much so that Billy barely stayed above .500 through the first year of his career. One particularly rough stretch in 1935 saw Conn lose four of the six fights he was in from April to August.

Ray kept working with Conn, and trainer Freddie Fierro said that Johnny taught Billy how to hold his hands in the ring and how to block punches. Just as Blackburn taught Louis the importance of the left jab, so, too, did Johnny teach Conn the same lesson.

"Ray," Fierro said, "explained the principle of the left jab, the punch that was to make Billy famous."

And just as Chappie taught Joe what has become known as the Blackburn Crouch, Johnny taught Billy the shell defense. Conn turned a corner in the Fall of 1935 by beating George Liggins at Duquesne Gardens and began winning more than losing. Ray's plan was working and by June 1941 he had crafted another master plan, this one on how to beat Louis.

"Take my word for it," Ray told *Collier's*, "it's a brand-new offense so far as Mr. Louis is concerned, and we believe it can't miss."

The reason was simple, said Ray. "Louis isn't the Brown Bomber anymore." Hadn't he been hurt by Tony Galento? Ray remarked that Joe's knees looked as shaky as "two helpings of grape jelly." Braddock knocked Louis down "with almost the first punch of the fight," Ray noted. Pastor hurt Joe and Natie Mann made the Bomber blink. "When Conn has a man hurt," Ray stated, "he never lets up."

Ray said he helped develop Conn's punching power by having Billy swing a sledgehammer. Ray arranged to have half a dozen sledgehammers weighing from 5 to 25 pounds each brought to camp and had Conn swinging them every day. Ray estimated those sledgehammers increased Conn's punching power by 15 percent. It showed when Billy knocked

Pastor through the ropes, hurt Lee Savold, and gave Al McCoy such a tough time that Ray figured they softened him up to become a Louis KO two victim months later.

"To Billy, Louis is just another guy named Joe," Ray said. "He'll keep after the Bomber . . . Billy is already telling people he's a cinch to knock Louis out."

It's precisely what Conn told writer Haskell Cohen for an article in *SPOT* magazine. "I'm going to whip Joe Louis," Conn stated, "and I'm counting on a knockout."

Many experts laughed at the notion that Louis could be beaten, but Billy boldly predicted that when he climbed into the ring with the Detroit Brown Bomber, it was the Pittsburgh Kid who was going to come out as heavyweight champion. Conn reminded doubters that experts "yelled their heads off" when Ray let him get into the ring with heavyweights.

One of those experts was Gene Tunney. The former heavyweight king called Conn "a credit to the game" but believed Billy would never make it as a heavyweight. Critics derided the Pittsburgh Kid as "a growing boy whose delight it is to punch around with mature men."

Conn scoffed at such statements. "I'm not just some pug a smart promoter pulled out of the bushes for some quick and easy money in one title fight," he said. "I'm a man who has been working all my life for one thing. Now I'm going to get it."

And what was the scheme devised by Johnny and Billy to stage boxing's biggest upset?

"I'm going to throw more lefts to his face than the champ ever saw before, and every left is going to have weight behind it," the Kid stated. "I'm going to show him footwork he never saw before and, I think, won't know how to handle. Then, as a finisher, I'm going to use a right that's been getting heavier with every punch I've thrown for ten years."

Conn and Ray believed Louis wouldn't know what to do with a fighter who had guts, a good left hand, and great footwork. "I know Joe

Louis is tough," Conn said. "I know he can hit like a mule. I think he's a great fighter. But I think I'm better."

Experts agreed that Conn was the best boxer of his day, a master craftsman. Like the ring generals before him, Billy was an expert boxer, but he could hit as well. Foreshadowing his fight plan for the Bomber, Sweet William said he'd rather punch than box.

"Louis," said Conn, "is going to learn some more about that when I get to work on him."

Billy thought Joe big but slow moving. "Nobody knows this better than Joe himself," he told reporters. "He's a dangerous fighter because he can punch and because he's been taught well. But he's a mechanical fighter, doing only what he's told [by Blackburn]. He can't think under pressure in the ring, and he knows it."

The Kid's comments angered the Bomber. "I never heard of him getting no college degree," Louis said. "He talks too much."

For millions of fans awaiting the start of this enormously publicized fight, the time for talk was all but over.

# CHAPTER FOUR

# PRELUDE TO A CLASSIC CONFRONTATION

On December 5, 1940, three days before George Halas's Chicago Bears enhanced their "Monsters of the Midway" reputation by beating the Washington Redskins 73–0 in the most one-sided NFL championship game ever and the first to be broadcast on national radio, Mike Jacobs made boxing history.

Uncle Mike made the stunning announcement that Joe Louis would defend his title against one challenger per month. Each bout would be held indoors and would lead to an outdoor fight at a ballpark in the summer of 1941. No heavyweight champion in history had fought so frequently, and with Christmas fast approaching, Jacobs's announcement amounted to an early present for fans wearied by war news.

More than 40,000 British citizens were losing their lives in the Blitz carried out by the German Luftwaffe against England's cities, ports, and commercial and industrial centers. German propaganda minister Josef Goebbels took pen in hand and wrote in his diary, "When will Churchill surrender?"

Across the ocean, some boxing fans wondered when Louis would surrender his title. Having coolly dispatched every contender to his crown, Louis was considered a fighter without peer. Joe had become too good for his own good. His dominance was such that some wondered if the Brown Bomber was bad for boxing.

Jacobs, of course, believed no such thing. Louis was worth a million dollars every time he stepped into the ring, by far the largest amount in boxing circa 1941. Max Baer was the next largest money earner but lagged far behind Louis at $300,000.

It was for this reason that Jacobs told the press, "If it could be done, I'd like to promote Joe Louis once a month. But of course, he must have some vacation, too."

Fall 1940 had seen the champion campaigning for Wendell Willkie, who was running for president against third-term candidate Franklin Roosevelt. Louis leaned toward Willkie because, as he said, "he promises my people better jobs."

Jacobs's plan to have Louis fight frequently ran contrary to the tradition of Tex Rickard, Jacobs's predecessor as boxing's top promoter. Rickard had held the opinion that *his* heavyweight champion—Jack Dempsey—shouldn't be seen in the ring too often. Eleven days after Uncle Mike's announcement, Louis entered the ring in Boston Garden to face the heavyweight champion of New England, Al McCoy. The challenger was 27, a year older than Louis, and had been fighting professionally for 12 years with 69 wins to his credit. Fighting mainly as a light heavyweight, McCoy had been knocked out four times.

A crowd of 13,334 filled the arena for the first heavyweight title fight in Boston and thrilled at the sight of their hometown champion emerging from his corner in a crouch that left his head at times below Louis's trunks.

Louis's right to the body dropped McCoy midway through Round One, but he arose and fought on. McCoy's exaggerated crouch could not prevent Louis's left jab from finding its mark, and by the end of Round Two Al's left eye was beginning to swell. Still, he jolted Joe in the fourth round and backed the Bomber into the ropes in the fifth. McCoy's eye was closed but the cheers of thousands in Boston Garden buoyed the local hero. He was, indeed, a real McCoy.

At the end of Round Five, Ray Arcel, McCoy's corner man and a trainer who worked with more than 2,000 fighters and 20 world champions ranging from Benny Leonard and Jim Braddock to Ezzard Charles and Roberto Duran, told referee Johnny Martin he was stopping the bout due to McCoy's badly damaged left eye.

Years earlier, Arcel and Jack Blackburn had sat beneath stately trees in Pompton Lakes, New Jersey, and dreamily talked about what it would be like to train a heavyweight champion. One day, Arcel and Blackburn met in Chicago and Jack told Ray, "I got the man now," meaning Louis.

McCoy was one of 14 fighters Arcel trained to fight Louis. The first was Braddock, the last Charles. Arcel's parade of challengers became known as "The Meat Wagon." He brought so many challengers against Louis that prior to one bout, when Arcel took yet another fighter to the center of the ring for prefight instructions, Louis looked at the trainer and asked, "You here again?"

The prospect of facing the Brown Bomber left many of Arcel's boxers beaten before the bout began.

"As soon as the bell rang," Arcel recalled, "they folded like tulips."

McCoy didn't, and neither did Louis's next challenger, Clarence "Red" Burman. A Dempsey protégé, Burman believed in the ancient ring adage, "Kill the body and the head will die." Burman studied McCoy's strategy of bobbing and weaving to get inside Louis's defenses and on January 31, 1941, Red was determined to take the fight to the Brown Bomber. Burman saw this as a once-in-a-lifetime opportunity. Here he was, making more money than he would for any other bout and fighting the heavyweight champion. Burman wasn't intimidated; in the ring he wasn't afraid of anyone.

A Madison Square Garden audience of 18,061 watched Burman tear a page from McCoy's playbook and charge the champ at the opening bell. Leaping from his crouch Burman nailed the startled Louis with a left hook to the face. The blow brought blood from the Bomber's right eyelid. Angry at being caught flat-footed, Louis began pummeling Burman. Red returned to his bob and weave tactics in Round Two, doubling up on his left hooks and landing to Louis's head and body. The champ was impressed; Burman was a pretty fair fighter. Red was such a tough out *The Ring* magazine noted that most of the top heavyweights avoided him.

Backed into a corner, the Bomber let loose with a left hook so wild it caused him to momentarily lose his balance and fall through the ropes.

Had he not gotten caught up in the middle strand Louis would have toppled completely out of the ring. The startling sight of the champion tangled in the ropes brought the Garden crowd to its feet; many believed Red responsible for Louis losing his balance. Burman continued to press Joe and it wasn't until Round Five that the Bomber seized control of the fight.

Stalking the challenger in his customary style, Louis backed Burman into a corner. A vicious body blow left Burman doubled over in agony; a second body shot had the challenger gasping for air; a third straight body shot dropped Red to the canvas. He lay motionless as referee Frank Fullam counted over his inert form. Burman's trainers carried him to his corner and finally revived Red with smelling salts. Louis told reporters his final body blow was one of the hardest punches he ever threw. It was enough to leave Burman passing blood in his urine.

"I always had the feeling I could beat anyone else in the world," Burman told Louis biographer Chris Mead. "He changed my mind that night."

Louis followed a month later with a fight against Gus Dorazio, a tough guy whom Billy Conn had beaten not long before. Scheduled for February 17 at Philadelphia's famed Convention Hall, the bout was considered such a mismatch that Senator John J. Hulaska of the Pennsylvania State Legislature stated he would start an investigation. Offended by talk of a mismatch, Dorazio promised to punch Louis into the senator's lap at ringside. Philadelphia's State Athletic Commission got into the act, stating that the senator was only complaining because he hadn't received complimentary tickets.

Fight night saw a crowd of 15,902 pour into Convention Hall. Like McCoy and Burman, Dorazio opened in a crouch; he was bent so far forward his head almost brushed the canvas.

Dorazio didn't straighten up from his turtle-like defense until early in Round Two and when he did Louis drilled him with a short right to the jaw. Down went Dorazio, who was counted out 90 seconds into the round. Louis knew Dorazio was the best Philly had to offer. "At least he tried," Joe said. Asked about Dorazio's crouching style, Louis shrugged.

"They need a new gag," he said. "This crouching don't go no more against me."

The champion returned home to Detroit for a March 21 bout against Abe "The Hulk" Simon. Unlike Louis's three previous opponents, the 6-foot-4, 255-pound Simon would not be fighting from a crouch. Boxing experts again believed the fight to be a mismatch. Jack Blackburn believed otherwise.

"I look for Joe to knock him out," Louis's trainer said, "but he ain't gonna have near the easy time doing it that a lot of folks think."

Cramming Olympia Stadium was the largest crowd in Detroit boxing history, 18,908 fans excited to see their hometown hero defend his title in a bout scheduled for an unconventional 20 rounds. Round One seemed to support those who saw Simon as being outclassed, Louis flashing a right to the New York giant's jaw that resulted in a knockdown with the first punch the Bomber threw. The fight was far from over, however. Like McCoy and Burman, Simon took the fight to Louis, champion and challenger exchanging wicked blows. Louis found Simon big but clumsy; he reminded Joe of Primo Carnera.

Simon survived Rounds Two and Three by using his reach advantage and sticking his long left in Louis's face. Slipping Simon's jab, Louis landed a right and left that felled the giant for a second time. From his kneeling position Simon winked at his corner to indicate he was fine.

Louis stepped up the pace in Round Seven, staggering Simon with a pair of rights that forced the big man to hold on. Another left and right caused Abe to try and clinch again, but Louis sidestepped Simon and the monstrous Manhattanite crashed to the canvas. He arose quickly and was met with right hands. Abe's ability to absorb the Bomber's best blows brought respectful cheers from the champion's hometown crowd.

Louis's right hands dropped Simon in Round 12 and again in Round 13. Climbing to his feet from his fourth knockdown of the night, Simon was stunned by a left hook so savage it left him senseless, the challenger turning his back to the champion and smiling in dazed confusion at the crowd. Louis looked imploringly to referee Sam Hennessy, who stepped in and stopped the bout at 1:20 of the round. Critics unimpressed with the Bomber's performance considered him lucky that night to have not been facing a skilled boxer like Billy Conn.

Three weeks later Louis was back in the ring, taking on Tony "Baby Tank" Musto. Tank stood 5'7½" and packed 198 pounds on his bulky frame. His record was 28-10 but that he had only been knocked out once was due to his durable chin. The bout was originally set for April 2 in Cleveland, but the city's boxing commission balked at sanctioning what they considered a mismatch. Jacobs moved the fight to St. Louis and reset it for April 8; it would be the first time Louis laced up the gloves for a pro fight in the Gateway City.

Following the same fight plan as McCoy and Burman, Musto presented problems like those posed by his predecessors. Louis viewed him as a local pro who was good in his steady way but too predictable. The first time Musto emerged from his crouch in Round Three, Louis dropped him with a left hook to the jaw.

Musto's constant pressure allowed him to fight Louis on largely even terms through six rounds. Louis's left jab began finding the range in Round Seven, and he opened a dangerous wound over Musto's eye, causing the fight to be stopped at 1:36 of Round Nine by referee Arthur Donovan. Musto was battered and bloodied but still on his feet. His sturdy jaw had survived even the jarring blows of Joe Louis.

The champion's road show took him to Washington, DC, for a May 23 meeting with Buddy Baer. Fought at Griffith Stadium, it was the first heavyweight title fight in the nation's capital. Like Carnera and Simon before him, the 6'6½" and 238-pound Baer towered over Louis. He had 50 wins under his belt, 45 by knockout, and had only been stopped once. His KO victims included tough guys Tony Galento and Simon. Though the fight was considered to be such a foregone conclusion there was little betting on the bout, Buddy proved to be a tougher opponent for Louis than his more famous brother Max had been.

With a much-anticipated mega bout with Conn in the offing, Jacobs received a fright in the first round when his champion was knocked through the ropes by a pair of left hooks. It was the first time since the Jack Dempsey–Luis Firpo fight in 1923 that a heavyweight champion had been knocked out of the ring in a title fight.

Baer returned to the attack, the 10–1 underdog thundering home right hands against an opponent he outweighed by 36 pounds. Louis's left eye swelled, and he was forced to grab and hold in Round Four after absorbing a series of rights. The following round saw Baer bulldozing forward and banging Louis with left hooks, bloodying the champ beneath the left eye in the process. Wary of Buddy's power, Joe fought a cunning, if cautious, fight.

Louis returned to form and fought savagely in Round Six, unloading bombs on the bigger man and corkscrewing him to the canvas with a right to the head. Buddy arose, but was unsteady on his feet, the announcer noting that the gigantic Baer looked like a "tree about to fall." The Associated Press reported that "Buddy went down as though one of Washington's Senators had just bounced a ball off his head." Another right returned Baer to the floor, and with the crowd in full voice, no one heard the bell ending the round. Louis let loose a head-rattling right hand that sent Baer crumpling to the canvas. Buddy's corner men, Arcel and manager Ancil Hoffman, dragged their unconscious fighter to his corner. Enraged at what they considered a late blow from Louis, Baer's corner demanded the champion be disqualified.

Hoffman stood in front of Buddy, who was slumped on his stool, as the bell rang for Round Seven. Donovan ordered seconds out, but Hoffman held his ground. Donovan shouted at Hoffman to leave the ring; the manager refused. With that, Donovan disqualified Baer because of Hoffman's stalling and named Louis the winner.

Louis's six fights in six months were disparaged in the sports pages as the "Bum of the Month Club." Jack Miley of the *New York Post* coined the phrase at the time of the McCoy fight.

"When he gets his 'Bum of the Month Club' rolling," Miley wrote, "Louis is going to cover more towns than the Ringling [Bros. Circus] show. The way he buffets 'em about, Louis could play five shows a day and get himself some real money."

"Smart ass sports columnist," Louis called Miley. Joe had pride as a professional and didn't feel the men he was fighting were bums. They were hard-working professionals trying to make a buck.

The facts back up the Bomber's opinion. The "Bum of the Month Club" included top 10 heavyweights in Simon, who was ranked sixth in 1941, and Buddy Baer (ranked eighth). Burman, Dorazio, and Musto were all ranked in the top 10 during their careers.

Like Louis, famed trainer Angelo Dundee strongly disliked the phrase "Bum of the Month." If a kid's a fighter, Dundee said, he can't be a bum. "You've gotta be a special individual to be a fighter."

In 1966, when Dundee's prize student Muhammad Ali was at the peak of his powers as heavyweight champion, he hired Louis as an adviser. During a TV interview, Ali asked, "Joe, do you think you would have stood a chance with me?"

Not missing a beat, Louis told Ali, "One time during my career, I fought on a 'Bum-of-the-Month' tour."

Ali was taken aback. "I would've been a bum compared to you?"

"You would've been on the tour," Louis deadpanned.

Decades later, Mike Tyson looked back on Louis's "Bum of the Month" campaign and echoed what the Bomber told Ali.

"If any of the fighters nowadays were around when Louis was fighting," Tyson stated, "even the Joe Fraziers and the Muhammad Alis would've been considered bums too."

Debate raged at the time whether Louis's "Bum of the Month" campaign helped or hurt him conditioning-wise. Conn and Ray believed the constant fighting dulled Louis's sharpness and left him overworked and stale; others felt it kept him primed and free of ring rust. In terms of legacy, casual fans look at the phrase "Bum of the Month" and figure Louis's opponents were less than top caliber. But each of the fighters in the "Bum of the Month Club" were contenders during their career. In truth, Louis was in a Catch-22. If the champ won too easily, critics downgraded his opponents as "bums." If Joe struggled in his bouts, those same critics said he was slipping.

Conn would be Louis's seventh opponent in as many months, and the fact that Louis was willing to put his title on the line so often is to his credit and stands in stark contrast to the heavyweight champions who preceded him. Many Black fans at the time were upset that Louis was putting himself at risk so often and pointed to the scarcity of title defenses made by white champions.

Jim Braddock took off for two years before making his lone title defense. Max Baer and Jack Sharkey each had one defense during their respective one-year reigns. Max Schmeling and Gene Tunney made two defenses each in two years. Carnera put his title on the line three times in one year, Dempsey six times in seven years, and Jess Willard two times in four years.

Miley's "Bum of the Month" phrase caught fire and sportswriters across the country picked it up and popularized it; forever will it remain a part of ring lore. Louis's controversial tour completed, boxing's Alexander looked for a new world to conquer. It came in the person of the cocky Irishman. Billy was nobody's bum, and Louis knew it. "I knew my next fight would be a rough one," Joe recalled in his autobiography.

Conn had been cleaning up on contenders, and the Bomber knew the Kid was young, arrogant, and tough. Conn, Louis said, had "all the stuff for a heavyweight champion."

Louis also figured that Billy, being Irish, was thinking of John L. Sullivan, James J. Braddock, and all the great Irish champions who had preceded him. "I knew I had to be ready for him," Louis said.

Writer James P. Dawson noted at the time, "Louis is fighting the world light-heavyweight champion because he has exhausted his available supply of heavyweight opponents. No more heavyweights remain. Repeats have not been highly successful and, anyway, few of the beaten heavyweights have wanted any more of the Louis game."

"It was the only fight that would draw big money," Freddie Fierro recalled, "and Uncle Mike knew that with this country headed for war, both Louis and Conn were ripe for the draft."

As it was a question of which would come first, the draft or the fight, Uncle Mike made the match. At the June 3 contract signing in Jacobs's Twentieth Century Sporting Club office near Broadway in Manhattan, champion and challenger shook hands for photographers, and the *New York Times* reported a brief but meaningful verbal exchange.

"You look good, champ," said Conn, nattily dressed in a suit jacket, white dress shirt, patterned tie, and white handkerchief protruding from the left breast pocket of his jacket. It might very well have been one of the expensive custom-made suits Uncle Mike had provided him.

"You do too, Billy," said Louis, who was dressed more casually in an open-neck shirt and coat. "You gaining weight?"

"You bet I am."

"Looking forward to seeing you in a few weeks, Bill."

Conn grinned. "You, too, champ. I'll be there."

The exchange was blood in the water to intellectual sharks in attendance. The Bomber's comment that he would see the Kid in a few weeks was a weighty one; for most fighters, a ring date with Louis was akin to a date with the executioner, minus the blindfold and cigarette. But Conn showed no fear and it was reflected in his response. Billy would not only "be there," he had every intention of beating the champ.

Standing between the two ring warriors was Jacobs. Uncle Mike had long been Joe's promoter, but he was now promoting Billy as well and had become a fan of the Kid. He sat ringside at Conn's fights, sweating through his silk suits as he cheered for Billy. Writer Mike Vaccaro stated that while Joe was Jacobs's meal ticket, Billy was his surrogate son.

Jacobs hinted that he wouldn't be heartbroken to see a changing of the guard in boxing's glamour division. Louis had been the dominant force on the heavyweight scene since 1935. Conn could breathe fresh life into boxing and Jacobs knew it. A Conn victory would ensure a rematch and generate enormous financial gain. Some suggested such a plan was in the works, hinting at a fixed fight. Dempsey dismissed it as an "ugly rumor."

Dempsey himself had been rumored to be in a fixed fight—his title-winning victory over Jess Willard in Toledo, Ohio, on July 4, 1919.

Willard, a Great White Hope who had knocked out Jack Johnson four years earlier to end the champion's tumultuous reign, dwarfed Dempsey by nearly six inches in height and 60 pounds in weight.

Dempsey came out blazing hotter than that afternoon's sun and delivered one of boxing's most vicious beatdowns. Willard was floored seven times in the first three minutes and only the bell saved him from a first-round stoppage. The victory ushered in the Age of Dempsey, a tiger who put the roar in the "Roaring Twenties" and stood alongside Babe Ruth, "Red" Grange, Bill Tilden, and Bobby Jones as immortals in sport's "Golden Age."

Willard was also involved in another title fight whose outcome was disputed. Johnson long claimed he threw his fight against Jess in Havana, Cuba, in a secret deal with US government agents to be allowed to return to American soil and have criminal charges against him dropped. Jack pointed to pictures of himself lying on his back, his gloved hands shielding his eyes from the Havana sun. As additional proof that he was taking a dive, Johnson noted that his legs were bent at the knees and raised to prevent them from being burned on the red-hot ring floor.

Willard rebuked Johnson's claim, remarking that if Jack was going to throw the fight why did he wait 26 rounds to do so? "If Johnson threw that fight, I wished he'd thrown it sooner," Willard remarked. "It was hotter than hell down there."

Dempsey disputed all claims of a "fix" in his fight with Willard and, perhaps addressing them as much as the rumors of a prearranged plan for the Louis-Conn bout, wrote in *Liberty* magazine, "In every great heavyweight championship contest the ugly rumor of a 'fix' is heard in irresponsible circles, and this fight is no exception."

Dempsey had heard rumors that the fight was fixed for Conn to win. "In justice to both Joe Louis and Billy Conn, I believe there is absolutely no truth to any such rumor," he wrote. "I do not believe that either of them would be a party to a fake."

Rumors of a fixed fight aside, Tom Meany stated in the New York afternoon paper *PM* before the bout that most fans were pulling for a

Conn victory. "This isn't because the public dislikes the Bomber, who has been an exemplary champion," Meany wrote. "It's merely because the public likes a change."

Louis set up training camp in Greenwood Lakes in the Catskill Mountains, Conn at Joe's former haunt, Pompton Lakes, New Jersey. It was a switch from Billy's usual site—the Pioneer Gym in New York City—when he was training for a fight in Gotham. There were days when Billy longed to leave the rustic retreat in Passaic County to visit his ailing mother in Pittsburgh. Maggie was dying of cancer and Billy was using the money he made fighting to pay her bills. As her condition worsened Billy paid for full-time care, and when he wasn't training, he would visit her and the two would spend long hours talking.

"Your mother," Conn would say, "should be your best friend."

Maggie was on Billy's mind; so too was Mary Louise. She was now 18 years old and the two planned to marry following the fight with Louis; they took their blood tests and applied for their marriage license. Mary Louise's father had other ideas.

Greenfield Jimmy Smith, 46 years old but still as feisty as he was during his days as one of Major League Baseball's most acid-tongued bench jockeys, threatened to kick "that mick fighter's ass." Smith told sportswriters that champion or no champion, "I'll punch the hell out of that fellow." Greenfield Jimmy wanted Conn to beat Louis and become heavyweight champion of the world, but he also wanted him to stay away from his daughter. "My girl has just turned 18, and that's a baby to me."

When Greenfield Jimmy's fighting words were relayed to Conn, the Kid shrugged them off. Billy's father, however, did not think Smith's words were to be taken lightly. "Who does this guy think he is?" asked Bill Sr. "There is one thing for certain, he hasn't ever punched a Conn. And it'll be a sorry day for him when he tries."

Louis, meanwhile, was having his own family problems. Joe and Marva spent a day in Detroit telling his mother of the difficulties they were dealing with in their marriage. Mother Barrow sided with Marva, cautioning her son about pride going before the fall. It was an ominous proverb to mention with Louis facing the prospect of his toughest fight in years.

The fast-approaching Louis versus Conn battle headlined a month filled with memorable sports news. On June 1 Joe DiMaggio hit safely in both ends of a doubleheader against Cleveland to extend his consecutive games hit streak to 18. The following day, retired Yankees legend Lou Gehrig passed away from ALS.

One day later DiMaggio doubled for one of his two hits off Bob Feller and his flame-belching fastballs. That same day Louis and Conn signed the contract for their much-anticipated showdown as Gehrig lay in state at Christ Protestant Episcopal Church in the Bronx. Thousands of grieving men, women, and children paid their respects at the casket of baseball's "Iron Horse."

On June 4 the *New York Times* issued the first printed reference to what came to be known as "The Streak" when it reported, "DiMaggio, incidentally, has hit safely in nineteen straight games." While DiMaggio was putting together his streak, Boston Red Sox star Ted Williams was also tearing the cover off the ball.

As opposing pitchers struggled to deal with DiMaggio and Williams, Louis and Conn sought to solve each other's ring style. Conn and Johnny Ray had plenty of opportunities to study the champion as he fought once a month; Louis and Jack Blackburn had fewer chances to observe Conn, Billy's recent schedule consisting of a tune-up bout in May against Buddy Knox. Conn's appeal was such that the event drew 27,000 fans to Forbes Field.

Louis felt that if Conn stayed cool and kept his head for 15 rounds, then the Kid could make it a long night for him. Joe, however, didn't think that was probable; he believed Billy's famed temper would eventually get the better of him.

"I know Billy will fight like a cornered cat when you hurt him," Louis told reporters. "He ain't got any better sense. He just naturally likes rough going and forgets to box."

Louis wasn't alone in his opinion. Jackie Zivic, older brother to Fritzie Zivic who had fought Conn, said the Kid was almost *too* fond of fighting. Jackie knew Billy and had seen him fight often enough to be able to break down his ring style. He had also seen Harry Greb fight, and though the fighting styles of Greb and Conn were vastly different, Jackie felt the two were similar in that they loved to mix it up.

"It's funny to say but Conn has too much guts," Jackie said. "With his boxing, he shouldn't get hit as often as he does, but he likes to fight so much he gives up a part of his defense to trade punches."

Freddie Fierro thought it was a matter of Billy being so sure of himself. The Kid not only said he would beat Louis but insisted he would knock him out. "He even named the round!" Fierro exclaimed.

Conn would seek to counter Louis's plodding style by making the champion lead with his punches and move out of his reach. The boxer's strategy for beating the slugger was not to let Louis hit him. "If they can't hit you, they can't hurt you," Conn reasoned. "Keep your hands up. Move. Mix them up."

While Louis was leaning on his belief that Conn would lose his cool, Billy believed Joe was no longer the awesome fighting machine that destroyed Schmeling in '38 and Galento in '39. Overuse had left Louis stale, Conn thought. In a span of 29 months from January 1939 through May 1941, Louis successfully defended his title an extraordinary 13 times. It's a pace that remains unmatched by any heavyweight champion and Conn was convinced it left Louis overworked.

"Louis is not the fighter he was a year ago," he stated. Daily did Conn hold court for members of the media. They loved the Kid; he was great copy. Quick with a quip, Conn put exclamation points on his colorful comments about how he would beat the Bomber with hand-drawn illustrations.

"I'll pop him with both hands and dance away while he's still blinking," Billy boasted.

"He ain't gonna hit me with those sucker punches."

"He won't get away from me when he's hurt."

Conn revealed to reporters that his fight plan included jolting shots to the heart, and Johnny Ray chimed in to say the champ "won't be able to take it downstairs for long."

When writers asked if he was worried about the prospect of facing the fearsome Louis, Conn brushed off such a suggestion and told them he left the worrying to his manager. Johnny, Billy said, was "vice president in charge of worrying."

Ray told reporters Billy wasn't just talking to hear himself talk. "He feels he's going to be the champ . . . Junior is gonna knock that son of a bitch out."

Sportswriters found themselves in quote heaven. They fed off the Kid, and he in turn loved the limelight. Conn's camp was jumping day and night and Billy and Johnny thrived on the energy. "Ain't it grand?" Conn asked and implored the hordes of reporters not to leave. Recalling his rather humble early years in the ring, Conn quipped, "I used to fight before crowds that were smaller than this."

The writers laughed along with the Kid and began to buy into Billy's confidence. Hadn't Louis's last three opponents—Buddy Baer, Musto, and Simon—lasted an average of 10 rounds each with Joe? And hadn't the Bomber been belted around a bit, getting knocked out of the ring by Buddy and bloodied by Burman? And what of the champ being confused by the styles of journeymen McCoy and Musto?

Others shared Conn's opinion. After Joe stopped Musto, Arthur Donovan, the third man in the ring that night, opined that Louis was slipping. McCoy had fought both Louis and Conn, and he felt Billy was going to give Joe problems.

"Conn is a much better boxer and faster so he's a lot harder to hit than Louis," McCoy stated. "Joe hits harder, I suppose, but he never hit me with the punches Conn did."

Fighters and ex-fighters picking Conn to win included Fritzie Zivic, Benny Leonard, Jim Braddock, Fred Apostoli, Gus Lesnevich, and Lew

Jenkins. Influential members of the media, including Hype Igoe, the dean of boxing writers at that time, and celebrated sports cartoonist Willard Mullin, also went with Conn.

Former heavyweight kings weighed in on Louis, each explaining how he would have fought the Brown Bomber. James J. Jeffries said he would have walked inside Louis's hooks and hammered short jabs to Joe's body. Jack Johnson stated he would have outboxed Louis. Willard said he would have waited for Louis to lead with his left jab and countered with his right. Dempsey remarked that he would have crowded Louis; Gene Tunney said he would aim left jabs at Joe's face.

Writing for *Liberty* magazine, Dempsey sized up the Louis-Conn fight. "Conn, in my opinion, has the skill and science to outpoint Joe Louis in fifteen rounds and take his heavyweight title from him. But I do not believe he can."

The reason, Dempsey stated, is that Conn had too much "Irish" in him. When he gets stung, "Billy gets angry, throws caution and boxing skills to the winds, and sails in to slug it out with his opponent."

If Conn had a real heavyweight punch this would be great strategy, Dempsey said. But Jack didn't believe Billy had enough firepower to survive a slugfest with the Bomber. Coolness under fire would be the deciding factor on fight night, wrote Dempsey, and there was no one cooler than Louis; "the champion is a veritable iceberg in combat."

Dempsey agreed that a quick, clever boxer like Conn could give Louis trouble. But Dempsey didn't consider Conn strong enough to deal with Louis's deadly punches. The champ's heavy blows would slow down the challenger, allowing him to catch Conn with the finisher.

Dempsey thought the Louis-Conn bout reminded him of his fight with Georges Carpentier in 1921. Carpentier was like Conn in that both were brilliant boxers. Dempsey and Louis had significant weight advantages over their opponent, and Jack believed that just as he had worn down Carpentier with hard shots before knocking him out, Joe's punching power would prove to be the difference.

"Unless I'm way off in my calculations," Dempsey wrote, "we'll see ring history repeating itself in this fight."

One thing was certain, Dempsey said. Louis wasn't taking Conn lightly. Billy was one of his more formidable challengers; Dempsey called Conn "an apt fighting machine" and warned that Louis would have to be "mighty fast on his feet and quick on the trigger to beat Bill."

What it all came down to, Dempsey wrote, was that Conn had the speed, Louis the power. "I look for a real contest when Joe and Billy face each other in the ring, and I believe the winner will know that he was in a battle.

"That winner, I believe, will be Joe Louis by a knockout."

Those favoring Conn believed Billy's speed afoot, agile dodging, ring generalship, and boxing skill would befuddle Louis, throwing him off his game and resulting in Joe not being able to use his punching power effectively. They pointed to historical precedents set by Corbett against Sullivan, Tunney against Dempsey, and more recently, by Tommy Farr and Bob Pastor against Louis.

Writer James P. Dawson doubted that Conn packed enough power to hold off Louis. The fighter who beats Louis, Dawson wrote, must be a combination boxer and hitter. Conn was clever, but he was also a stand-up fighter and Louis's toughest fights had come against opponents who employed bobbing, weaving styles. Joe acknowledged as much. "I like to fight a man who will stand up," he said.

He would face such a fighter in Conn. "Billy is fast," Dawson wrote. "He is clever. He is shifty. He loves to fight. He has an amazing confidence in his ability to conquer. Yet Conn has had no really stern test against a heavyweight.... He tires under pace and pressure."

Dawson rated Conn only an outside chance to upset Louis. It all depended on certain factors. "If his legs carry him at top speed, if his marksmanship is unerring, if he does not tire or expose himself to fire," said Dawson, "he may stick and stab his way past Louis for fifteen rounds."

But because Billy would be fighting in a stand-up style, "one false move will be his undoing," wrote Dawson. "He cannot afford to give Louis even the tiniest opening for a shot at his jaw. We all know what happens when Joe gets one clean crack at a vital spot."

Daniel M. Daniel of *The Ring* saw the fight from a different angle. "If the Louis of 1941 were the Louis of even 1939, we'd say—Four heats, bring the stretcher for poor Bill, and make a series of dates with his doctor and dentist."

Conn, wrote Daniel, was "a skilled technician ... who may bring some angle into the fight which will baffle the champion."

Billy was a stand-up boxer but not a stand still boxer. "He will move here and there and will throw a big burden on Joe's heavy legs," Daniel opined. He noted that Conn was a quick hitter and fast on his feet. Billy would stab with the jab and stab again. "He is a tantalizing fighter," observed Daniel.

If Conn could keep moving, keep stabbing with the left, "Billy will have a fine chance to last the limit and take the championship on points."

Daniel thought the incentive in this fight lay with the challenger. After all, what did Billy have to lose?

If Louis could rouse himself one more time, his incentive being that with war looming and the possibility of joining the armed services, the champion could leave fans with the bright memory of being arguably the greatest of all champions. "It's conceivable," Daniel said, "that against Conn we will have the last chance to see the real Joe Louis."

What almost everyone agreed on was that when Louis and Conn finally met in the ring, it would be a classic confrontation. Ever since David had stood in against Goliath, the matchup of a good little man versus a good big man had proved intriguing. So, too, had bouts matching a master boxer versus a stalking slugger. The irresistible force meeting the immovable object has long served to excite the public.

As fight night drew near, Jacobs expected a near-capacity crowd of 54,000 to jam New York's historic, horseshoe-shaped Polo Grounds. For the first time since Louis's rematch with Schmeling three years earlier extra ringside seats were being built, and Uncle Mike priced the prize seats at $25 apiece.

Interest was such that Jacobs had his sights set on a gate of $450,000. Fans thought enough of Conn's chances that they bet the odds down to 18–5, the shortest odds placed on Louis since the second Schmeling fight.

"This match was made chiefly for the reason that in the heavyweight ranks, no man stood out as likely to draw flies with Joe Louis in an outdoor bout," Daniel declared. "Conn was lifted out of the light heavyweight ranks to make the only match which Mike Jacobs had a chance to cash in handsomely."

Louis versus Conn was indeed the best of all possible matchmaking. It has always been that way in boxing, championships between the boxer and puncher, the matador and the bull, thrilling fans since Corbett fought Sullivan in 1892. Similar style fights followed—Jeffries-Corbett, Jeffries-Johnson, Dempsey-Carpentier, and Dempsey-Tunney.

Now came Louis-Conn, a rightful heir to the classic slugger-boxer confrontation. Daniel theorized that if Louis was the same fighter who had shown signs of vulnerability during his "Bum of the Month Club" campaign, then Conn's chances of winning were good.

But if the Bomber reverted to the form he flashed in 1938?

"If you remember what happened to Schmeling," Daniel said, "you shudder for Conn."

## CHAPTER FIVE

# THE BALLPARK AND THE BROADCASTER

Fight night, and Gotham was aglow with the flaring stadium lights of the Polo Grounds.

It was a pleasant evening; skies were clear and close to 55,000 fans made their way to Upper Manhattan for the ballpark situated in Coogan's Hollow, the bottomland between Coogan's Bluff and Harlem River. Many stepped from the 155th Street Subway and took the Bushman Steps to the Polo Grounds ticket booths. Others crowded the John T. Brush Stairway, named after the owner of the New York Giants baseball team, on West 157th Street between Edgecombe Avenue and St. Nicholas Avenue.

The Polo Grounds served as the site for three stadiums that from 1880 to 1963 were primarily used for baseball but also for boxing and football. The original Polo Grounds hosted the New York Metropolitans from 1880 to 1885 and the New York Baseball Giants from 1883 to 1886. The Giants also played in the second Polo Grounds in the 1889 and 1890 seasons, and the third Polo Grounds from 1891 to 1957.

Two other New York baseball teams, the Yankees and Mets, also called the Polo Grounds home, the Yankees from 1913 to 1922 and the Mets in their first two years of existence in 1962 and 1963. Each edition of the Polo Grounds hosted a World Series, and Major League Baseball All-Star Games were held there in 1934 and 1942.

The New York Giants of the National Football League used the Polo Grounds as their home field from 1925 to 1955, and the New York Titans (later renamed the Jets) of the American Football League played their home games there from 1960 to 1963.

Fifth and Sixth Avenues bound the Polo Grounds on the east and west, 110th and 112th Streets on the south and north. The Grounds got its name due to the original site being built for polo when it opened in 1876. The ballpark was known for its quirky attributes—a great green expanse of outfield, which measured 483 feet from home plate to center field, 450 to left-center, and 449 to right-center; extremely short distances to right (258 feet) and left (279) fields; and a horseshoe or bathtub-like shape. The comparison to the latter led to the ballpark being called by many "The Bathtub."

Whatever name it went by, the Polo Grounds oozed history. Columbia University and Yale University drew sizable crowds for their Thanksgiving Day games in 1883 and 1887. In the 1884 World Series, "Old Hoss" Radbourn hurled three consecutive scoreless games for the Providence Grays against the Metropolitans at the Polo Grounds.

On August 16, 1920, Ray Chapman of the Cleveland Indians was hit in the head by a pitch from the Yankees' Carl Mays and died 12 hours later, the only player to die from an injury that occurred in a major-league game. Four months later, on December 4, the Polo Grounds hosted the first pro football game played in New York City, the Buffalo All-Americans edging the Canton Bulldogs 7–3.

In 1920, the Yankees' new slugging star, Babe Ruth, awed spectators when he hammered a home run over the Polo Grounds' right-field deck, a blast estimated at more than 470 feet. The Babe's power was prodigious, and he took advantage of the Polo Grounds' short porch in right field. Ruth's home run total jumped from the 29 he hit for the Red Sox in 1919 to 54 in his first year with the Yankees in 1920.

The Yankees sublet the Polo Grounds from their New York neighbor, but Giants owner Charles Stoneham evicted his co-tenant in 1920, though he allowed them to continue to play in the Polo Grounds while their new stadium was being built across the Harlem River. Originally named "Yankee Ballpark," the new cathedral was renamed "Yankee Stadium" prior to its opening in 1923.

The most famous and dramatic home run hit in the Polo Grounds came thirty years after Ruth's upper deck drive. On October 3, in the third and deciding playoff game for the National League pennant, the Giants' Bobby Thomson delivered baseball's "Shot Heard 'Round the World," a game-winning line drive into the left field seats off Brooklyn Dodgers reliever Ralph Branca.

College and pro football played significant roles in making the Polo Grounds hallowed grounds. The Army-Navy game was played there in the 1910s and 1920s, and in 1924, Notre Dame's upset of Army in the Polo Grounds inspired sportswriter Grantland Rice to immortalize Knute Rockne's Fighting Irish backfield of Jim Crowley, Elmer Layden, Don Miller, and Harry Stuhldreher as the "Four Horsemen."

The New York Giants hosted NFL championship games at the Polo Grounds in 1934, '38, '44, and '46. The '34 game, played between the Giants and Chicago Bears on December 9, is remembered as the "Sneakers Game." The playing field was frozen by a cold rain the night before, and with New York trailing 10–3 at halftime, Giants end Ray Flaherty told head coach Steve Owen the team could get better traction on the ice-slicked field if they converted from cleats to sneakers. Owen dispatched Abe Cohen, a friend and tailor who assisted on the Giants' sideline, to Manhattan College in search of sneakers. The college's athletic director, Brother Jasper, gave Cohen nine pairs of sneakers. Outfitted in their new footwear, the Giants outscored the defending champions 27–0 in the fourth quarter to claim a 30–13 win.

Two years later, in Game 2 of the 1936 World Series, Yankees center fielder Joe DiMaggio made a spectacular grab of a long drive that foreshadowed the catch-and-throw made by the Giants' Willie Mays against Cleveland's Vic Wertz in the opening game of the 1954 Fall Classic. DiMaggio tracked down Hank Lieber's long fly 440 feet from home plate. The momentum of DiMaggio's long run carried him up the clubhouse steps in center field. The Yankee Clipper stopped and stood at attention as the crowd cheered Franklin Roosevelt as the president's car left the ballpark. Displaying his jaunty grin, FDR waved to DiMaggio in acknowledgment of his gift for grab.

On May 24, 1940, the New York Baseball Giants played their first night game at the Polo Grounds. One year later, the New York night was again abuzz with anticipation. That afternoon DiMaggio had extended his hit streak to 31 games with a single off Thornton "Lefty" Lee. That the hit came against the clever southpaw of the Chicago White Sox and Yankee killer, a man who would post 22 victories that season and a league-leading 2.37 ERA, made DiMaggio's accomplishment even more special.

As day turned to dusk, fans streaming to the Louis-Conn title bout felt the excitement and energy in the city streets. There was something special about a big fight in a stadium on a summer evening. The Polo Grounds, Yankee Stadium, Soldier Field, Sesquicentennial Stadium, Braves Field, and Fenway Park all hosted major bouts during boxing's golden years. Boxers booked into bouts in ballparks knew they had reached the big time.

"Anytime you fight in a big stadium, you know it's special," said Hall of Famer Carlos Ortiz, who once headlined a fight card at Shea Stadium.

A big fight outdoors proved as compelling to fans as it did to fighters. When Gene Tunney took Jack Dempsey's title on September 23, 1926, 120,757 spectators filled Philadelphia's Sesquicentennial Stadium. Nearly one year to the day later, the Tunney-Dempsey rematch drew 104,943 to Chicago's Soldier Field.

A spectacular draw, Dempsey brought 91,613 to Boyles Thirty Acres in Jersey City, New Jersey, for his July 2, 1921, fight with French champion Georges Carpentier. Dempsey's subsequent bouts with Luis Firpo in the Polo Grounds on September 14, 1923, and with Jack Sharkey on July 21, 1927, each packed in more than 80,000 eyewitnesses. An audience of 102,000 watched Max Schmeling stop fellow German Walter Neusel in Round 9 of his August 26, 1934 fight in Hamburg, Germany, and Schmeling's rematch with Louis in 1938 brought more than 70,000 to Yankee Stadium.

In the 1954 Academy Award–winning film *On the Waterfront*, Marlon Brando's character, former fighter Terry Malloy, explains to his gangster brother Charlie the magic of an outdoor fight in a ballpark: "Remember that night in the Garden you came down to my dressing room and you said, 'Kid, this ain't your night. We're going for the price on Wilson.' You remember that? This ain't your night? My night! I coulda taken Wilson apart! So what happens? He gets the title shot outdoors in a ballpark and what do I get? A one-way ticket to Palooka-ville!"

Fans filling the Polo Grounds were aware of the old ballpark's history of hosting memorable matchups. They hoped Louis versus Conn would equal the excitement and intensity of previous Polo Grounds classics. From the time it first opened its doors to boxing with a small show on October 12, 1922 to its final fight card in 1960, which featured Floyd Patterson becoming the first man to regain the heavyweight title when he knocked out Ingemar Johansson in the fifth round—a vicious left hook that left the Swede's feet twitching as he was counted out—the Polo Grounds had a huge impact on ring history.

In 38 years of hosting boxing events, the Polo Grounds was the site for 33 fight cards and 25 championship bouts. The ballpark did not prove favorable for reigning kings, titlists losing their crowns nearly half of the time. The list of fighters who climbed the ring steps inside the Polo Grounds reads like a Who's Who of boxing greats.

Now came Louis and Conn, and their confrontation seized the imagination of the public, tens of thousands of whom would be in attendance while millions listened on radio. *Time* magazine estimated that 55 million people listened on radio when Louis fought. *Time* noted that apart from President Roosevelt's two most recent radio addresses in 1941, Louis's championship fights were attracting the largest audiences in radio history. Three years earlier, more than 100 million people listened to the Bomber's rematch with Max Schmeling. It was the largest radio audience in history to that point and included an estimated 64 percent of radios in the United States being tuned in. That total was exceeded only by FDR's addresses, which attracted 73 percent of America's radio owners.

Radio reached its zenith in the 1930s and 1940s, the airwaves bringing the world closer than it had ever been before and helping create the "global village" Canadian theorist Marshall McLuhan would write of in 1962. Radio allowed fans to sit in on major sporting events ranging from championship fights, World Series, and All-Star Games to college football bowl games and NFL championship games.

The medium also allowed national figures and world leaders to broadcast their speeches to millions of people worldwide. The impact of radio on the world was vividly illustrated by *Life* magazine in its issue published the week before the Louis-Conn fight. *Life* reported that on the day following FDR's historic broadcast from the East Room of the White House on May 27, a short-wave listening post in the United States heard the BBC in London rebroadcasting an excerpt from the president's speech. Roosevelt's reassuring voice and his measured diction was followed immediately by the shrill, guttural, frenzied speech of Adolf Hitler. A third voice, that of the British announcer, stated "We leave it to you listeners to judge which voice is the voice of calm strength and which that of hysterical violence."

Don Dunphy was among those who knew the important role radio played in 1941. The young broadcaster was teaming with veteran color analyst and one of the country's top sports columnists Bill Corum on the Mutual Radio Network broadcast of the Louis-Conn bout. A graduate of Manhattan College in New York, Dunphy began his career in the media as a part-time journalist for the *New York Journal-American* and *New York World-Telegram*. He moved on to be the public relations director of the New York Coliseum in the Bronx. It was there that Dunphy became interested in boxing and started his radio career broadcasting fights for WINS.

"That was my first break," Dunphy once recalled. WINS aired the Diamond Belt Bouts and Dunphy, outfitted in a stiff tuxedo, broadcast 24 three-round fights in one night. Most big fights were network broadcasts—NBC, CBS, and Mutual. WINS did a Saturday boxing program before the big fights, and Dunphy's interviews with boxing insiders were part of the show. Because the networks had Ted Husing, Bill Stern, and Sam Taub to do title fights, Dunphy found it difficult to get a prime assignment.

His second big break, however, came weeks before the Louis-Conn fight. Dunphy heard that Husing had a scheduling conflict and couldn't broadcast the bout and that an audition would be held to find a suitable replacement. The audition would be held the night of the light heavyweight championship bout between Gus Lesnevich and Anton Christoforidis. Auditioning along with Dunphy were Jimmy Powers, sports editor of the *New York Daily News*, local sportscaster Bert Lee, and Paul Douglas, who would enjoy renown as an actor.

Each sportscaster was scheduled to broadcast two rounds apiece of the title fight, and Dunphy decided to avoid the possibility of tripping over the fighter's tongue-twisting surnames and simply call them Gus and Anton. The strategy worked, and while his fellow broadcasters were struggling with names, Dunphy's descriptive account drew praise for being clear and concise.

In the weeks and days leading up to the fight of the year, Dunphy digested the prefight coverage in the New York newspapers. He read that Louis was favored to win, that the Bomber had been eliminating contenders to his throne for years, and that Conn just seemed to be the most available challenger.

Dunphy studied Conn's credentials and found them impeccable. Winner of 18 fights in 1936, including a victory on points over tough Fritzie Zivic; conqueror of former middleweight champs Babe Risko, Vince Dundee, Teddy Yarosz, and Young Corbett III in '37; two non-title wins over middleweight king Fred Apostoli in '39; decision over light-heavyweight boss Melio Bettino in '39; three combined title defenses against Bettina and Gus Lesnevich spanning 1939–1940; KO of heavyweight Bob Pastor in 1940; and unanimous decisions over heavies Al McCoy and Lee Savold.

In time, Conn took down 10 men who held titles, fighters whose surnames spanned the alphabet from A to Z—Apostoli, Bettina, Corbett III, Dundee, Krieger, Lesnevich, Risko, Yarosz, Zale, and Zivic. Billy was awarded the Edward J. Neil Trophy as the Boxing Writers Association of America Fighter of the Year in 1939 and was named by *The Ring* as its Fighter of the Year in 1940.

The *New York Daily News* touted Conn, stating "The Irishman is indeed a beauteous boxer who could probably collect coinage by joining the ballet league if he chose to flee the egg-eared and flattened nose fraternity."

Newspapers carried comments from Conn that he was going to beat the champ. The Pittsburgh Kid was tough and brash, but Dunphy wasn't sure Sweet William could pull off what he promised; despite his credentials it seemed an idle boast. In Dunphy's view, the Kid wasn't big enough, strong enough, or skilled enough to stand up to the Bomber.

Still, the broadcaster believed, as did others, that Conn did have one thing going for him. The Kid was quick, Dunphy thought; he could hit and move. Still, as one sportswriter noted, "Nobody can keep moving long enough to stay away from Joe all night."

Despite what sportswriters were saying, the Kid left little doubt that he would not only beat the Bomber, but he would also stop him inside the 15-round distance.

"I'm going to knock Louis out," Conn declared, "and be the champion for the next 20 years!"

The drama built for weeks, and on the morning of June 18, Dunphy pored over the early editions of the New York newspapers for the latest on Louis and Conn. He left his home in Jackson Heights to go to the weigh-in. Dunphy then had lunch and headed to WINS. Station manager Cec Hackett was going to the fight and invited Dunphy to have dinner with him and his wife. The Hacketts offered to drive Dunphy to the Polo Grounds after dinner and Don accepted.

The Hacketts' apartment was on 70th Street and Fifth Avenue, and even with the expected traffic Dunphy figured they could make it to the ballpark in less than 45 minutes. The main event was scheduled for 10:00 p.m., and with Dunphy planning to be at ringside no later than 9:00, he and the Hacketts were confident they could leave at 8:00 and make it in plenty of time.

Dunphy and the Hacketts reached 125th Street and were only a mile and a half from the stadium when their drive stalled. There was construction on Eighth Avenue for the next half-mile and all traffic was being rerouted. Cars were gridlocked and by 8:45 Dunphy was growing alarmed; by 9:00 he was in a near-panic. He knew the executives of Mutual and its sponsor Gillette were at ringside and wondering where he was.

Dunphy's mind raced. Would his station and its sponsor wonder if he was in an accident, or worse, had chickened out? At 9:15, Dunphy and the Hacketts reached 145th Street. They were inching closer, but Dunphy could wait no longer. He thanked the Hacketts for dinner and the drive, hurried from their car, and hustled down the subway steps. A train arrived almost immediately and was jammed with fans heading to the fight. Dunphy squeezed aboard and within minutes the train arrived at the stop for the Polo Grounds.

With ticket in hand the broadcaster ran to the ballpark's press gate; it was packed but he got in. He should have entered the field by way of the bullpen in right field and headed to the ring that was set up over the pitcher's mound. Trying to make better time, Dunphy instead took an alternate route, ducking beneath the stands and out to the field through the box seats. His shortcut worked and he was just 70 feet from his seat when a policeman stopped him and examined his ticket.

"This ticket calls for entrance through the bullpen," the officer said. "You can't get out this way."

Dunphy could see the Mutual and Gillette execs at ringside looking for him. He told the policeman who he was and that he was there to broadcast the fight. The officer remarked that he had never heard of him and ignored the broadcaster's pleas to enter the field through the gate. It was 9:30, and Dunphy had to retrace his steps under the stands and back to the bullpen entrance. He was not only fighting time, but also the huge crowd that was pushing against him.

Finally reaching the field, a fatigued Dunphy suddenly felt invigorated by the sweet scent of the outfield grass; it was tonic to the tiring announcer. Racing to ringside, Dunphy reached his seat at 9:40; only 20 minutes remained before the start of the main event. The look of relief on the faces of the executives who had been anxiously awaiting him was a sight that stayed with Dunphy the rest of his days.

While fans packed the Polo Grounds, Louis was feeling the ill effects of trimming down to 199 pounds. The day before the fight was usually one of rest or light work; instead, it had seen the champ training as hard as he had throughout his preparation. In so doing he defied his trainer, and Chappie Blackburn was fuming. "Mad as hell," Louis remembered. Knowing the Bomber needed some pumping up, Bill Bottoms, one of Louis's corner men, prepared a meal of steak, black-eyed peas, and salad before the champion's entourage departed for the ballpark.

When Louis arrived at the Polo Grounds, he saw the stadium filling up. "Good house," he thought. He followed what had become his standard routine in the final hours before a fight—he climbed onto a locker room table and fell asleep.

Not far away in his dressing room, Conn was keyed up. Earlier that day he and his brother Jackie had engaged in a wrestling match in Billy's hotel room. Freddie Fierro finally separated the Conn boys, but their antics had Johnny Ray just as mad as Jack Blackburn.

Billy was on edge for several reasons. Days before the fight he had flown back to Pittsburgh to visit his mother one final time before the fight. He presented her with a diamond bracelet, but she gave it back to him. "It's beautiful, Billy. But don't give it to me. Give it to Mary Louise."

Kissing his mother goodbye, Billy told her, "I gotta go now, but the next time you see me, I'll be the heavyweight champion of the world."

"No, son," she replied. "The next time I see you will be in Paradise."

Billy took his leave, and now he was in his dressing room, thinking of Maggie, of Mary Louise, of Louis. A notoriously slow starter in the ring, Billy began shadowboxing and pacing to get his muscles warm.

Inside their rooms the fighters and their trainers could hear the stands above filling up. Fans congratulated DiMaggio on his way to his ringside seat; Bob Feller was nearby as well. J. Edgar Hoover, Bob Hope, and Al Jolson took their places at ringside, as did General of the Army George Marshall.

DiMaggio's appearance caused quite a stir. Fashionably attired in a double-breasted blue suit, French cuff shirt, hand-painted tie, and Italian shoes, Joe D. attracted so many autograph seekers that he had almost as many of New York's Finest around him as Louis and Conn. The debonair DiMaggio dragged on a Camel cigarette as his close friend George Solotaire, a Broadway ticket holder, stood nearby and thought the celebrity of the Yankees star was close to starting a riot.

Fans thumbing through their 25-cent souvenir program scanned the names involved in the undercard, a four-round bout followed by four fights scheduled for six rounds each leading up to the main event. There were single-page biographies of Louis and Conn. Of Louis, writer Jersey Jones said:

"No champion ever has compiled such an amazing list of 'firsts' as this spectacular load of two-fisted machinery. No heavyweight has boasted the remarkable punching percentage that has established Louis as one of the greatest clouters, if not THE greatest, the prize ring has uncovered."

Jones noted that over the course of Louis's pro and amateur careers, he had recorded 88 knockouts in 107 starts, a KO percentage of .822. The Bomber was the "fightingest" champion in heavyweight history, but when asked in the article how much longer he would continue in the ring, Joe wasn't sure.

"Can't say," he answered. "Maybe three or four years. Maybe only a couple of months. Maybe Uncle Sam wants me for the army. If he does,

I'm ready. If he don't, I'll keep fighting as long as Uncle Mike finds me opponents."

Conn's bio, penned by Jack Miley of "Bum of the Month Club" renown, acknowledged that many believed Billy to be a boy on a man's errand. "As a matter of fact, Conn has had more actual ring experience than Joe. He has had more fights than the champion he seeks to dethrone . . .

"Billy Conn had to fight tooth and nail for everything he's got, and he has now pummeled everybody out of the way except the head man, Louis, who is next man on his Hit Parade."

Miley quoted Billy and Johnny as saying that if they're wrong in their belief that Louis was ready to be beaten, they didn't want sympathy afterward. "Because if That Man licks us nobody can say we didn't ask for it. Only we know we're going to win, see? Otherwise, we wouldn't be fooling around with the fellow."

Down the hall, the champion awoke from his short nap. "Got to get to work," Louis said. Millions of US radio owners in living rooms, bars, and social clubs turned their dials to the broadcast. In Forbes Field, the host Pittsburgh Pirates and New York Giants were preparing to halt their game, exit the expansive grass and dirt grounds of the brightly lit ballpark and head to their respective dugouts to listen to the broadcast that would be boomed throughout the ballpark.

At 5435 Fifth Avenue in Pittsburgh, the young colleens of the Conn clan sat shoulder-to-shoulder around one of the three radios in their home. In her bedroom upstairs Maggie prayed for her boy in this, his crucible hour. Downstairs, Billy's sister Mary Jane and young cousin Davey Herr leaned forward in their seats to catch every crackling word coming from New York.

At 10:00 p.m. Eastern Standard Time, Dunphy began what would become an historic broadcast:

> "From the Polo Grounds in New York City . . . the
> heavyweight championship of the world. Joe Louis,
> the champion, versus Billy Conn, the challenger . . ."

The sudden explosion of crowd noise inside the ballpark told Dunphy that one of the fighters could be seen making his entrance from beneath the packed stands. The broadcaster was struck at the sights and sounds of nearly 55,000 spectators standing and screaming and whistling.

Dunphy strained to see Conn making his way to the ring; the Kid was "marching down the aisle," Dunphy noted. The smiling Irishman had his dark hair covered by a white towel; his smile, however, shone bright.

Wearing a cream-colored satin robe trimmed in Celtic green and with his name embroidered in script across the back, black leather boxing shoes, and white socks, Conn raised his right arm high in the air to acknowledge the deafening roar of his fans, many of them clad in Irish green. Inside the collar of Conn's robe was a manufacturer's label for the Benlee Sporting Goods Company.

Dunphy watched the challenger dance up the ring stairs; he thought Billy "confident and sure of himself." The broadcaster told his radio audience that the fearsome reputation of the Brown Bomber had not damaged the Pittsburgh Kid's self-confidence.

Dunphy: "Conn approaches the ring, climbs over the ropes, dances to his corner and begins loosening up."

Corum: "Billy is wearing those purple trunks...."

Billy bowed to his fans, blessed himself in the Sign of the Cross, and moved to ring center. A huge ovation, erupting from the right field seats where Giants great Mel Ott launched home runs, signaled the first sighting of Joe Louis.

Corum: "Here comes Joe! Julian Black precedes him into the ring. Listen to that cheering...."

The champion moved carefully as he threaded his way through thousands of fans. He was wearing black shoes, white socks, and as was his wont, a white flannel robe beneath a blue satin robe with red trim.

Corum: "Joe's got on his famous blue-and-red bathrobe with JOE LOUIS on the back, and he's got another dressing gown and robe underneath that, a white one ... He's holding a towel around his head."

Louis was confident but not demonstrably so. When he first started fighting, Louis was afraid he might lose. After he won the title, he no longer thought about defeat. He knew that if he kept on fighting, someone would come along and take the title from him. But in Louis's mind, it was never this guy, never this night.

Like many champions before him, Louis was a creature of habit. He favored the blue-and-red robe over a white robe just as Jack Dempsey always wore a dirty, maroon-colored sweater when he entered the ring. "That sweater," Dempsey once told George J. Pardy of *The Ring*, "has been with me ever since I began fighting." Dempsey bought the sweater in St. Louis out of his first ring earnings and was never beaten while wearing it. He believed it brought him luck. Prior to the Firpo fight, Dempsey's manager Doc Kearns replaced the old maroon sweater with a new white one. After Jack had to rally from a near knockout, he handed the new sweater back to Kearns.

"Here Doc, take this. I don't want to see it again. For my next bout give me that old coat you wouldn't let me wear tonight. That Firpo fellow nearly put me out because I didn't go out in my old coat."

Heavyweight champs Jim Corbett and Bob Fitzsimmons were also superstitious, as was middleweight king Stanley Ketchel, who would never enter the ring without wearing his favored cap. Once in the ring Ketchel would place his grimy hat on top of a ring post for good luck.

Dunphy noted that Louis's face was nearly buried beneath a white towel. The Bomber took off his satin robe and threw a series of short, quick punches into the night air.

Corum: "Conn is putting on the gloves first, and Billy looks in great shape, doesn't look as big as Louis naturally, a 174-pound man couldn't. Twenty-five pounds have got to show...."

Finally, Louis and Conn were in the ring together. Both men wore brown Benlee brand boxing gloves. Fans were on their feet as tuxedoed ring announcer Harry Balogh began introducing the celebrities in the crowd. Balogh was an announcer with few peers. The New York native got his start at Grupp's Gym on Eighth Avenue; Grupp's was famous as the site where numerous notable fighters and trainers began their careers. At the time, leather-lunged Joe Humphreys—renowned for working without a microphone—was the country's most celebrated boxing announcer. Humphreys's retirement in 1933 allowed Balogh to become the voice of boxing.

Balogh was the first boxing announcer to work in a tuxedo, beginning a tradition that continues still. He worked bouts at the Polo Grounds, Yankee Stadium, and Madison Square Garden and was known for speaking out against racism. Addressing fight crowds, Balogh told fans to judge boxers not by their skin color but by their skill.

"Regardless of race, creed, or color," he implored into the ring microphone, "let us all say and mean it, 'May the better man emerge victorious!'"

Balogh's call was far more forward-thinking than others. His predecessor, Humphreys, served as guest ring announcer for the Joe Louis–Max Baer fight, and introduced Louis in the following manner:

"Although colored, he stands out in the same class as Jack Johnson and Sam Langford as an idol of his people."

On this night, as Louis and Conn warmed up in their corners, Balogh called for the crowd's attention as he began his introductions for the main event.

Balogh: "Attention, please. Thank you, ladies and gentlemen. The officials as the judges—Marty Monroe, Bill Healy, the timekeeper is George Bannon. Counting for the knockdowns at the bell, Jed Gahan. The referee is Eddie Joseph."

The crowd was restless and Balogh again called for their attention.

Balogh: "The feature attraction on this evening's program . . . Fifteen rounds for the heavyweight championship of the world!"

Bannon rang the bell several times as Balogh, his dark hair slicked back and outfitted this night in a white tux, white shirt, black bow tie, black pants, and shoes, prepared to introduce the principals. The champion was announced first, and Balogh barely got through his introduction before Joe's supporters made their presence known.

Balogh: "Presenting the present world's heavyweight king, from Detroit, Michigan, weighing 199 and a half, he's wearing black trunks ...Joe Louis!"

Louis's satin trunks were dark purple rather than black, and they were trimmed with a navy-blue waistband and navy-blue stripe on each side panel. It was customary for the champion to don the color of royalty, but Conn, perhaps seeking to offset any psychological advantage Louis could claim by wearing the color of a king, was also wearing purple trunks. Fitting, since Conn in Gaelic is related to the Old Irish "cenn" (chief) or "cond" (king).

These were two kings of the ring and Balogh, turning toward Conn's corner, extended his left arm toward the challenger.

*"From Pittsburgh, Pennsylvania, weighing 174 . . ."*

The crowd gasped. Conn weighed 180¼ for his most recent fight, against Buddy Knox in Pittsburgh less than a month earlier. Fans couldn't believe he weighed in six pounds lighter and wasn't even in heavyweight range. They would have been even more shocked had they known that Billy's actual weight was just 169.

Dunphy thought Conn seemed so much smaller than Louis that people were afraid for Billy. Conn didn't appear concerned. He felt good as he loosened up; his dark locks shining beneath the bright ring lights. "Yeah, I figured I could beat him," Billy said later. "I was in good shape. I figured I could move around and outpoint him."

Balogh: "Wearing purple trunks, the very capable challenger ... Billy Conn!"

The cheers were deafening. It seemed to Dunphy that the challenger had twice as many supporters as the champion. Conn stepped forward from his corner and acknowledged the applause with a wave of his gloved right hand. The crowd noise filled the air and rose like a tidal wave across the ballpark and out beyond the streets. "All New York had to hear it," Dunphy thought.

Balogh: "May the better man emerge victorious!"

Referee Eddie Joseph, wearing a light gray, long-sleeved, button-down shirt with two breast pockets, the left one housing his scorecard and pen, cuffed gray slacks, black belt, black bow tie, and ankle-high black ring shoes, brought the fighters and their handlers to ring center for their final instructions.

Johnny Ray smiled as Billy, preening like a peacock, pranced out to meet Louis. Ray loved the way the Kid walked out there to get his instructions from the referee, Billy's cocksure manner letting everyone know he wasn't afraid of anybody. No matter who Billy was fighting, Ray thought the Kid made it clear before the first bell that he was boss of the ring.

"Let's have a good clean fight. Shake hands and go to work," Joseph said.

As was his custom when the referee spoke, Louis looked down at the canvas. Conn grinned at the expressionless champion. At the conclusion of Joseph's instructions, the fighters touched gloves.

Corum: "They're going back to their corners, Johnny Ray rubbing Conn, patting him on the back. Jack Blackburn with his hand over Louis's shoulder."

From his seat behind the Mutual microphone on the ring apron, Dunphy could feel the tension in the air. His voice and throat went dry for an instant. A deep breath and the broadcaster felt fine again. Dunphy knew he'd be ready when the bell rang.

Louis and Conn were ready as well. "Once the bell rings, you're on your own," Louis said once. "It's just you and the other guy."

In past fights the "other" guy facing Louis often froze with fear. This time, however, Billy the Kid was in the opposite corner.

As the bright lights inside the ballpark dimmed, Louis looked resolute, Conn nervously cocky.

One of the greatest fights in ring history was moments away.

Corum: "There's the bell!"

## CHAPTER SIX

# "HE CAN RUN, BUT HE CAN'T HIDE"

What would it feel like to get hit by Joe Louis?

The question had to be on the mind of Billy Conn in the final seconds before the opening bell of their championship fight. The Pittsburgh Kid had heard the frightening firsthand stories from past opponents of the awesome punching power of the Brown Bomber.

"Nobody hits like Louis," former heavyweight champion Jim Braddock said. "That man is dynamite. I've never been hit so hard in my life.

"That first jab he nails you, you know what it's like? It's like someone jammed an electric bulb in your face and busted it."

Asked about Louis's right-hand punch, Braddock said, "It ain't like a punch. It's like someone nailed you with a crowbar. I thought half my head was blown off. I figured he caved it in. After he hit me, I couldn't even feel if it was there."

Other former champs agreed with the Cinderella Man about the Bomber's power. "That guy can hit, there's no lying about that," Jack Sharkey stated. "You can't afford to make mistakes against him."

Max Baer, another former champ who couldn't deal with the dynamite in Louis's gloves, said he was hit so hard by Louis, "I couldn't see straight."

Eddie Simms lasted less than a minute with the Bomber before referee Arthur Donovan mercifully stopped the carnage. "Louis might have broken Simms' neck," Donovan said.

"He's a hell of a puncher," Tony Galento said of Louis. Johnny Paycheck's legs still quivered for several minutes following his knockout by Louis. "How that man can hit," said Paycheck. "I don't remember anything after the first knockdown."

Louis hit Nathan Mann so hard Mann was concussed and wasn't even aware he had hit the canvas several times. "I didn't know I was down," Mann told startled reporters. "Was I?"

Following his brutal stoppage, Red Burman remarked, "I was doing all right until I was knocked out!" Jack Roper, stopped in the first round, lamented, "I zigged when I should've zagged."

The Bomber drove Paulino Uzcudun's teeth through his mouthpiece, immobilized Max Schmeling with a right hand to the kidney and paralyzed him with a left hook to the solar plexus. Max's nervous system was jarred; his vision blurred. Louis hit Schmeling so hard in the body it caused him to lose sight for several seconds. "He hurt me so much," Schmeling said.

Tommy Hearns's trainer Emmanuel Steward studied film of the Louis-Schmeling rematch and thought the Bomber's body blows "unbelievable." A physician during the champion's reign stated publicly that the human body was not built to absorb punches from Joe Louis. Nat Fleischer wrote in the April 1939 issue of *The Ring* magazine, "No human body can take the punishment that Joe dishes out once he goes after his prey. That has been proven conclusively."

Eddie Futch, who trained future heavyweight champs Joe Frazier and Ken Norton, sparred with Louis at the Brewster gym in Detroit. "Joe's punches could paralyze you," Futch said of Louis. "Anywhere he'd hit you, you'd feel it."

Futch recalled catching Louis's lefts and rights on his arms and shoulders and thought their impact as jarring as an automobile accident.

Louis left Arturo Godoy's face a grotesque mask of welts, bruises, and bloody cuts. Perhaps the only person not awed by the Bomber's power, speed, and accuracy was a slick boxer sitting ringside at the Godoy fight.

"He wouldn't do that to me," Conn told reporters. "I'd be dancing all around him, shooting for his chin."

To others, the Kid boasted that even if Joe did land one of his bombs, he'd deal with it. "Few of Louis's opponents were kayoed with one punch," Conn told writer Sam Andre in 1940. "Most of them went down a couple of times, had a chance to recover but got panicky instead and were goners."

Decades later *The Way It Was* host Curt Gowdy praised Louis as the greatest heavyweight champion ever and remarked to Conn that despite the fact that he was fighting a legend who was 25 pounds heavier, stronger, and hit infinitely harder, Billy still thought he could beat him.

"Sure," Conn stated matter-of-factly. "That's my business."

Fleischer placed Louis's boxing style and abilities in historical context. "He sails in, crashes his blows to the body and head, gives the opposition little chance to get set for a counterattack and wards off blows with the cleverness of a Jack Johnson." Fleischer thought only Johnson and Jack Dempsey compared to Louis in fighting ability.

Louis was a ring rarity, a puncher-boxer with the hardest punch and fastest hands ever seen among heavyweights to that point. Writer Monte D. Cox calls Louis "without doubt the greatest combination puncher to ever lace on the gloves. No one could put their punches together as beautifully as did Louis."

Cox believes Louis threw every punch—jab, cross, uppercut—with textbook perfection. The Bomber made his punches more murderous by placing them perfectly to vital parts of his opponent's anatomy—behind the ear, chin, floating rib, heart, and liver. "In this extremely important category of punching efficiency," wrote Cox, "Louis has no peer."

Boxing writer William Detloff states that all the punches in the Bomber's arsenal were so perfectly and precisely thrown every time "that you get the sense watching him that he couldn't have been wild or sloppy if he tried."

British ring historian Gilbert Odd noted that Louis's straight left was so powerful it would "snap a man's head back with sickening monotony until he wavered under the steady punishment, then he was speedily finished off with swift and accurate hooks from both hands, or a finely-timed right cross that carried such knockdown force that few who took it could survive."

Sportswriter Hype Igoe thought Conn could survive and would beat the champ. But Igoe had reservations. Writing in the February 1941 issue of *The Ring*, Igoe contended that if Louis fought every foe with the same fury he showed against Schmeling, none of Joe's opponents would survive the first round.

Louis was a fast starter, his record number of first-round knockouts were proof of that. Conn, by contrast, required a couple of rounds to warm up due to his slow heartbeat. This contrast served to make the opening moments of their showdown even more meaningful.

Knowing fans leaned forward in their seats: be they inside the Polo Grounds, listening to the public address system in Forbes Field, or huddled around radios. A huge roar accompanied the opening clang of the bell; Louis versus Conn was now reality.

Emerging from his corner in his familiar fashion, the champion's stance was both stylish and sound. Hall of Fame trainer Freddie Roach, who has worked with more than 20 champions including Mike Tyson, Manny Pacquiao, Oscar De La Hoya, Bernard Hopkins, and Julio Cesar Chavez Jr. calls Louis the best textbook fighter of all time.

Louis's style in the ring was so classical it could be set to music and often was. No other athlete has ever inspired as many songs as the Brown Bomber. Joe was still two years away from winning the heavyweight championship when Memphis Minnie sang in August of 1935 that Louis's punches were like "a kick from a Texas mule" and "a jolt of dy-nee-mite." Memphis Minnie, in her husky voice, sang of a Louis fight film being shown at a local movie house and declared, "If you ain't got no money, honey, go tomorrow night!"

As writer David Margolick pointed out in the *New York Times* in February 2001, "To be immortalized in a single song is a kick; to have a couple written about you is extraordinary. But to have dozens is homage of almost biblical proportions, and in the world of sports only Joe Louis has that distinction."

Rena Kosersky, whose job has been to locate music for documentaries on sports greats Muhammad Ali, Jack Johnson, Jackie Robinson, and Joe DiMaggio, spent nine years researching musical tributes to Louis. She discovered a startling 43 songs about the Brown Bomber and added that there are likely many more.

William H. Wiggins Jr., an authority on Louis, said that no other athlete and certainly no other fighter has inspired the number of songs that Louis has. Musical tributes to Louis include virtually all genres, from jazz to blues, Tin Pan Alley to ballads, gospel to hard rock. Song titles included "Joe the Bomber"; "Joe Louis Is the Man"; "Winner Joe, the Knockout King"; and "Champ Joe Louis (King of the Gloves)."

Tributes were produced by legends Count Basie and Cab Calloway, as well as famous white composers like Irving Berlin. Margolick wrote in the *Times* that the Louis of these songs is someone who deals out ambidextrous destruction in the ring. "But out of it, he is decent, hard working, gentle. . . . The songs describe Louis's famous poker face, his natty clothes, his love of a nice thick steak. Several stress how good he is to his mother—the type . . . to buy her a brand-new home with his earnings."

They were part of a distinctive soundtrack to the 1930s and 1940s—radio broadcasts of Louis's fights; Major League Baseball games; college football bowl games; FDR's Fireside Chats; Bing Crosby; Billie Holliday; Count Basie.

Louis liked listening to Basie and attended the Count's performances in clubs in New York City. Basie's trademark sound—a unique brand of swinging blues—could have served as a soundtrack for Louis's fights. Just as Basie's band battled other bands in ballrooms—bands would play opposite each other to see who received the greater applause—Louis battled in the ring. And just as Basie's band was never beaten, neither did Louis endure defeat.

"Louis was so impressive," William Detloff says. "His technique was perfect, his mechanics were perfect, and he threw those short punches."

In his opening advance on Conn, Louis led as he always did, with his left foot. As instructed by Jack Blackburn, the Bomber closed in on

Conn a few inches at a time, his right foot following to maintain proper balance. In his book *How to Box*, Louis told readers, "Boxing is built upon punching and footwork." If Louis found his stance too narrow, he moved his right foot a few inches to the right to widen his stance. If Joe thought his stance too wide, he would glide his right foot forward a few inches.

Unlike some champions, most notably Muhammad Ali, Louis's style never changed in a career that spanned three decades and was challenged by more varying styles than perhaps any fighter ever.

Conn's slick, standup style was the latest test to Louis, and in those opening moments a pattern was established that would last for almost the entire fight. Despite his remarks that Louis was no longer the fighting machine of 1938, Conn remained respectful of the Bomber's power. Don Dunphy observed that the challenger would not slug with the champion; "No man in his right mind would," he stated. Instead, the Kid would box and move; he would snake out long left-hand leads and try to keep the Bomber off balance.

Louis would counter by relentlessly stalking Conn, seeking to get inside Billy's defenses and hammer his lean flanks with body blows to slow him down. Knowing this, the Kid quickly retreated to avoid the advancing Bomber. Billy's wavy hair bounced in concert with his movement. Sportswriter Vincent Flaherty thought Conn "looked like Oliver Twist invading the den of 40 thieves with a cap pistol." Billy moved backward, Randy Roberts wrote, "for no other purpose than to avoid serious injury."

As the Kid backpedaled the Bomber moved forward in brisk fashion, his patented poker face an expressionless mask. Writer Gay Talese watched film of the Louis-Conn fight years later and noted the "menacing, solemn image of Joe Louis" moving across the screen toward Conn. Nat Fleischer, editor of *The Ring* magazine, was at the fight and saw Louis as a "cold, calculating fighter with fixed eyes, mercilessly and systematically going after his taunting rival."

Louis's cold stare unnerved opponents. "It's his eyes when you're in the ring with him," a sparring partner said. "They're blank and staring, always watching you. Always that blank look—that's what gets you."

Confronting Louis for the first time, Conn looked shaken; the challenger issued a couple of jabs that fell harmlessly short. The Kid was nervous, and his anxiety showed just seven seconds into Round One when while backing toward the ropes near his corner Billy's right foot slipped and he nearly went down.

Dunphy: "Conn almost slips, moving around very fast . . ."

Conn's rapid retreat recalled the exchange Louis had with sportswriters prior to the bout. When Hype Igoe mentioned that Billy the Kid would try to keep the Bomber at bay by employing a "hit-and-run" attack, Louis offered a sobering and soon-to-be-famous response.

"He can run, but he can't hide."

Some sources credit Joe's remark to his rematch with Billy in 1946, but Louis told Gowdy on *The Way It Was* that Igoe told him before the 1941 fight that Conn was "going to do a lot of running."

"For no reason," remembered Louis, "I said, 'He can run, but he can't hide.'"

*The Ring* magazine likewise stated that Louis issued the quote in the lead-up to his 1941 fight with Conn. The June 1946 issue of the *Coshocton* (Ohio) *Tribune* quotes Louis as making the remark in response to a reporter asking the champ, "If (Conn) runs, will you chase him?" The following day's *New York Times* coverage of the fight included a headline reading, "Louis Proves His Own Prediction: Conn Could Run but Couldn't Hide."

Quotation expert Ralph Keyes said Louis was likely repeating a line he had originally made years before and was used as street talk. Barry Poplik said Louis made a similar statement prior to facing boxer Bob Pastor in 1939.

"It's all right to have good legs," Louis said of Pastor, "but remember one thing—when you're in the ring you can run, but you can't hide."

The phrase was so popular Louis later co-authored a song titled "You Can Run (But You Can't Hide)," recorded by soul singer Solomon Burke. Joe introduced his composition on the January 4, 1957, airing of *Tonight on the Steve Allen Show*.

Louis had a sharp wit; he's said to be the author of another famous quote, "Everyone has a plan, until they get hit." It's a saying Mike Tyson popularized decades later. It's also a quote that seemed fitting for Joe's fight with Conn, particularly when 10 seconds into the fight Louis landed the bout's first blow, a left jab that landed high on Conn's forehead and snapped his head back.

Photographer's flashbulbs popped from the ringside as Conn felt for the first time the dreaded blow that Braddock said felt like a lightbulb being busted in his face, that writer Gilbert Odd saw snap a man's head back in sickening fashion. Described as "piston-like," Louis's pumping left jab was a product of his formative days in Detroit, the jab first taught to him by Holman Williams.

Williams was a member of "Black Murderer's Row," a title given to talented Black boxers who were never given a shot at a world title. A future boxing Hall of Famer, Williams worked with Louis in Motown, and helped improve Joe's left jab.

The worth of Williams's work in developing Louis's punches, particularly his left jab, was evident when Blackburn took over as Joe's trainer. Chappie saw a fighter who he thought was likely to trip over his own feet but could kill an opponent with his left jab. "Man, if he can hit you that hard with a jab," thought Blackburn, "wonder what he can do with his right?"

By the time Louis stalked Conn, Blackburn's years of working with Joe had turned the champion into a consummate puncher-boxer who outslugged heavy hitters and outboxed tacticians. This was the complicated puzzle the masterful Conn was seeking to solve.

Dunphy: "Louis jabs with his left . . ."

Conn's columnar neck and sturdy chin stood him in good stead throughout his career and would do so now again against the Brown Bomber.

Says Tim Conn, "Melio Bettina told me, 'Your dad had a great chin. I couldn't hurt him.' My father had a thick neck, 17½ inches. That was the only measurement he beat Louis in."

Three seconds following Louis's landing his first jab, Conn countered by connecting with his first punch, a left jab to Joe's left eye. Billy stayed on his bicycle, circling to his left to stay away from Joe's jab. What was startling in seeing Conn and Louis squaring off was that Billy at 6'1½" looked as tall or taller than the 6'2" Louis, because Billy's stance was straight up and Louis was bent slightly forward at the waist.

Dunphy: "The wraithlike Conn keeps moving around the ring. Louis is trying to get him into a corner. Still trying to crowd him and get that crushing blow in if he can . . . Louis just waiting for Conn to lead so he can counter with that right."

Moving forward in measured steps, Louis kept his right hand cocked. Louis and Blackburn saw the straight right hand as one of the most dangerous blows in boxing. In Louis's repertoire, the right hand was always preceded by the left jab and carried, in the Bomber's words, "a lot of force."

The straight right was one of the more deadly punches in the champion's arsenal; the right cross was another, Louis throwing the punch with all the energy and strength he had. Joe's right hand stopped Bob Pastor in their rematch. "I didn't even see the punch coming," Pastor said. "The next thing I knew the referee was counting nine."

Dunphy: "Louis still stalking Conn. Conn moving around very fast, from right to left."

The Kid's nervousness was evident a second time in the first minute of the fight when he tossed another straight left and slipped again, this time stumbling backward onto the canvas. Louis was in the process of aiming a right hand to Conn's head when he went down amid more flashing bulbs, but Eddie Joseph correctly ruled it a slip and stepped between the fighters to wipe the rosin from Billy's gloves without issuing a count.

Dunphy: "Conn is down but it's not from a punch. He jabbed at Louis and slipped. And Louis didn't even hit him on the way down. It's not going to be a knockdown."

Louis and Conn clinched for the first time in the fight and the champion hooked hard to the challenger's head. Billy fired a left to the body but was tagged with a left and right to the head as Joe caught him in a place Conn wanted to avoid—along the ropes.

Dunphy: "He's got Conn on the ropes. He rips a hard right to the midsection and a left hook to the jaw."

"My plan was to catch him in the corners," Louis later told Gowdy. "I knew he was going to do a lot of running; I wanted to keep him from the center of the ring."

Conn hooked twice to Louis's head but got tagged again, the Bomber landing a pair of hard rights and a left to the ear as Billy backed away. Conn continued to dance and poked a left into Joe's face before the two clinched for the second time.

Dunphy: "They clinch. Louis gets a left and a right free and pounds Conn twice and Conn seems to be hurt. But he's out bouncing around in the center of the ring."

"I was trying to keep him from getting a good shot at me," Conn told Gowdy. "I knew he could take you out with one punch, so I had to keep moving."

Spectators could see in these two celebrated fighters their distinct contrasts in style and motive. Billy would dart left, dash right, and look to outbox the Bomber; Joe was on an urgent seek-and-destroy mission. The Kid was snaking out left jabs that the Bomber brushed away with his right glove. This championship contest would be as much mental as physical; Louis and Conn both being pragmatic strategists. Billy would be reading Joe, and the Bomber would set traps for the Kid with feints and false leads.

Dunphy: "Louis had Conn on the ropes but Billy kept moving away and got out of range . . . Louis is trying to get Conn into a corner."

Louis's swift advance and Conn's quick retreat made the pace of the first round very fast. It was enough to keep even the well-conditioned referee on the go.

Dunphy: "Eddie Joseph is moving around. A very fast fight . . . Louis is trying to get Conn in there and Conn won't accommodate."

With 10 seconds left in the round Louis landed again, a hard left to Conn's eye.

Dunphy: "And there's the bell for Round One!"

Dunphy turned the microphone over to Bill Corum for analysis.

Corum: "That was a good round but a feeler-out round."

Round One belonged to Louis. Billy the Kid was moving quickly but the Bomber had still caught him with a couple of hard shots. Corum thought Conn's strategy was evident. Billy would move and try to tire Joe out. Louis's last eight fights had ended inside 15 rounds, and the Kid was hoping the Bomber might struggle to go the distance.

Louis considered Conn's movement mosquito-like. "He'd sting and move," Louis remembered in his autobiography.

Conn told author Peter Heller his strategy was not to get hit. "That's the game," Billy said. "Get out of the way." Sweet William's fight plan was to move side to side, keep the Bomber turning. The Kid knew the Bomber was, as he put it, "a real dangerous man."

Dunphy: "Everybody wonders just how long Billy Conn can keep away from the champion. Louis continually tries to get him in close . . ."

Round Two followed the same script as its predecessor. Billy was backing up, moving away from Joe, who continued his stalking tactics. Conn thought Louis too slow, too methodical and robotic, to beat a boxer as stylish as he was. He also believed Joe could be outfoxed and struggled to make in-fight decisions; many agreed and pointed to the first Schmeling fight as proof. The Kid's confidence was bolstered when he scouted the Bomber in person.

"Get me in the ring with this guy!" Conn pleaded to Johnny Ray. "He won't be able to hit me with a handful of rice!"

What some failed to realize was that even though Louis did not cut the ring as aggressively as other fighters, the Bomber was so efficient a stalker that there wasn't a boxer in the world during his near 12-year reign who held a stylistic advantage over him.

Dunphy: "They're out in the center of the ring again . . . Louis, as usual, just moves around; watching Conn do all the motioning . . ."

Louis's footwork lacked the dynamism of Conn, so Joe wasn't overly aggressive in trying to cut the ring as Billy backed up and circled. What the Bomber did do was pressure the Kid psychologically; he moved with Sweet William in whatever direction Billy was going, boxing's ultimate predator forcing upon Conn the realization that one false move could lead to a sudden ending.

By keeping his front foot perpendicular to Billy's back foot, Joe was able to follow his own maxim to "move the body easily at all times so that balance will not be disturbed." This was clever footwork, and while most fans equate footwork with speedy boxers, Louis did not. "Clever footwork," Louis said in *How to Box*, "does not mean hopping and jumping around." The purpose of footwork, Louis learned from Blackburn, was to give opponents false leads, and that was what Joe was looking to do to Billy.

Unlike the pressure-cooker approach applied by Louis's contemporary, "Hurricane" Henry Armstrong, the Bomber's pressure was slow and psychological. Joe was economical with his punches; he sought quality not quantity. Where Armstrong would swarm an opponent and break him down physically, Louis looked to force a confrontation that was psychological first, physical second.

As a fighter with power and patience, Louis owned an advantage over opponents because he had 15 rounds to figure out their style and capitalize on their mistakes. From a strategic standpoint, the Bomber didn't have to do anything other than apply slow pressure and measure his man for the knockout. As the champion, Louis could be patient and pace himself.

Conn, meanwhile, was under pressure as the challenger to step up and tag the champion with enough punches to pile up points. This made for risky business for Billy; the Kid would have to move into the Bomber's hitting zone to tag him.

Dunphy: "Louis trying to get him to exchange blows. Louis jabs with his left and Conn goes back out of range. Louis moving around, tries to get Conn into the corner once again. Billy still on the move . . .

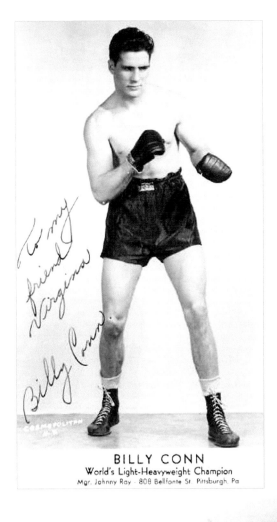

**BILLY CONN**
World's Light-Heavyweight Champion
Mgr. Johnny Ray · 808 Bellfonte St · Pittsburgh, Pa

Handsome Billy Conn, the "Pittsburgh Kid," was admired by men and adored by women.
*COSMOPOLITAN* VIA WIKIMEDIA COMMONS

Renowned photographer Carl Van Vechten took a series of Joe Louis portraits in September 1941. This photo captures the somber visage that terrified opponents.
LIBRARY OF CONGRESS, PRINTS & PHOTOGRAPHS DIVISION, CARL VAN VECHTEN COLLECTION

En route to winning the heavyweight championship in 1937, Joe Louis earned celebrity status that brought him into contact with some of the biggest sports stars of the decade. Here, he hams it up with Detroit Tigers slugger Hank Greenberg in 1935.

The enormous interest the Louis-Conn fight generated required a venue that could hold the nearly 60,000 fans who would eventually pay to see it. New York's Polo Grounds, seen here in 1921, fit the bill and served as the site for several celebrated bouts.

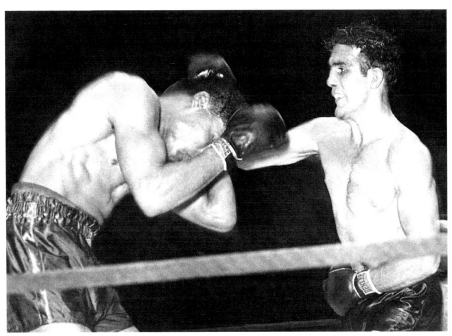

Billy Conn's barrage of blows fueled furious assaults and forced Joe Louis to cover up on several occasions. Conn's aggressiveness impressed ringside judges who had him leading Louis late in their memorable fight. ASSOCIATED PRESS

The iconic stances of slugger Joe Louis and boxer Billy Conn were on vivid display in their dramatic confrontation.
LIBRARY OF CONGRESS, *NEW YORK WORLD-TELEGRAM & SUN* COLLECTION

The popping flashbulbs of ringside photographers in New York's Polo Grounds illuminate Conn, who slipped to the canvas in the first round, and Louis, who towers ominously over his opponent. LIBRARY OF CONGRESS, ASSOCIATED PRESS

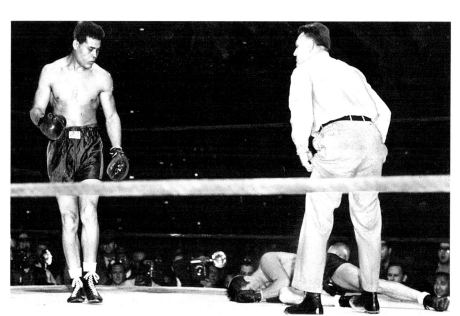

In the 13th round, champion Joe Louis strides toward a neutral corner as referee Eddie Joseph begins counting over gallant challenger Billy Conn. LIBRARY OF CONGRESS, *NEW YORK WORLD-TELEGRAM & SUN* COLLECTION

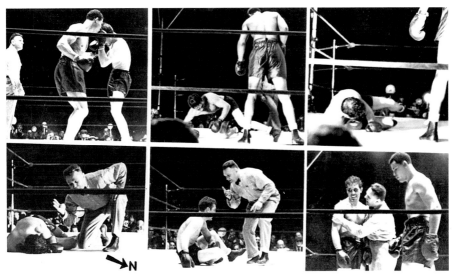

This photo montage captures the climactic moments of the classic fight. From upper left, Louis lines up Conn for the final blow, a devastating right hand. Billy drops to the canvas and referee Eddie Joseph tolls the 10-count over the fallen fighter. The Pittsburgh Kid looks to be out cold in the bottom left photo, but the courageous Conn begins to climb to his feet. In the final photo, Joseph consoles Conn, who appeared to some to have beaten the count, as an expressionless Louis heads to his corner.

LIBRARY OF CONGRESS, ASSOCIATED PRESS

Joe Louis brandishes his famous left fist after finally felling Billy Conn in the fateful 13th round of their epic 1941 world heavyweight championship fight in New York City.

LIBRARY OF CONGRESS, *NEW YORK WORLD-TELEGRAM & SUN* COLLECTION

The 1941 Louis-Conn championship fight was so spectacular the sporting public demanded a rematch. Billy's injured hand and America's involvement in World War II caused the much-anticipated title bout to be delayed until 1946.

Heavyweight champion Joe Louis was very active in doing his part to help the United States and its allies win World War II. A casual remark he made at a charity dinner in 1942 led to the creation of this propaganda poster by the US Office of War Information.

After completing his service in the Army, Billy Conn (fourth from left) celebrates V-E Day with Bob Hope (center) and other Hollywood luminaries. TIM CONN

Billy Conn, fourth from right, and Mary Louise Conn, second from left, at the wedding of Pittsburgh family friends David M. H. Jones and Emily Burk on April 22, 1948. Jones's brother, Thomas Mifflin Jones IV, stands on Billy's right. BLYTHE JONES LYONS

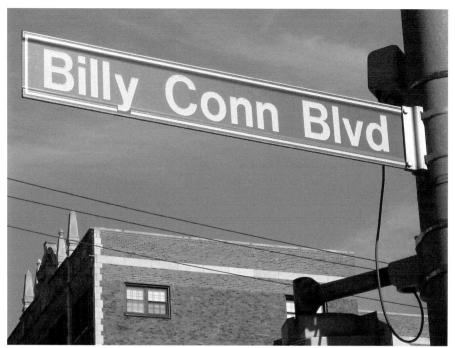

In honor of its native son, the city of Pittsburgh renamed a portion of North Craig Street in the Oakland neighborhood after Billy Conn. WIKIMEDIA COMMONS

In 1979, Detroit opened the $57 million riverfront sports arena named after Joe Louis. Nicknamed "The Joe" by Detroit Red Wings fans, the venue had a 38-year run before closing in 2017. WIKIMEDIA COMMONS

Louis trying to get him in close so he can rip home a punishing blow . . . Billy keeps on the move, circling around the champion."

This deadly game of cat and mouse was vividly illustrated when Conn bounced a jab off Louis's nose and the champ was wild with a right-hand counter. Twice more Billy jabbed and backed away. The two exchanged left jabs to the eyes; the Kid flicked another jab to Joe's nose but the Bomber backed him into a corner and fired a pair of left-right combos to Conn's head. It was evident Louis was trying to end this night early.

Dunphy: "Conn beats Louis to the punch with a left hook to the jaw, a stinging blow. Louis is jabbing a left, hooks a left to Conn's chin, drives him into the ropes, he's pummeling him with rights and lefts. Conn tries to hold on, takes a right to the jaw. Louis's blows pack a lot of steam. Louis on top of him with a right and left to the body."

Ringsiders thought Billy appeared hurt, but Conn lashed back with a hook of his own. Louis landed lefts and rights to head and body before Billy fired both hands to Joe's head and hooked hard to the body.

Dunphy: "Conn fights back with a hard left hook to the body. Billy is stung and he's hurt but he's fighting back . . ."

The crowd was in an uproar, but cheers turned to gasps when the Bomber dug two hard lefts to the ribs, raising angry red welts on Sweet William's whitish skin. Joe was tattooing Billy's body, but instead of folding as previous opponents had done, the Kid battled back, hooking a left to Louis's eye.

Dunphy: "Louis hooks a left to the body and Conn appears to be hurt. Another left hook to the body and Louis crosses a right to the jaw."

Louis delivered his right cross with his body bent slightly forward. Joe put all of his power into the blow, bringing his right arm up, over, and across. It was the punch that had overpowered Pastor; it nearly did the same to Conn.

Dunphy: "Conn is staggering a bit but he's fighting . . . A left hook to the jaw by Louis staggers Conn . . . Louis has him on the ropes just above us . . . Conn's face is very, very red . . . A left and right to the body by Louis and Conn fights back with a left and a right to the jaw, another left hook to the jaw by Conn brings the crowd up screaming . . . Plenty of excitement in that flurry . . . Conn hooks another left to Louis's head, and there's the bell for Round Two!"

Corum: "That left that Billy hooked at the end of the round is about as good a punch as he got over in the entire round because Louis was hurting him, pounding and pummeling. Right over my head he hit a terrific right hand that really shook Billy and Conn suddenly stopped going in those big, wide circles. There's one thing very obvious. While Louis turns in a little circle in the middle of the ring, Conn trying to cover a lot of ground was naturally tiring himself a little. He fought back as gamely as any fella could fight back."

The Bomber had staggered Billy with two right hands, but the Kid kept dancing. "Keep away from him," Conn said of his strategy. "Just move in and out."

The Kid was quick; there was no denying that. The challenger would make the champ chase him around the ring. Conn, Dunphy noted, was hoping to wear the heavier man down.

In his corner, Louis listened to instructions from Blackburn and received some loosening up of his muscles by trainer Mannie Seamon. Louis knew that while he was pressuring Conn, he couldn't quite catch him. "Just too fast," Louis thought. "Too much speed for me."

The Bomber had brought the battle to Billy the first two rounds. He figured he had the Kid when he staggered him; at that point the champ believed the fight would soon be over. Louis looked across the ring at Conn. "That tough Irishman," he thought, "is standing up to my fists."

Louis won the first two rounds on the Associated Press scorecard, but with the third round about to begin, the Bomber could feel the effects of the Kid's speed, his flicking left jabs, and his own drying out and weight loss. Conn, by contrast, was just getting started.

"The first rounds don't count," Conn later told Gowdy. Buoyed by the fact that he had withstood the Bomber's power, Billy jauntily told Johnny Ray in his corner, "All right, Moon, here we go."

Corum: "There's the warning whistle. Johnny Ray is pleading in Conn's ear. Blackburn is patting Joe lightly on the chest and Joe is glancing over this way, seems very cool. And there's the bell!"

At the start of Round Three, Louis continued to try to corner Conn. Dunphy thought the pattern of the fight was firmly set: "Conn moving back, away, ducking the champion's punches; Louis moving in, looking for his opening, throwing punches, waiting for that one spot where he can land the killing blow."

Louis and Conn exchanged hooks, Billy hooking to Joe's ear but taking a hard hook to the head in return. The Bomber dug a right to Sweet William's stomach and aimed another right to the head.

"I thought if I could get him in the corners, I could cut his speed down," Louis recalled.

Conn had been hurt in Round Two, even staggered on a couple of occasions. But there was a marked change in him in Round Three.

Dunphy: "Conn looks as spry as ever after the minute's rest between rounds ... Conn still circling Joe Louis ... Louis moving in faster now, he senses he has his prey and his quarry is right where he wants him. He's trying to get Conn into the corner or on the ropes where he can batter him at will ..."

Billy bounced a left off Joe's chin and Louis leaped forward with a left hook to the head. Conn connected with two lefts to Louis's head and the Bomber retaliated with two lefts to Billy's body. Sweet William whacked another left to Joe's jaw and the two fell into a half-clinch.

Dunphy: "Referee Eddie Joseph has the boys break, which they do. A very clean fight and a very sensational one ..."

Louis landed another hard right to the ribs and champion and challenger traded stiff lefts. Halting his retreat, Billy brought his fans to their feet by boring in and belting the Bomber in the head with both hands.

Dunphy: "Conn shakes up Louis with a left hook to the jaw ... Louis is having a bit more respect for Conn's punching power ... Conn keeps on the move. Now Conn is actually dancing around the ring, trying to befuddle the old master ..."

Conn's rapid-fire outburst raised a small mouse under Louis's left eye. The Kid was flicking left jabs, flashing left hook leads to the head, and firing right-left combos before flying free of danger.

"Feint him out of position," Conn said of his strategy, "whack him and just keep going."

Dunphy: "Conn comes in, crosses a right to Louis's jaw, rips a right to the body, a right to the jaw, and another left hook to the jaw by Conn … Conn's best rally so far … Again, the crowd comes up screaming … Conn with a left hook to the jaw, drives Louis into the ropes with another left hook to the jaw."

The champ was holding on, something he rarely had to do in his 17 previous title defenses. At round's end, an aroused Louis unleashed a left that appeared to skin Billy's right eye.

Dunphy: "And there's the bell!"

Having won his first round of the night on the AP scorecard, the Kid smirked at the Bomber at the bell. Returning to his corner to a chorus of cheers from fans, Sweet William winked at Moon.

Corum: "Now there was a round! And how that boy Billy Conn did fight. He came back as fresh as a daisy … As Don says, he's a slow starter … Conn shook Joe pretty good … When Bill wasn't fighting, he was dashing away and as I say, he couldn't have looked fresher."

Stanley Woodard of the *New York Herald* scored Round Three for Louis, "on a small margin." The AP scored it for Billy. The discrepancy among ringside observers showed how difficult scoring a battle between a boxer and a puncher can be. Does a boxer who's landing three punches to one deserve to win a round, or should the round be scored in favor of the puncher who lands the more damaging blows?

What was clear was that through three rounds referee Eddie Joseph was enjoying a relatively easy night. Louis and Conn had clinched sparingly and broke cleanly. Joseph was one of the top referees of his era, a Staten Island native and former boxer with blue eyes, broad shoulders, and as one observer noted, muscles upon muscles.

Be it moonlighting as a boxer or working on boilers in his day job as an ironworker, Joseph enjoyed physical activities. He skipped rope, hammered a heavy bag in a makeshift gym in a firehouse, and walked rather than drove from his home in West Brighton's Bement Avenue to various stores.

As a referee or fighter, Joseph always held his own in the ring. In 1921 he forced future heavyweight champion Gene Tunney to fight the full 12-round limit. In 1938 he refereed two title fights; he was the third man in the ring when Louis stopped Abe Simon and was there when Jake LaMotta gained a decision over Fritzie Zivic for the middleweight crown.

Joseph would also referee the Raging Bull's loss in February 1945 to Sugar Ray Robinson. Joseph's career was not without controversy. In 1949 Joseph was embroiled in a dispute following Willie Pep's points victory over Sandy Saddler at Madison Square Garden. Charlie Johnston, Saddler's trainer, was so upset he pushed to air his complaints against Joseph before the New York State Athletic Commission.

When he wasn't refereeing big fights, Joseph was serving as timekeeper. He was ringside for the Louis-Schmeling rematch, serving as timekeeper for referee Arthur Donovan.

Now Joseph was on center stage for another big bout, the third man in the ring for arguably the most dramatic fight ever.

# CHAPTER SEVEN

# CONN-FIDENCE

Ego, Norman Mailer wrote in 1971 in his coverage of the first Ali-Frazier fight in *Life* magazine, was the great word of the 20th century.

"If there is a single word our century has added to the potentiality of language, it is ego," wrote Mailer. "Everything we have done in this century, from monumental feats to nightmares of human destruction, has been a function of that extraordinary state of the psyche which gives us authority to declare we are sure of ourselves when we are not."

Ego was indeed at the forefront of many events in the 1930s and 1940s. It was ego that convinced Billy Conn to surrender his light heavy-weight championship to take on the heavyweight king, and it was ego that led Joe Louis to believe that someone might eventually beat him, but not while he was in his peak years.

"Every good prizefighter must have a large ego," Mailer wrote, "because he is trying to demolish a man he doesn't know too much about, he is unfeeling—which is the ground floor of the ego; and he is full of techniques—which are the wings of ego."

For the first two rounds of his fight against Conn, Louis had walked his man down in a style called the "Blackburn Crouch." Attributed to Jack Blackburn, the man many believe to be the greatest trainer in boxing history, the Blackburn Crouch was taught by the wily old strategist to Louis, Sugar Ray Robinson, and Jersey Joe Walcott. Each of the three champions was directly influenced by Blackburn; Jack trained Jersey Joe and Louis, and Robinson recalled in his autobiography going to Louis's training camps to watch Joe train and to talk boxing with Blackburn.

The Blackburn Crouch calls for its practitioners to advance on their opponent with head tilted, chin tucked, and torso bent slightly forward.

The tilting of the head makes it a less inviting target; tucking the chin behind a slightly upraised lead shoulder lowers the number of punches that can filter through. The lead hand is extended slightly toward the opponent, thus shortening the distance of the jab to its intended target. The other hand is kept close to the chin to parry opponent's punches or block blows outright. Modern proponents of the Blackburn Crouch include trainer Freddie Roach and retired champion Bernard Hopkins.

Confronting the Blackburn Crouch for the first time, Conn seemed confused. Billy was a well-schooled, scientific boxer, but in the early going he had difficulty dealing with the Blackburn Crouch and its head movement that allowed Louis to slip the Kid's rapid-fire jabs and punches. The educated footwork Louis had learned from Blackburn caused Sweet William to retreat to further study the steady advance of the Bomber. Louis's forward movement forced Conn to back straight up; when Billy bounced left or right, the Bomber slid with him, Joe's small steps effectively cutting off the Kid's escape route.

In winning the light heavyweight crown and then beating heavyweights, Conn had proved adept at confusing opponents by giving them angles. Blackburn studied Billy and prepared Louis against the day. Joe's footwork wasn't as fast as Billy's, but Blackburn's teachings allowed Louis to cut off the angles of his smaller opponent. Once the Bomber blocked Billy's fights to freedom, he would plant his feet and try to power punch Conn to the canvas.

That was the Blackburn plan for dealing with Sweet William. For the first two rounds Jack's strategy proved effective as Louis blunted Billy's attempts to establish his attack, parrying the Kid's punches and avoiding others. Louis looked relaxed in walking Conn down and entering the "pocket," the hitting zone. By continually closing on Conn, Louis backed Billy into the blind alleys of the corners and along the ropes, thus forcing the Kid to attack and provide openings for damaging counters.

While Conn was confronting the Blackburn Crouch, Louis was looking to solve the shell defense Johnny Ray had taught Billy. Joe was starting to understand just what he was up against. The Kid had fleet feet and fists, almost too fast for the champ to cope. When Joe did connect to Conn's head, the Kid took it and fought back. When the Brown Bomber dug both gloves to the body and raised red blotches on Billy's ribs, Sweet William sneered.

"Conn stood up to Louis's punches," William Detloff says. "A lot of guys couldn't."

Louis looked at Conn and wondered what was keeping the Kid up? Sitting in his corner, getting rubbed down between rounds by Mannie Seamon and lectured by Blackburn, Joe stared across the ring at Billy. The Kid was smiling; he was full of confidence. The Detroit Bomber was making his record 18th title defense, but he had never encountered a contender like the Pittsburgh Kid.

Billy, in typical bonhomie fashion, smiled and winked and thought boxing the Bomber was a breeze. Having won Round Three in the eyes of many, Conn came out for the fourth round and resumed his stylish movement.

Dunphy: "Round Four and they're out in the center of the ring. Conn still moving around and Louis trying to crowd him. Louis looks a little bit more determined than he has at any point in this fight. Now he's going after Billy just a little bit faster, he didn't like that flurry of blows that Conn landed on him in the previous round . . . Conn keeps those hands up high, ready to shoot either one . . ."

The grinning challenger tagged the grim champion with a left to the stomach and a right to the ear. This was the Conn his supporters had come to see. If Louis's ring style could be compared to the music of contemporary Count Basie, Conn's attack could have been accompanied by the rousing sounds of Irish War pipes.

To his followers, Billy the Kid was a Celtic god, and his furious assaults on the favored champion stirred memories of Irish battle music. The crowd's boisterous reaction was such that it seemed as if Sweet William's fans could hear the bagpipes, flutes, and harps of the Highlands.

It was as if a Celtic horn had sounded and Conn, a son of Erin, was fighting for Celtic pride. Knowing that, as St. Dominic once said, "(i)t is better to be a hammer than an anvil," Billy brought the fight to the Bomber. The Kid's strong showing was making it clear he was not only there to take part in the fight; he was there to take *over* the fight.

"He's out-boxing Louis from the third round on," Tim Conn says.

Conn stepped up his attack, aiming a hook to the body and catching Louis with a hard right to the head. The Bomber's knees buckled. No longer backing away, Billy was now moving in, unleashing two straight lefts and a snappy right to Joe's eye.

Dunphy: "There's Conn, beating Joe to the punch . . ."

Conn was carrying out his strategy—"Keep away from him. Just move in and out. Feint him out of position and whack him and just keep going"—and Louis was struggling to find a solution.

"I remember [*Pittsburgh Press* sportswriter] Joe Williams saying, 'Louis never saw such speed,'" Tim Conn says.

The Kid was taking command of the fight. He stuck two more lefts into the Bomber's bewildered face and in a half clinch worked his right hand free and fired a series of punches to the champ's head. Conn was connecting with short shots; this was the flashy fighter that fascinated so many.

"Billy's just too fast," Louis thought. "Can't catch him."

Dunphy: "Conn keeps circling around . . . Crosses a right to Louis's head, which shakes up the champion! A terrific right cross by Billy Conn . . . Louis is not the aggressor he was a few moments ago. Conn crosses another right to Louis's jaw, left hook to the jaw by Conn, a right cross to the jaw by Conn . . ."

For the first time in the fight, Louis was forced to hold on. The sight of David taking it to Goliath pulled the Polo Grounds crowd to its feet. The crowd was clearly with Conn and feeding off the fan's frenzy, Billy bore in again.

Dunphy: "Conn in close with a left hook to the jaw, and the complexion of the bout is turning . . . Conn showing more fighting ability than he did in the first three rounds . . ."

The blurred gloves of champion and challenger flashed beneath the ballpark's bright lights. Louis delivered a left to Conn's ear; Billy bounced a right off the champ's chin; Joe landed a left to the head in return. The Kid rushed in again, this time with a right to the Bomber's eye and Louis countered with a hard hook to the head. The Associated Press reported that the crowd was "in a continuous uproar."

Dunphy: "What a fight this has turned out to be!"

Returning to the attack, Conn cut loose with two more rights to Louis's eyes.

Dunphy: "Round Four rapidly coming to a close . . . Billy continually on the move; shakes off a left jab thrown by the champion . . . Louis trying to get him into a corner to get home a cruel, crushing blow if he can . . . Conn bounces off the ropes and goes back into the center of the ring . . . Louis hooks a left to Billy's chin and drives into him the ropes. And there's the bell for Round Four!"

The Bomber nailed the Kid at the bell with a smashing hook to the nose, but Billy was unfazed. The AP noted that Sweet William "returned to his corner with a grin on his face." More than that, Conn was literally laughing as he turned from Louis. The Kid's confidence was sky high. "This is a cinch," he told Johnny Ray with a jaunty smile.

The challenger had won two consecutive rounds on the AP card to pull even with the champ. Those who thought Billy had run a "con" game on the public prior to the fight had to think again. The Kid was giving the Bomber his toughest test in years; he had seized the momentum of this back-and-forth bout.

Corum: "Conn was the real McCoy in that round . . ."

In their corner, Louis and Blackburn knew they had a fight on their hands. Blackburn waved smelling salts under Joe's nose and the Bomber headed out for Round Five with Chappie's urging to take the play away from Sweet William ringing in his ears. A straight left caught Conn and the Bomber followed by crossing a right to the head.

Dunphy: "Louis is trying to stalk him in that corner or on the ropes, as he has been throughout the fight. Conn tries to keep on the move. Joe's after him now, jabbing a left to Billy's chin . . ."

Louis's proficiency with his lethal left jab was such that he could change its speed, power, and distance. Among heavyweights, only Sonny Liston could boast a straight left jab in the same class as Louis; Sonny's jab, however, was not nearly as polished nor as consistently punishing as Joe's. Ali, Larry Holmes, Mike Tyson, Gene Tunney, and Jack Johnson all owned excellent left jabs, but none had a force comparable to Louis.

Sitting ringside, Corum watched Louis's left snap forth from the shoulder and thought it the "most destructive jab boxing has ever seen." It was one punch, Corum thought, for which there was almost no defense.

Joe used his jab to control distance and create openings for more powerful punches. What Conn saw coming at him were the repeated sharp thrusts of Louis's left hand. The Bomber aimed his jab at Billy's jaw and would punch through his target, not at it, thereby producing a follow-through frightening to behold.

The power behind Louis's jab came from the slight turning of his left shoulder to the right. At the same time, Joe would turn his body to the right and raise his right hand to parry Billy's countering blow. Louis would double- and triple-jab, each time returning his left hand quickly to position to jab again.

Being belted by Joe's jab got Billy's Irish up; he hooked two lefts to Louis's ear. The two traded jabs and the Kid danced away. Conn came back with a hook to the head; Louis answered with a hard left to the stomach. The Bomber was looking to execute the theory that if you kill the opponent's body, the head will die.

Dunphy: "Louis crosses a hard right to Billy's midsection, which shakes up the challenger ... Louis rips a left and a right to the body, digging in hard, punishing shots. Another right to the body by Louis ..."

Joe was frustrated by Conn's quickness and his ability to stand up to his punches. Still, the Bomber believed that if he continued to pound away at Billy's body, his power would slow the Kid down and turn him into a stationary target.

Dunphy: "Louis digs a right hand into the midsection and hooks a left to the body ... Conn takes a right hand to the body ... He's got

Conn on the ropes now, ripping in a right to the body. A hard right to the body thrown by Joe Louis and the crowd is yelling for Billy to get off the ropes ... A left hook to the jaw thrown by Louis gets in there, a crushing right hand to the body. It's apparent now that Louis is trying to slow down Conn with body blows ..."

Six months earlier, Louis had knocked out Red Burman with a straight right hand to the heart. The devastating punch left Burman sagging into the ropes, his body gone limp. Burman later called Louis's body punch "the killer-driller."

The punch was so unexpected that the Madison Square Garden crowd let out what the *Lewiston Morning Tribune* reported as an "audible gasp." The Bomber, the *Tribune* added, had "revealed this new way of arriving at the old result." Louis's 12 previous title defenses prior to Burman had ended in knockouts, but all had come via blows to his opponent's head. Trapped along the ropes, Burman was suddenly bent in half by the hammer to his heart.

"A funny look spread over [Burman's] face," the *Tribune* stated. "Then he toppled."

Louis was typically a headhunter, evidenced by the fact that this was the first stoppage by a body punch during his championship reign. But his blows to the body were renowned and feared, even by former champions; they brought a scream of pain from Max Schmeling, a look of horror from Primo Carnera, a grimace from Jack Sharkey.

Louis looked at body punches as a means to weaken his opponent. Joe would take a punch or two if he could work his way inside and continue his assault on Conn's ribs, and that's precisely what happened in their next exchange. Louis took a right cross to the jaw but slammed four punches to Billy's flanks in a half clinch. Left uppercuts were traded in mid-ring before Conn uncorked a hard left to the body and a right to the head as they came out of their clinch.

Billy followed by sticking two straight left jabs to Joe's face, but as Conn came back with a third straight left, this aimed at the body, Louis smashed a tremendous right to the head. Returning to his body attack, the Bomber belted Billy's ribs and a vicious right rocked him. The Kid staggered, and in rapid succession the champion landed a half dozen more punches. The challenger reeled. "Conn was hurt," the AP reported. "Louis was all out now."

Dunphy: "Conn staggers into the ropes! He's trying to cover up . . . Louis crosses a right to Conn's chin, ripping a right and a left to the chin. Conn is taking the blows without fighting back. He's hurt . . . Joe comes back with a left hook to the body . . ."

Billy wilted a bit from the Bomber's rib-bending blows, and Louis looked to finish Conn before the bell. Back in the Kid's hometown a funereal quiet gripped family and friends. Fans in his hometown ballpark, Forbes Field, feared the worst. Silence descended on the Pittsburgh stadium as the crowd hung on the announcer's every word.

Dunphy: "Conn takes a right uppercut to the jaw and seems pretty badly hurt . . . Louis won't let him go . . ."

Conn grimly tried to hold on until round's end. Louis worked his arms free and landed a short hook to the head just before the bell. The blow brought blood; Conn was cut over the right eye. The Kid wiped away the blood with his right glove.

Dunphy: "[Louis] crushes a right to the body of Billy Conn, hooks a left to the jaw, and there's the bell!"

Corum: "That was as tough a round of fighting as any man will see. Louis just tore the body practically out of Billy and had him dog-tired . . ."

Louis headed back to Blackburn bolstered by the fact that he had accomplished what he had set out to do three minutes earlier—wrest momentum away from Sweet William.

Conn, meanwhile, weaved toward the wrong corner. Johnny Ray and Freddie Fierro worked feverishly over their battered boxer, reviving him with smelling salts, spraying him with cold water, and working on the cut over Conn's eye.

Corum: "His eye is cut but he is certainly a game youngster and he fought when it looked as if he just couldn't hold up his hands . . . They're busy in Conn's [corner], dressing that eye. It's not badly cut but he's hurt. Billy is a little tired and it begins to look as if maybe we're not going to get 15 rounds out of this fight. But you never know . . ."

Now leading on the AP card three rounds to two, the champ rested imperiously in his corner and then returned to the riotous fray for Round Six.

Dunphy told his audience that Conn was wet from the water his seconds had poured on him between rounds. Anxious to follow up on his strong fifth round, Louis was three-quarters of the way across the ring when the bell for Round Six clanged. Billy was barely off his stool and appeared startled at the champ's hurried advance. There was an exchange of left hooks to start the round, and the Kid, perhaps still feeling the effects of the Bomber's punches in the previous round, quickly danced away. Writer Joe Williams thought Conn "an elusive shadow."

Dunphy: "Louis trying to get Conn on the ropes . . . Conn going back to his tactics of the earlier rounds, disdaining to mix with the champion and keeping on the move . . . Louis still stalking his prey . . ."

Blood leaking from the cut above his right eye, Conn poked a left to Louis's head and hooked another left to the head. When Billy stepped in Joe jolted him with a left, right, and left to the body. The two clinched, and as Conn cuffed a right to the ear Louis cut loose with shots to the midsection. Aware that the Bomber's body attack was aimed at softening him up, Billy broke from the clinch and tossed a left-right-left to Joe's head.

Dunphy: "Now Louis has Conn on the ropes, ripping a left and a right, another hard right is dug into the ribs of Billy Conn, still another by Joe Louis! A left hook to the body by Louis. Conn unable to fight back, trying to tie up his opponent . . . Louis digs a hard right into Conn's midsection and is slowing up the challenger once again . . ."

His knees buckled by a body blow and once again in real danger, the gritty Conn went on the offensive. He hooked a left to the eye and landed a left on the jaw. The champ fired both hands to the body, but the challenger stood his ground. Billy belted Joe with a hard left to the eye and landed another hook to the head. The Kid was reclaiming the momentum that the Bomber held in Round Five.

Dunphy: "Conn rushes Louis into the ropes, actually bulls him there ... Conn's back in with a left hook to the body ... Conn fighting back ... A left and a right to the jaw by Billy Conn ... Louis takes another left and a right to the body ... Conn on the move and his right eye is pretty red ..."

Bloodied but defiant, Conn returned to his hit-and-run tactics that he later explained to Curt Gowdy. "Keep away from him," Conn said. "Make him miss and hit him."

Williams could see the Kid's strategy unfolding. The mercury-footed Conn would lead the Bomber on a spirited chase, the idea being to wear the bigger man down as the rounds piled up.

"When you do most of the forcing against a will o' the wisp," Williams reasoned, "it takes a lot out of you."

Conn's corner was caught up in the throbbing excitement. "Stick and run!" Johnny Ray and Freddie Fierro yelled to the Kid. "Keep movin'!"

Dunphy: "Conn dancing around, continually on the move, circling and circling ... Conn hooks a left to Joe's chin, a very hard blow. A left jab to the jaw thrown by Billy Conn gets in there ... Conn hooks a left to Joe's jaw ... Conn's up on his toes now, going back out of range ... Louis trying to get him on the ropes again, he almost has him, but Conn jabs a left to the jaw ..."

Conn and Louis swapped lefts, and Joe tried to turn the tide as the final seconds ticked away. He delivered a left to the body and right to the head before Billy danced away from further damage as Round Six ended.

Dunphy: "Whatever Bill Corum said of Conn's gameness goes for me too. And there's the bell and here is Bill ..."

Corum, sitting at Dunphy's right elbow on the ring apron, was beginning what he would later call "one of the happiest associations of my life." Over the next eight years, Corum and Dunphy would team to broadcast more than 500 fights. The two were always splendidly dressed, sporting dark suits, white shirts, and knotted neckties.

A month from his 46th birthday in June 1941, Corum was short, stout, and debonair. His pal, Damon Runyon, described him as a man who looked cheerful and lived cheerfully. Corum, Runyon wrote, reported on sports events as he saw them, and he always saw them more clearly than everyone else.

"No more popular chap than Bill Corum ever lived in this man's town," said Runyon. "He is one of the ablest journalists of these times and one of the grandest guys."

A product of Speed, Missouri, Corum graduated from the University of Missouri in 1917 and enlisted in the US Army upon America's entry into the First World War. He distinguished himself in his military service, serving as commander of Company D, "Dirty D" he called it, the 101st Infantry Battalion of the 96th Infantry Division.

At age 24 he was one of the US Army's youngest majors during World War I. Corum was three times cited for gallantry in the summer and autumn of 1918. He would write in his autobiography *Off and Running* that neither words nor writing skill could adequately describe the "ear-splitting hells of Chateau-Thierry and Belleau and Croisette Woods."

Many recognized Corum's heroism in the Great War, but he routinely downplayed it. "Hero nothing," he would say, "there was no other choice."

Colonel John C. Greenway recommended Corum for the Distinguished Service Cross and he earned three Silver Star citations as well as a Purple Heart. Corum was a victim of mustard gas attacks that damaged his eyes, leaving him, in the estimation of doctors, 10 percent disabled.

Discharged from the army Corum headed to New York to attend the Columbia University School of Journalism. He was hired as a copy editor at the *New York Times* and eventually left the copy desk to become assistant sports editor. Corum left the *Times* the following summer to cover the New York Baseball Giants for·the *New York Evening Journal*. Corum's first sports column appeared in the July 26 edition of the *Journal*. He typed close to 10,000 columns over the next 32 years, writing for the *Journal* and the *Journal-American* following the merger of Hearst's morning and afternoon papers.

Corum witnessed firsthand many of the greatest moments in American sports history, and in an era that included sports writing legends Runyon, Ring Lardner, Grantland Rice, and Red Smith, Corum earned fame as one of the country's foremost sports columnists. Like contemporary Walter Winchell, Corum was renowned as both a columnist and broadcaster. He called the Kentucky Derby on radio for close to a quarter-century and in 1925 coined the expression, "Run for the Roses."

Corum first started following boxing on July 4, 1910, the day Jack Johnson jolted White America with a knockout of former undefeated champion Jim Jeffries at Reno, Nevada. Corum was 15 at the time but recalled poring over newspapers of the day to read reports of an event whose "sparkle and color" dwarfed even holiday fireworks.

On July 2, 1921, Corum saw his first major championship fight, the Dempsey-Carpentier bout. Corum saw the prime Dempsey in action, was ringside at Jack's fights with Tunney and Rocky Marciano's wars with Ezzard Charles and knew all about the legendary champions in boxing's greatest division. In Joe Louis Corum saw a fighter he believed to be the best ever.

"Louis," Corum wrote, "was almost without faults in the ring. He was the greatest fighter of all time, in my opinion."

He based his opinion on the fact that Louis was one of the few fighters who brought *two* dynamite fists into the ring. "He had a devastating hook and cross in either hand," Corum wrote. Corum compared Louis's defensive skills, his ability to avoid opponent's punches, to that of Corbett and Tunney. He had covered many of the great fights of the past quarter-century, and halfway through the Louis-Conn bout in 1941 Corum knew he had a ringside seat for another history-making event.

"This," he exclaimed, "is a great fight!"

With the AP having scored the sixth round for Conn, a fight that was expected by many to be one-sided in favor of Louis was once again even. Louis and Conn had become tethered together in a push-me-pull-you existence; their ego—Mailer's great word of the 20th century—at play because neither man believed he could be beaten.

Their belief in their invincibility being expressed in their body language.

"There are languages other than words, languages of the body," Mailer wrote. "And prizefighting is one of them ... Boxing is a dialogue between bodies. [Fighters] ... address one another in a set of *conversational* exchanges which go deep into the heart of each other's matter."

Louis and Conn were locked in such an exchange. Halfway through their fight they had delved deep into the heart of each other's matter; they would delve deeper still before this night was over.

# CHAPTER EIGHT

# BLACK MOSES

The Pittsburgh Kid wasn't just fighting Joe Louis, heavyweight champion.

Billy Conn was taking on a man whose superiority, Bill Corum stated, extended far beyond the confines of the ring. Louis, wrote Corum, "was as great a person and an American as he was a champion."

Corum never forgot the groans, growls, and hisses aimed at the mere mention of Jack Dempsey's name, and the contempt many held for Gene Tunney, the educated Marine who read Shakespeare and allowed his tongue to linger lovingly over three long words when one short word would have sufficed.

No one ever said such things about Louis; Corum thought Joe's lack of pretense, his sincerity and integrity made it impossible and unthinkable to do so. He never uttered a word of alibi for himself, never disparaged an opponent, and in his years as titleholder lent a sense of honesty and dignity to a sport for which those two words, Corum noted, "are not synonymous."

While Corum recognized the greatness in other boxers, most notably Sugar Ray Robinson, no other fighter affected him the way Louis did. Corum was far from the only person to feel so strongly about the humble champion.

*Time* magazine, in its September 1941 cover story on Louis, described him as "a living legend to his people, a black Moses leading the children of Ham out of bondage."

Louis was viewed by millions of Blacks as a champion of his race and Joe saw himself as such. "I want to fight honest," he said, "so that the next colored boy can get the same kind of break I got. If I 'cut the fool,' I'll let my people down."

*Time* stated that Louis was "an ambassador of racial good will . . . Negroes are grateful to him for remaining his own natural self and thereby doing much to bring about better racial understanding in the U.S.—doing more, some of them say, than all of the race leaders combined."

Louis's popularity crossed racial lines; *Time* noted that radio broadcasts of Louis fights averaged 50 million listeners. The Black man from the poor red clay of the South was the biggest radio draw in the United States outside of the patrician serving as president, Franklin Roosevelt.

Like Corum, the *Time* cover story commended Louis for his exemplary sportsmanship. Louis, the magazine stated, "took on all comers, fought 20 times in four years, was never accused of a fixed fight, an unfair punch, a disparaging comment."

It was for these reasons that writer Edward Mallory, who would work with Louis on his book *How to Box*, called the Brown Bomber "the idol of the sports world. . . . The youth of the world have acclaimed Joe Louis their favorite personality. He, in turn, has given a perfect example of true heroism. He has been commended for his honesty, loyalty, utter simplicity, and profound dignity, always shown both in and out of the ring."

Louis, wrote *Time*, was "not only an idol of his race but one of the most respectable prize-fighters of all time. From the sorry pass to which a series a second raters had brought it (Sharkey, Carnera, Baer, Braddock), he restored the world's championship to the gate and almost the vigor that it had in Dempsey's day."

Louis's reputation in and out of the ring resonates through time. "Joe Louis is an incredible fighter and individual," said Mike Tyson, who calls Louis his favorite heavyweight champion.

This was the giant of a man whom Conn came out to meet in Round Seven. Louis was as much living legend as he was flesh and bone; Billy knew it, and knew that to beat Louis, he had to *beat* him. The challenger was fixated on the belief that he would knock out the champ. That way, when Billy and Mary Louise walked the boardwalks on the Jersey beaches, passersby wouldn't just say, "There's the man that defeated Joe Louis." They would remark, "There's the man that *knocked out* Joe Louis."

Conn started Round Seven, in the words of the Associated Press, "looking stronger." Billy jabbed to Joe's nose and the Bomber countered by poking a pair of lefts to the head and following with a right cross that fell short of its intended target.

Louis dug a left to Conn's body and the next minute saw Joe stalking and Billy circling. The Kid was staying out of range of the Bomber's fists. Louis tried to pin Sweet William in a corner, but Conn danced away.

Dunphy: "Conn flicking his punches at Louis, moving, moving, moving ... Louis looking a little annoyed, reached out with a left hand, misses ..."

Dunphy thought the challenger was working the champion with great speed. Joe would be close to cornering Billy, but the Kid would elude the trap and cuff the Bomber about the head as he brought the fight back to center ring. Conn followed with a right hand to Louis's heart and another combination to Joe's stomach.

Joe Williams saw the same strategy from the Kid as did Dunphy. Conn, Williams wrote in the *Pittsburgh Press*, "would rush in on Louis, smack him sharply, and dance away before the Bomber knew what happened."

Louis was still stalking Conn but now Billy was stepping back and gliding left or right. What the Kid was doing was making the Bomber reestablish his position. The delays destroyed Joe's timing; he had to reset before stepping forward to return to hitting range. Conn was not only defeating Louis; he was also defeating Blackburn's carefully crafted fight plan.

Chappie wanted his champion to get into the pocket by means of his weighted jab, which derived its power from Louis driving off his back leg. Joe was to fire his jab once, sometimes twice in a double jab aimed at blinding Billy, and then follow with the right hand or left hook. If either punch landed flush and stunned Conn, Louis would proceed into the patterned punch combinations he was famous for.

By instructing Louis to keep his lead shoulder as close to Conn as possible, Blackburn was looking to negate Billy's advantage in hand speed. Having Joe stride forward in the Blackburn Crouch would allow him to parry Billy's blows and counter with heavier shots. But the Kid was clever; he was avoiding the traps Blackburn baited by strategically matching his footwork with that of the Bomber, thus forcing Joe to re-adjust his planning while on the move. At the same time, Conn was tagging Louis with stinging rights.

"I think the Blackburn Crouch was effective from an offensive stand-point because it put the fighter in range to land short punches," William Detloff says, "but it also left him vulnerable to straight right hands."

Swirling cigarette and cigar smoke and popping flashbulbs framed the fighters as Louis and Conn traded hooks to the head. The Bomber caught the Kid against the ropes and ripped a hard hook to the ribs. Billy absorbed the blow, bounced back, and nailed Joe with two hooks to the head and a left and right to Louis's bronzed body. The champion responded by digging another left to the ribs.

Conn came back headhunting, lashing a left that tagged Louis's left ear and nailing Joe's other ear with a right. Working as carefully as a man diffusing a live bomb, the Kid darted in and out of the Bomber's reach and then flashed inside to unfurl flurries at Louis.

Dunphy: "Conn hits Louis with a hard left hand to the ribs and the champion is forced back a little . . ."

Dunphy believed Conn was gaining more confidence as he discovered he could tag Louis and move away before the Bomber could retaliate with countering shots. Billy stuck a hard left hand to Louis's face and followed by adding insult to injury.

"How'd ya like that one, Joe?"

The champ never answered. Instead, he maintained his relentless pursuit of his challenger. Dunphy watched as Louis kept moving forward, following the dancing Conn and waiting for an opening. Conn caught Louis with a short right to the chin and Joe retaliated by resuming his withering offensive against Conn's ribs. The Bomber's body attack was such that it moved the AP to report that Louis "smashed away" at Sweet William's midsection. The two-fisted action brought fans to their feet again. Joe's fury was evident as the round ended. While he prided himself on his short, accurate punches shot straight from his shoulders, a frustrated and tiring Louis was wild with a left uppercut at the bell.

The AP awarded Round Seven to Conn, and for the first time in the fight the challenger was leading. It was rare for Louis to be behind in a bout, and concern was creeping into the champion's corner.

"By the time the eighth round came up," Louis recalled, "I was tired as hell."

Joe Williams said it was known prior to the fight that Louis had ignored Blackburn's counsel to ease up in training, to work out on alternate days rather than daily. "I wanted to break 200 (pounds) to get more speed," he later told Ron Olver, "but in doing so weakened myself." It was the only argument Louis and Blackburn ever had, and Jack was being proven right. Louis was dehydrating, and as Williams looked at the tiring champion, he thought Joe's ignoring Chappie's instructions was now handicapping him.

The Bomber was also in pain. He'd hurt his right wrist in Round Seven punching down on Conn's head. "It nearly killed me," Louis said of the excruciating pain.

Weary and wary, Louis looked to even the score in Round Eight. In a half-clinch he clipped Conn's head with a left and right. Louis let loose with a two-fisted pummeling of Billy's body. His curly hair slick with sweat, the Kid countered with three right hands fired in close. Once again Louis and Conn went toe-to-toe, Joe hooking a solid right to the jaw and Billy bouncing his right hand off Louis's eye.

Dunphy: "Conn comes out faster than he did in any previous round of the last four. He jabs a left to Joe Louis's chin; Louis is back with a left to Conn's button. Louis is again trying to get Conn in a corner. Conn jabs away with the left hand and continually keeps moving around . . ."

Joe and Billy went to long range and exchanged lefts. Conn closed in again and scored a right and left as Louis lashed away at the ribs.

Dunphy: "Louis in close; rips a stinging left to the body, followed by another left dug into Conn's midsection. There's another left thrown in there by Joe Louis. Conn scores with a left to the body . . . Conn in close, has the right hand free and pounds it once to Louis's body and once to the head . . ."

Louis tried using his jab as a range finder to reestablish momentum, but Conn's constant movement was negating the most potent punch in the champion's arsenal.

Dunphy: "Louis jabs twice with his left, they're short of the mark. Conn is a very elusive target; keeps moving away from Louis . . ."

As Conn and Louis circled one another, Dunphy described the classic fighting styles being illuminated by the ring lights.

Dunphy: "Conn and Louis out in the center of ring. Conn keeps his left hand out in front of him. Louis's hands are near more his chin . . ."

Planting his feet, Billy brought over a terrific right that brought a spray of water from Joe's head, a big roar from fans, and as reported by the AP, "brought the crowd to its feet."

Dunphy: "Now Conn gets going with a left hook to the body and a left to the jaw, all thrown with almost the same motion, and another left hook to the body and a right cross to the jaw thrown by Billy Conn and the crowd seems to like it . . ."

Williams thought Billy's performance "magnificent." Conn returned to the attack, sticking two lefts into Louis's face and following with two more rights to the jaw. The fight was now all Conn. He was moving into Louis for the first time since Round Four, peppering the champ with repeated one-twos.

Dunphy: "There's Conn jabbing a left and crossing a right! Conn hooks a left to Louis's jaw and the champion shakes his head. Conn in with another right to the jaw, misses a right, which was intended for a haymaker . . ."

Sweet William hooked hard to Joe's head and flailed away with both fists before the two men fell into a clinch. Referee Eddie Joseph separated the fighters, and the Kid resumed his attack. Conn landed another hook to the head and fans were frenzied; the AP noting "the crowd went wild."

Dunphy: "The battle is taking on quite a tone . . . Billy's right eye is cut but not bleeding; they did a fine job in the corner. Louis jabs with his left and crosses a right to Conn's chin. Conn doesn't seem to mind the blows . . ."

The Kid felt the Bomber's power, but he realized during the fight that Louis wasn't the hardest hitter he had ever faced. That honor still belonged to Oscar Rankins. He had knocked down Conn in the second round of their fight with a punch so hard that it left Billy in a fog for 12 hours. Conn courageously pulled himself up from that knockdown against Rankins and was just as courageously coming back from the battering Louis had given him earlier in the fight.

"Louis hurt him with body punches in the fifth and sixth rounds," Tim Conn observes. "From the eighth round on, my dad really takes control of the bout."

Conn's war with Louis was following a similar pattern to his fight with Rankins. The early rounds had seen Billy hurt and staggered, but the Kid was rallying back and raining blows on a stronger but startled opponent.

Dunphy: "Conn keeps that left hand up very high, ready to jab . . . He hooks a left to Louis's chin, jabs a left on Louis and crosses a right to the champion's jaw! . . . There's Conn, back with a right and a left to the head, and another right and a left to the head by Conn!"

Billy was beating Joe to the punch and the champion was baffled by Conn's circling movement, hit-and-run tactics, and rapid-fire combinations. Williams thought Conn was making Louis look bad but believed Billy might have been able to do the same to any of the great champions of the past. In Conn's corner, Freddie Fierro marveled over the Kid's fleet feet and flashing fists. Poetry in motion, Fierro thought.

Dunphy: "Louis hooks a right to the body and Conn blocks the blow. Conn back with a left hook to the jaw, comes in with a left hook to the body. Another left and a hard right to the body thrown by Billy Conn, and he's still punching . . . A left and a right to the head."

Conn's combinations of punches—left hook and right cross, left hook to the body and left hook to the chin—had Louis off balance. "Bing, bang, boom!" Conn later told Peter Heller. "Real fast, like a machine gun, then get the hell out of the way."

Sweet William was succeeding where so many others had failed. He was bombing the Brown Bomber, and the proud champion was forced for the first time in years to employ his entire repertoire of defensive maneuvers and tactics—blocking, clinching, ducking, feinting, parrying, slipping, slide-stepping, and weaving—in a desperate attempt to survive Conn's guerilla attacks.

Dunphy: "What a fight this has turned out to be! There's the bell and they're still slugging it out at close quarters!"

Having swarmed the Bomber with rights and lefts, Sweet William returned to his corner in a euphoric state. "I did it!" he hollered to Ray and Fierro. "I did it!"

The Kid had opened a two-round lead on the AP scorecard. Louis bowed his head as he heeded Jack Blackburn's increasingly urgent advice.

Dunphy: "Round Nine and the crowd wondering if Billy Conn can keep it up. Conn soaking wet as he comes out after every intermission ..."

His long muscles glistening with water and sweat, Billy's confidence was soaring. He began the round by banging a hard right cross off Joe's jaw. Moving in, he popped Louis with a pair of lefts to the face.

"Joe, I got you," the cocky Kid told the champ as they clinched.

Coming out of the clinch Conn hammered away with both hands. Louis covered up and Sweet William was suddenly laughing at the Bomber. They traded straight lefts before Billy opened up again, hooking a left to the jaw and ramming two rights to the head.

Dunphy: "Conn's in, crossing a right to Louis's jaw. Conn seems to be out to make more of a fight of it than he did in the previous rounds ..."

Fighting back, Louis launched two left jabs against Billy's bloodied eye. Conn answered with a hard right to the head and fired another right to the head. The Bomber caught the Kid with a stiff left. Conn triple-jabbed Joe's nose, but in a half-clinch Louis landed a hard double-hook, the first blow catching Billy's jaw and the second nailing his head.

Seemingly no longer fazed by the Bomber's power, the Kid landed a hook to the head. Joe knocked Billy off balance with a right to the head, but Conn doubled up on his hooks, digging to the head and body. Louis's face, usually a dour mask, expressed pain and amazement.

"He surprised me," Joe told Curt Gowdy years later.

Dunphy: "Conn jabs a left to the jaw, another left to the jaw by Billy Conn ... Louis jabs twice, he's got Conn on the ropes now, but Conn fights out of a clinch with a left and a right to the body and a left to the jaw ... Louis takes a left and a right thrown by Billy Conn ..."

Conn continued to circle Louis, pounding the proud champion with a startling assortment of lefts and rights, jabs, crosses, and hooks. Tim Conn would recall Joe Williams remarking, "Billy Conn was the most natural fighter I ever saw."

The sight of the Kid stinging Louis with an electric left and dancing away had Conn's corner ecstatic. "Box him, Billy!" Ray and Fierro screamed above the crowd. "Box him!

Dunphy: "Conn keeps that Irish grin on his face, he jabs a left to Louis's chin ... Conn keeps on the move ... feints with his left hand, trying to befuddle the champion ... Conn jabs a left to Joe's jaw. Louis trying to get Conn in a corner, Conn beats him to the punch with a right cross to the jaw ... Conn dancing around, he's up on his toes. Louis stalking him ..."

It was a delicate dance the Kid was doing, trying to stay one step ahead of the ever-advancing Bomber. Conn and Louis traded lefts at the bell and a beaming Billy pranced back to his corner with a commanding lead, having won his third straight round.

Louis was in trouble, and he knew it. Conn had doubled him up in rounds, 6–3, and was in firm control of the fight. The challenger was too quick, too slick; even when the Bomber cut off escape routes and pounded him, Sweet William would wink and smirk and dance away.

And when Louis least expected it, Conn would close in, bang away with both hands, and circle out of range.

The Bomber had a range he liked to work in. He would move forward in a deliberate manner, setting traps for Conn and trying to lure the Kid with false leads. Louis alternated his forward movement between a slow shuffle and a quick movement a few inches at a time. Pursuing Conn, Louis slid his black leather boxing shoes along the white canvas. When Billy's attacks forced Joe to back up, Louis kept his balance by sliding his right foot slightly backward. As Conn circled to his right, Louis circled to his left, gliding with his left foot in the lead and his right foot following. When Billy circled left, Louis followed by circling to his right, moving his left foot toward Conn's right foot.

There were limits to Louis's footwork, and no fighter ever exposed them to the degree Conn was doing. One reason is that Conn's footwork was every bit as disciplined as Louis's. Billy used the same small moves going backward that Louis used going in. By doing this, notes writer Matt McGrain, Conn "minimized dramatic errors and dented Joe's momentum." When Billy substituted small moves for larger ones, McGrain states that they were "brilliantly judged and perfectly executed."

Conn carried out a brilliant fighting retreat. Even while backing up, Billy belted Joe at every opportunity. The tactic kept Louis honest and prevented the champion from closing in on Conn unimpeded.

Dunphy watched Conn continue to poke away at Louis as the night wore on and the bout moved through the middle rounds. The broadcaster studied the challenger and saw blood coming from his nose. Still, Dunphy thought the Kid had gained the upper hand in the fight.

Bill Corum was also watching Conn closely. He saw the big Irish grin Billy continued to flash throughout the fight and recalled how he had seen a similar smile in a title fight halfway across the country from New York's Polo Grounds. It was the second Jack Dempsey–Gene Tunney title bout, and it was held in Chicago on a memorable September night in 1927. Corum had been ringside that night as well and thought the event and the evening the crowning achievement of Tex Rickard's promotional genius.

More than 105,000 fans streamed into Soldier Field, described by Corum as "a Grecian structure on Chicago's lakefront." The massive crowd dropped $2.65 million to watch Dempsey try and regain his title from the upstart Marine. The night skies were clear, and Corum was struck by how "the glow from the busy Loop a mile away silhouetted the stately columns atop the concrete horseshoe" that was Soldier Field.

Corum's seat for that classic encounter was situated directly beneath Tunney's corner. He was so close to the champion that he believed the only ones closer were Gene's four corner men, fronted by Jimmy "Bow-Tie" Bronson. Just before the opening bell, Corum stood up to ease his tension and look over the "fabulous sea of faces" surrounding him on all sides.

While he was drinking in the unmatched atmosphere of a big title fight, Corum heard a voice above him call out. "Sit down, Bill, there's nothing to get excited about."

Corum looked up into the smiling face of Tunney. Some 14 summers later, Corum was again looking into the beaming visage of a master boxer. From his seat across the ring, Louis looked at the same smiling Irish face as Corum. "Conn sure knew what it's all about in a ring," Louis later said. "He was one clever fighter."

Clever enough to employ a strategy that was proving successful in wearing down what was thought to be an indestructible fighting machine. Louis's ring reputation was such that three months prior to his bout with Conn, ABC radio aired a National Urban League program that saw two actors appearing in a skit about fictional fighter Eddie "One-Round" Green and his manager preparing to take on Louis. Decades later, DJ Jazzy Jeff & The Fresh Prince took a similar approach in their 1989 hit song, "I Think I Can Beat Mike Tyson."

In 1941, the radio skit went as follows:

**Manager:** "It's the first round. Joe Louis climbs into the ring like a tiger. What do you do?
**Green:** "I climb out of the ring like another tiger."

**Manager:** "It's the 15th round and you're crawling around the ring on your hands and knees. What are you doing on your hands and knees?"

**Green:** "Looking for a trap door."

**Manager:** "The crowd is yelling, 'Stop it! Stop it!' And what do you say?"

**Green:** "Okay by me."

**Manager:** "I throw in the towel, and they give the fight to Louis."

**Green:** "Let him have it. I don't want it."

**Manager:** "But you fought so well they give you a reward."

**Green:** "Oh yeah. What do they give me?"

**Manager:** "They give you a return fight with Joe Louis."

**Green:** "Oh no they don't!"

While comedic, the reality of this skit was closer to truth than to fiction. Louis was considered by boxing experts and sports fans in general as being otherworldly in his ring skills. When the Bomber ruled the boxing world, he saw the terror in his opponent's eyes. Sportswriters fueled the fears of otherwise brave fighters by declaring the Bomber's invincibility. Lester Scott penned a piece in the *New York World-Telegram* that was headlined, "There Should Be a Law Against Putting Men in Ring with Louis."

Conn and Johnny Ray, however, were executing a daring fight plan that saw Billy make Joe expend energy by following him around the ring. Sweet William's expert footwork allowed him to sidestep Louis's left jabs and when Joe did get into hitting range, the Kid was beating the Bomber to the punch with flashy combinations that forced the champ to cover up.

Dunphy recognized the effects Conn's tactics were having on Louis. Chasing the fleet-footed challenger was tiring the champion. Billy's punches weren't doing a lot of damage, Dunphy thought, but they were succeeding in annoying Louis. Williams watched Louis trudge back to his corner and thought the champion looked "pathetic." The Bomber,

Williams wrote, "looked slow, and as the fight wore on, he looked tired and discouraged."

In his corner following Round Nine, Louis listened intently to Blackburn's advice. Chappie's strategy was based on Billy trying to slug it out with the Bomber. But the Kid was fast; he moved like a mosquito and was just as tough to swat. *Billy's surviving on speed*, Louis thought.

Conn was setting a torrid pace, and Blackburn knew his Chappie was tiring trying to keep up with the Kid. Williams thought Louis's legs looked heavy from the energy he was expending trying to corner his quarry. "He was beginning to pick 'em up and lay 'em down with some effort," Williams wrote.

Louis's right wrist continued to pain him as well. Yet it wasn't just Louis who was feeling pain and frustration. Joe was the most famous Black person in the world, and writer Chris Mead noted in his biography of Louis that many sportswriters in the 1930s and 1940s suggested that the Bomber "had a symbolic importance beyond the prize ring."

Media personality Ed Sullivan wrote in his column "Little Old New York" that Louis's fists were the "microphones and megaphones" of his race on nights he defended his title. As the symbol and standard-bearer of his people, Louis was to an extent no longer an individual—"he is all the sorrows and joys, and fears and hopes and the melody of an entire race," Sullivan stated.

Sullivan called Louis a compound of every small cabin in America's Southland, every tenement or apartment in Harlem and in all Northern Black cities and communities. Black Moses was, said Sullivan, "the memory of every injustice practiced upon his people and the memory of every triumph."

Thus, every blow delivered by Conn upon Louis was felt by millions of Black people listening to Dunphy and Corum on radio.

Every Conn left jab that stung Louis stung his people down South.

Every right cross from Billy that shook Joe shook Harlem.

Every left hook landed by the Kid that rocked the Bomber rocked people of color in Detroit and the Midwest.

Every ounce of pain felt this night by Black Moses was likewise being felt by Blacks listening on radios in living rooms, tenements, and apartments across the country. And in these Black communities, they knew—as did Chappie and the champ—that the heavyweight title was slipping away.

## CHAPTER NINE

# "KNOCK THIS SOB OUT!"

The largest crowd to see a fight since 1938 was standing and cheering wildly inside the Polo Grounds.

Celebrated as he was, Billy Conn was not supposed to have survived nine rounds against Joe Louis. Most experts and fans expected Sweet William to have already been stopped by the Brown Bomber, but here he was, not only still standing as timekeeper George Bannon counted down the final seconds prior to the start of Round 10 but leading Louis on all scorecards.

That the champion was feeling the pressure of being behind in the scoring was evident in his rushing from his corner at the bell. The AP declared that the Bomber was "intent on catching the dancer and doing damage." Don Dunphy noted the same and alerted his radio audience to Louis's grim resolve.

Dunphy: "Louis jabs twice with the left hand to Conn's chin, Conn takes the blows and goes into a clinch . . . Louis going after Conn more seriously than he did a few rounds ago . . ."

The jabs Joe landed on Billy were not the flicking jabs used by some fighters; the Bomber put his 200 pounds behind every punch and Conn felt their power. Joe jolted Billy early in the round, bouncing two hooks off the challenger's body. Conn countered with a right hand that missed but followed with a hard left to the jaw. Louis landed a solid left to the head and then rifled a right hand and two lefts to the head. Startled, Billy backed up in the face of Joe's aggressive attack, but Louis caught Conn with a long left.

Dunphy: "Louis is after him, jabbing a left to Conn's jaw ... Louis has him on the ropes now, ripping a right to the body and a right cross to the jaw thrown by Louis catches Conn as he comes off the ropes."

Round 10 was all Louis thus far. The Bomber continued his assault on Sweet William's slight frame. Louis landed a hard left to the challenger's midsection, "probably the hardest left of the fight," the Associated Press stated. Stepping up his offensive, the champion jabbed to Conn's face.

Dunphy: "Louis jabs away with his left ... Conn takes a left hook to the jaw ... Louis gets the right hand free in close and rips it to Conn's jaw ... Louis trying to stalk Conn into a corner again, jabbing twice with the left and hooking a left to Conn's jaw ..."

Suddenly Billy was on the canvas. He had slipped again; both fighters had trouble with traction at times during the fight. Conn clambered up immediately and referee Eddie Joseph correctly ruled no knockdown.

Dunphy: "Conn slips to the canvas once again and very gentlemanly, Louis doesn't even try to land a blow. Very nice, Joe, and the crowd appreciates it."

It wasn't only the crowd that appreciated the champion's sportsmanship. Writers at ringside noted that the Bomber stepped back and allowed the momentarily defenseless Conn to regain his footing. Chris Mead wrote that Louis's gesture toward the helpless Conn reflected not only his ingrained sportsmanship but also his deep confidence.

"Even while he was losing control of the fight," said Mead, "Louis never lost his calm and did not feel desperate enough to take advantage of Conn's slip."

Billy and Joe touched gloves in a gesture of mutual respect and sportsmanship before the Bomber resumed his body attack, driving both hands to Billy's ribs. Conn fought back, and he and Louis swapped hooks to head and body.

Dunphy: "Now they're fighting again ... A left hook to the jaw thrown by Billy Conn. Louis comes back in, jabs a left to Conn's chin ... Conn dancing around and Louis is after him, jabbing a left ... Conn moving from side to side, hooking a left into the midsection of Joe Louis and crossing a right uppercut as he gets in close . . ."

Conn hooked a left to Louis's head but was tagged in return with a right and left to the jaw.

Dunphy: "Louis comes back with a left hook to the jaw, digs a hard left hand and a right into Conn's midsection. Louis, still punching, rips a left to the jaw. Conn finally ties him up, but Louis gets his hands free, another left and a right to the head, another left and a right to the head by Louis! Conn comes out fighting out of the clinch with a left and a right to the body."

As the round's final seconds melted from the clock, Louis and Conn were at close quarters, hammering away at one another. The Bomber was boxing's king of pain, but the Kid was defiant; *give me your best punch* was the gritty Conn's mindset as he warred with Louis at close range. Dunphy saw blood seeping from Billy's nose; he also saw Joe wincing from Conn's hard left hooks to the head.

Dunphy: "Louis hooks a left to the body and crosses a right to the jaw. Believe me, when Billy stops walking, he really fights; a left hook to the jaw by Conn and a left to the body and a right uppercut scored by Conn! In close, Louis comes back with two hard left hands to the jaw and a right uppercut on Conn's chin. There's Conn coming back with a left to the body, and they really mixed it in that round . . ."

Round 10 went to Louis, tightening the scoring and moving the champion within striking distance of the challenger's lead. Corum watched the Bomber desperately trying to turn the tide of events back in his favor; he had seen this scenario played out before, had seen a slugger struggle to solve a clever boxer. In 1926, Corum was talking with his friend Harry Greb, who had sparred a few rounds with Jack Dempsey prior to his title defense against Gene Tunney in Philadelphia.

Following his sparring sessions with Dempsey at the champion's headquarters in Atlantic City, Greb urged Corum to pick Tunney to pull the upset.

"Dempsey hasn't got it, Bill," Greb said. "He won't win because he's just not there anymore."

Corum considered the fierce-fighting Greb a "pleasantly disarming fellow with a soft, sincere voice that belied his profession." He knew Greb was not given to hyperbole, and Harry was proven right in his prediction when Tunney easily outboxed Dempsey over the full 10 rain-soaked rounds and took Jack's title to the amazement of fans.

Two decades later it appeared as if ring history was repeating itself. Yet Louis's strong showing in Round 10 gave the Bomber's supporters hope of a comeback against the Kid.

Corum: "Louis picked up a little bit in that round, seemed to have a little more dash, and shook Conn with his best punch."

Corum thought Louis's solid 10th round tied the fight at 5–5. At the same time, Corum knew the Kid had won four of the previous five rounds and that the Bomber was tiring; chasing Billy around the ring was taking a toll on Joe. If Conn could maintain his brisk pace for five more rounds, Corum believed a new heavyweight champion would be crowned that night.

Corum also knew that the Bomber hadn't yet let loose that killer right hand of his in full force; Louis's right hand lurked like an assassin in the shadows. If Louis could catch Conn, Corum believed Joe could still change the course of the fight.

Louis looked to do that in Round 11, drilling Billy with a short right. The Bomber closed the distance and ripped two lefts to the body and another right to the jaw. Conn came back with a left and right to Joe's body. The Kid then dug two lefts to the midsection.

Dunphy: "Round 11 and with each passing minute it takes on more the appearance of a tough fight ..."

In a fierce exchange, Joe whistled a left and right to the body and Billy responded with a combination of his own, sending a right to Louis's head and digging a right to the ribs. Conn followed by hooking a left to Joe's ear. They remained at close quarters, their flying fists electrifying the crowd. Louis landed a right to the ribs and Conn countered with another left to the side of the head.

Dunphy thought the crowd noise was increasing with every blow; it was impossible for him to tell if fans were cheering for Joe's comeback or for Billy to continue his successful strategy. Either way, Dunphy felt fans were being carried away by the action. Amid the tumult and shouting, the young broadcaster kept his concentration on the fight.

Dunphy: "Conn dancing around, Louis into the attack with a left hook to the body, another left hook to the body scored by Joe Louis . . . There's Billy fighting back with a right to the body, crossing a right to the jaw, another right to the body by Billy Conn and now the tables have turned . . ."

His left arm slightly extended, his right glove held high to protect his chin and parry punches, Conn cut a dashing figure as he darted around Louis. Billy would move forward behind a series of punches, and then dance out of hitting range. Joe Williams thought Louis was not only facing the fastest fighter the Bomber had ever seen but possibly the fastest anyone had ever seen. Conn's quickness "would make Louis or anybody else look slow in comparison," wrote Williams.

Conn's constant movement kept Louis twisting and turning. Frustrated and angry, the Bomber aimed a right uppercut at Billy's jaw. Conn not only survived the vicious blow but answered with more than a half-dozen punches.

Dunphy: "Conn hooks two left hands to the body . . . Conn crossing a right to the head and Louis hooking a left to the body. Conn gets in another shot to the body, he seems to be befuddling the champion in close . . . Conn hooks two left hands to the body, brings in a right to the body . . ."

Like a riverboat gambler, the Kid was dealing aces with every blow. Louis was so stunned by Billy's body blows he didn't deliver a single meaningful counter. Two Conn hooks staggered Louis, and the ballpark rocked with cheers.

Dunphy: "Conn comes back with a right to the body, another right to the body, a left hook to the body by Conn. A right to the body, left hook to the jaw, another right and Conn is still swinging. Louis hasn't landed a blow in this flurry. A left hook to the body, a right cross to the jaw and Louis is worried. A left hook, another left hook by Billy Conn and now it's Joe Louis who's a little bit tired. The battle has turned again!"

Pulling the trigger on his pistol-like punches, the Kid's combinations were something to behold—lefts, rights, jabs, hooks, crosses, and uppercuts. Writer Roy McHugh, studying the fight film in hindsight for an article on the 50th anniversary of the bout, characterized Conn's combinations as "*Bing-bang-bing.*"

Conn told Peter Heller that when it came to combinations, "There's a set that comes natural to you if you know how to fight."

Billy knew how to fight, and he was convincing the champion of that very thing. Louis later acknowledged that Conn "knows how to take care of himself in the ring better than anyone I've ever fought."

Williams thought Conn's performance was reinforcing the fact that Billy in 1941 was one of the best boxers the fight game ever saw. In his mind's eye Williams could see Conn swarming recent heavyweight champions Jimmy Braddock, Max Baer, Jack Sharkey, Max Schmeling, even Gene Tunney. Speed, Williams wrote, comes close to being the main essential in any sport, "and Conn is Mr. Swift himself, both on his feet and with his hands."

Dunphy: "Conn beats Louis to the punch with a left hook to the jaw. The fight gets more dramatic every minute! Conn comes in with a left hook to the body and drives Louis into the ropes . . ."

This was swashbuckling Billy at his best. Having seized the advantage, Conn rushed in with another blow to the Bomber's body. Staggered a moment before, Louis now stood his ground and nailed Conn with a right to the jaw. The Kid and the Bomber traded punches in the final seconds, climaxing a round that had fans in a frenzy.

"The crowd," the AP reported, "had gone mad."

Says William Detloff, "It was very dramatic because Conn was doing what no one thought he could do."

Dunphy: "A left hook to the body by Billy Conn ... Louis hooks a left to Conn's body and Conn rips his own right to Louis's head ... Louis hooks a left to Conn's head at the bell! Oh, boy!"

Corum: "There's excitement for you. Listen to that crowd! Louis was definitely hurt in that round. He's very tired, goes back to his corner completely dispirited. Conn dances back to his corner, waving to the crowd, still looking like a million dollars ..."

The Kid had reclaimed control of the fight; now it was the Bomber on the defensive. At the end of the round, Freddie Fierro rushed into the ring to hug him. Conn, equally excited, thrust his gloved right fist into the night air.

Corum: "He really hurt Louis, there's no question about it. He hurt him and he had him hanging on and he also had him very tired ... Conn simply outfought him with sheer Irish fight, grinned and punched and punched, hooked and slammed and knocked Joe around ..."

In Irish pubs in Pittsburgh and around the country, patrons raised a pint to praise Conn's "Irish fight." It would not have been surprising for them to listen to Dunphy and Corum describing how this son of Erin was unleashing Celtic thunder on the champion and think of the lyrics from "God Save Ireland."

*(T)hey met him face to face*
*With the courage of their race ...*

Conn's spirited rally stole the show, giving the challenger the round, and regaining momentum that had been lost. A frustrated Louis leaned back in his corner as Blackburn pressed an ice pack to the back of his neck.

Corum emphasized that the Bomber was being punched around the ring by Billy the Kid and that Joe's punches, even when they landed, didn't have as much on them as those thrown by the smaller Conn. To

Corum, Louis looked far more tired than Conn. The champion also appeared to be completely confused by the Kid's style.

Corum: "He seemed to be befuddled by Conn. He couldn't tie him up, he couldn't get away from him, he couldn't punch at long range. He just got pasted in that round."

"You look straight at the fellow, and you just take the lead away from him," Conn would say of his strategy. "You try to mix him up, befuddle him."

Sweet William was turning the Brown Bomber inside out. Louis had chased Conn down a rabbit hole; now they were through the looking glass. Billy the Kid had become the banger, the Bomber the boxer; roles had been reversed and champion and challenger were suddenly in a world where up was down and down was up.

"From the 10th round on my dad is coming down off his toes, outslugging Louis, and really beating him at his own game," Tim Conn notes.

Dunphy: "Round 12, four to go. The boys are out in the center of the ring. Heavyweight championship of the world at stake . . ."

Round 12 opened with Joe jabbing hard to Conn's nose and then catching Billy with a glancing right to the head. The Bomber hurled a right to the head, but the Kid planted his feet once more and landed a left and right to the body.

Dunphy: "Louis jabs away with the left at Conn's chin, Conn dances around . . . Louis is after him; he's a very serious young man now the champion is, as he crosses a right to Conn's jaw . . ."

Louis dug a vicious hook high on the body and Conn answered by whipping a hook to the midsection. Louis fired back with a left to the jaw.

Dunphy: "The bout is going to get faster as it goes along, we can see that . . ."

Conn had abandoned his dancing, circling, and moving; the Kid was instead standing toe-to-toe and trading blows with the Bomber. "Conn," the AP reported, "was now staying at close quarters and just keeping on punching."

Dunphy: "A hard left hook to the body scored by Billy Conn, a hard left to the jaw by Conn as he rushes Louis to the ropes . . . In close they batter the body with lefts and rights . . . Conn hooks a left to Louis's head, hooks another left to Joe's jaw . . ."

The Kid had become the little giant. Louis was weight drained; if he had fought at his normal 200-plus pounds, he might not have been staggered by Billy's blows. Seeing Louis hurt, Conn thought the champion a spent fighter. His two-fisted attack had fans frantic. As Conn punctuated the air with punches, his followers filled the sky with hats and fight programs tossed in wild celebration.

The Kid's strategy was courageous but scary, especially when dealing with a proud and powerful champion. Louis hammered a left to the head; Conn drove a right to the jaw. Joe pumped two jabs to the face; they were range finders, advance scouts sent to determine the distance of the enemy target. With his target sighted, the Bomber moved in and exploded two right hands off Conn's ear. Joe and Billy exchanged hard left hooks and the Kid again brought the fight to the Bomber, digging both hands to the body.

Conn then reached back to Ireland, to a land whose soil was stained with bloody battles and landed two wicked left hooks to Louis's head.

Dunphy: "Louis is staggered by a left hook! Conn staggers Louis! Louis is reeling around and holding on! A left hook to the jaw followed by a right cross and the champion is hurt. A left hook to the jaw by Conn. Louis is trying to hold on . . ."

Billy's "Irish" was coming out, just as it had in the third round and again in the middle rounds. Sweet William was wading into the Bomber and blasting away with both fists.

Dunphy: "Conn is battering him with a left and right . . . Conn hooks two lefts to the jaw, another left hook to the jaw by Conn finds the mark . . ."

The Kid was in command; he had the Bomber staggering and holding on.

"Louis did a little dance," Freddie Fierro noted. "He felt the punch and Billy knew he did."

Conn cut loose with a hard hook and Louis looked hurt. Another hook by Billy and the Bomber, weakened by dehydration and the Kid's power, was again wincing in pain.

Dunphy: "Louis is hurt, make no mistake of that . . ."

Decades would pass and Louis would still recall Billy's left hook catching him flush and snapping back his head. The blow energized Conn. Sensing the kill, the Kid closed in. Conn had flipped the script; the challenger was now the hunter, the champ his quarry. In the Conn household six-year-old Davey Herr became so excited at his cousin's furious rally that he jumped up from his seat and toppled a table upon which sat a stack of phonograph records. The records shattered on the floor at the same time as Billy was shattering the myth that he was overmatched against Louis.

"Two swinging left hooks in the 12th round staggered Joe," Sid Feder wrote in his Associated Press story, "and for a few moments, the crowd, which packed the upper and lower grandstands and filled every one of the 14,000 infield seats went wild. The fans jumped on chairs, tossed hats or anything else handy and let out a roar as Joe fell back into the ropes and came out covering up and trying to hold on."

The Blackburn Crouch was designed to be not only a viable option for offense but for defense as well. Because Billy's blows were so fast and accurate, a startled Louis was employing every defensive strategy he knew to survive Conn's attack. The Bomber would duck when the Kid led with a left to the chin. When Billy banged to the body, Joe would tuck in his elbows to block the blows. When Conn ripped a hook to the head, Louis would use his shoulder to try and block it, dropping his arm and turning his body so that his shoulder took the shot.

Louis also tried parrying Sweet William's punches. When Conn aimed a left jab or hook, Louis would bring up his right hand to brush the blow aside. Slipping punches was another of Louis's defensive tactics. As the Kid led with a left, Joe would shift his body to the right of the jab; at other times the Bomber moved his head slightly to slip Billy's punch.

Hurt and tired as he was, Louis would clinch, calling into use a tactic that not only helped Joe but hurt Billy, the Bomber using his weight advantage and superior strength to tire the Kid. When the champ wasn't clinching, he was sidestepping in a desperate attempt to avoid Conn's combinations.

As Conn delivered punch after punch, Louis lowered his head under the piston-like movements of the Kid's arms. Joe was weaving at the waist, crouching and ducking in desperate attempts to avoid Conn's quick combinations.

Dunphy: "Conn hooks a left to the jaw and Louis paws with his left . . . A left hook to the jaw scored by Billy Conn! "

With time running out in Round 12, Billy moved in again. At the bell, Conn and Louis swapped stinging left hooks, their gloves flashing.

Dunphy: "There's the bell and here's Bill Corum."

Corum: "There was drama for you if you ever saw it in any ring. What a fight this is turning out to be! Conn hooked Louis with a left and Joe did just miss going down!"

On the AP's card Conn was clearly in control, Billy had won the last two rounds and eight of the previous nine. He had doubled up Louis in rounds, 8–4, and by the AP's unofficial count at least had already clinched a victory by decision should the fight last the full 15.

Two of the three officials' scorecards also had Conn leading Louis but by smaller margins. Referee Eddie Joseph scored it 7–5 for Conn, and Judge Marty Monroe had it 7–4–1 for Billy. Judge Bill Healy saw the fight even at 6–6.

As the bout was being scored on a round-by-round basis with a majority vote of the three official scorers, if Conn won even one of the final three rounds, he would be crowned the new king as he would have won eight rounds on the scorecards of Joseph and Monroe.

Such an outcome would give Sweet William a split decision victory at the very least. If Billy won two of the final three rounds, he would also be declared the winner on Healy's card and would take the title by unanimous decision.

How was it, wondered Dunphy, that a light heavyweight, even one as skilled and courageous as Conn, was beating a man considered the greatest heavyweight of all time?

Could Louis be tired and overworked from his "Bum of the Month" campaign, as Conn and Johnny Ray had proclaimed?

Might the Bomber have underestimated the Kid, a light hitter who was believed by some to lack a devastating punch?

Or was it simply that Louis was used to fighting bigger, slower heavyweights and thus could not cope with Conn's quickness?

Dunphy didn't have answers to his questions; no one did. But the broadcaster knew Louis had never dealt with a fighter as fast and fearless as Billy Conn. Among recent opponents of Louis, Tony Galento shared Conn's courage and Bob Pastor came close to matching Billy's boxing skill. But Conn was a better boxer than Pastor and more sophisticated in his strategy than Galento.

The Kid's abilities impressed Dunphy, who realized that Conn's speed was not in his feet alone; Sweet William's hands flashed like lightning. Dunphy thought that once Billy had rid himself of the tension he felt in the early rounds he fought like he, and not Louis, was the champion.

Dunphy had heard of the "One-Two" in boxing, a phrase used to describe a combination left jab/right cross. But Conn came up with a combination Don had never seen before—a left hook to the body, left hook to the head, and a right hand to the head. The Kid would then repeat the combination, which was new to Dunphy, and the broadcaster felt it was new to Louis as well since Joe seemed unable to cope with it.

Those celebrating what seemed to be a certain victory for Conn almost overlooked that Louis had landed several punches in the 12th that shook the challenger, and his slashing fists had Billy bleeding from several cuts on his face. At round's end, the Kid startled some by heading to Louis's corner; Fierro rushed to Billy, who pivoted quickly and the two headed in the correct direction. Corum thought Conn's confusion an indication of the cumulative effect the Bomber's blows was having on the Kid.

Conn stated in a 1950 interview for *National Police Gazette* magazine, "Louis hurts you every time he hits you. He punches you numb."

Corum knew this to be true and knew the Bomber's heavy blows were having a cumulative effect on the Kid.

Corum: "Don't think because Conn has been drawing the cheers and forcing the fighting that he's been doing all of it. Louis hurt him two or three times in that round and cut him a little bit about the mouth and about the eye, and when the round was over Billy tried to go to Louis's corner..."

Other observers saw it differently. To some, Conn heading to the wrong corner at the end of Round 12 was due more to the Kid being sky high with excitement after he had Louis holding on. Hype Igoe thought Conn was simply excited at the end of Round 12 and that was why he lost his bearings.

"Corum advances the thought that, despite Conn's great twelfth round, in which he had Louis rocking and almost going to the floor, Billy was weak and 'going' himself because of the early body punishment," Igoe later wrote. "Corum points out this fact, as proof that Billy was badly hurt. When the bell ended the twelfth, Conn started to go to the wrong corner. This, Corum tells us, is physical evidence that Conn didn't know where he was.

"With this, I can't agree. How often have great fighters done the same thing? The bell finds them in the middle of a furious onslaught. They hear the gong!

"They know the minute's rest will be important. They must take advantage of every single second of it and without looking up they start for the nearest corner for the precious rest. Should they head for a wrong corner, it doesn't prove that they are groggy, weak or even flabbergasted."

The Polo Grounds crowd was in an uproar. The sight of the former light heavyweight champ taking it to the heavyweight king made Louis versus Conn an instant classic.

Corum: "The big punch was that left hook that Conn landed which definitely all but shook the champion off his throne ... Louis was

completely dazed. He's so tired in his corner, more tired than Conn ...
A terrific round, a terrific fight!"

Corum's analysis of the champion's physical condition, his fatigue,
was correct. "I was completely exhausted," Louis revealed in his autobiography, "and he was really hurting me with left hooks."

Louis had been looking for a knockout that would end it. But the
12th round had turned into the 12th of never for the Bomber. The champion was in trouble, Corum thought. He awarded Rounds 11 and 12 to
Conn, giving Billy a two-round lead with three remaining. The Bomber
later admitted that he was hoping the Kid would lose his cool and gamble. If not, thought Louis, "I could see myself saying, 'Bye-bye, title.'"

Across the ring, Conn was confident. "Did you see that, Fat?" he said
excitedly to Fierro. "I staggered him! I'll knock him out next round."

"Don't go nuts, Billy! You have the title in your hands."

Conn didn't reply. Instead, he stared across the ring at Louis, saw
Jack Blackburn and Mannie Seamon shove smelling salts under Joe's
bloody nose and press an ice pack behind his neck. Years later, Conn
recalled his mindset at that point in the fight. "I hurt him in the 12th
round, so I figured I'll try and knock him out."

Billy couldn't have known that the Louis-Blackburn strategy was
based on Conn trying to slug it out with the Bomber. Fierro figured
it that way, however. "That's just what he wants you to do," he shouted
when Conn told him he was going for the knockout.

Chappie knew his champ was tiring; he also knew Joe was hoping
for the slugfest Conn was contemplating. Hurting as he was, Joe had
been studying Billy all night. "If he starts to throw that long left hook,"
the Bomber thought, "I have him."

Blackburn and Seamon continued to work on Louis. Above the raucous crowd, Chappie yelled into Louis's ear. "You're losing on points.
You've gotta knock him out to win!"

Longtime Louis friend Freddie Guinyard was in the champion's corner and believed Blackburn the only one besides Louis who was keeping

cool. Co-managers Julian Black and John Roxborough were in a panic. "He's way behind! What's he going to do?"

Conn's corner men were preaching caution. Billy was so confident of impending victory he was laughing as he sat on his stool. "I can take this son of a bitch out this round," he stated to a startled Fierro and Ray. "Don't worry about it!"

"No, no," Ray pleaded. "Just box. You've got the fight won. Just stay away from him. Stick and run. You got the fight won. Stay away, kiddo. Just stick and run!"

Years later Conn could still hear his corner men's pleas. "They were telling me, 'Just stay away from him. Keep boxing. You're way ahead of him.'"

Ray was aware that his fighter was leading on points and well on his way to pulling the upset of the century, if only he followed the fight plan and boxed. Conn had other ideas. The Kid knew his mother Maggie was sick but still getting reports on the fight from family members. Billy was aware, as he said later, that his mother "held on to see me leading Joe Louis in the stretch."

Mary Louise would say that on the night her future husband fought Louis, "Billy just had too much to win for."

Dunphy wondered if he was sitting in on what he thought would be "the greatest upset of all time." As referee Eddie Joseph called for "Seconds out!" Blackburn blistered Louis's ears one more time.

"I'm tired of going up and down these steps," the aging trainer screamed as he waved smelling salts under Louis's nose. "Go knock that son of a bitch out!"

In his corner Conn was shouting strikingly similar words to Johnny Ray, who was pressing ice packs to Billy's forehead and on the back of his neck. "I'm gonna knock this son of a bitch out!"

Conn and Louis were no longer fighting for just the heavyweight championship of the world. They now found themselves fighting for the championship of each other.

## CHAPTER TEN

# "YOU'VE GOT A FIGHT TONIGHT!"

The New York night belonged to Billy Conn.

Don Dunphy looked up from his seat on the ring apron and saw brash Billy brandishing a broad smile as he headed to center ring to meet Joe Louis. Sid Feder saw the same from his ringside seat and noted it in his Associated Press story. "Billy . . . was grinning and confident."

Dunphy figured Conn knew he had the title won if he could keep away from Joe for three more rounds. The broadcaster thought the Bomber looked tired; Conn, meanwhile, still had some steam.

Truth was, as Conn later admitted, by Round 13 he was bruised and tired from the cumulative effect of Louis's punches.

"Listen," he said later. "Sometimes it may look as though that guy ain't punching at all. But every time he lands on you hurts, and don't let people kid you about that."

Jack Blackburn believed Louis's ferocious body attack had taken Conn's legs away and forced the Kid to fight flat-footed. If so, Billy put up a brave front, telling Johnny Ray, "We've got him!" The Kid's corner was a frenzied mix of confidence and concern. "Stay away! Box! Coast in!"

Conn shrugged off the advice. "No! I'm gonna fix him up! I'll knock him out. Don't worry!"

The manager shook his head in dismay. "You're on your own!" Ray yelled.

Louis emerged from his corner feeling roused as well. "Blackburn said I was fighting a bad fight and to keep Billy against the ropes," he told Curt Gowdy. "For some reason, and I don't know why, I said, 'Forget about it. I'll knock him out this round.'"

At the opening bell for Round 13, Billy the Kid walked up to the Bomber, landed a right cross to Louis's head, and punctuated his punch with a pithy comment.

"You've got a fight tonight, Joe!" Conn said in his cock o' the walk fashion.

"I know it," Louis responded.

Billy said later he ribbed the Bomber with those words several times that night, during Round Nine in particular. The challenger's remark made it plain he was conscious of the champ's "Bum of the Month" campaign. The Bomber murmured his response but remembered thinking, "We'll see."

Louis also recalled that Conn had more words for him at the start of the 13th. "Let's have a fight! *I'm gonna knock you out!*"

Conn's confidence doesn't surprise Douglas Cavanaugh. "Billy," he says, "was a killer."

The Kid was dragging this fight from the bright lights of grandiose New York into the grimy back alleys of Pittsburgh he was accustomed to. The glamour matchup had become a gutter war.

Louis, like Conn, was experiencing the effects of the long, tough fight. He felt fatigued and acknowledged later that Conn hurt him in Round 12. But Billy's brashness buoyed the Bomber. Conn's saying to him "Let's have a fight" at the start of Round 13 "was playing right into my hands," Louis told writer Ron Olver.

Conn would tell his son Tim that his success in the 12th round fueled his confidence going into Round 13. "My dad had a different tactic in the 13th than in other rounds," Tim states. "Dad told his corner, 'I'm going to knock him out this round!' I watched the fight with my dad several times and I asked him, 'Why did you change tactics in the 13th? Why did you do that?'

"He said, 'A fighter's instincts are that if he has the other guy hurt, he wants to go after him, he wants to knock him out.' Dad said, 'If I hadn't landed that left hook in the 12th round, I would never have tried to knock him out in the 13th.'"

Their epic battle rejoined, Conn and Louis landed solid hooks to the head. The Associated Press noted the Bomber "had his right hand cocked, apparently ready for any opening."

Dunphy watched as the two great fighters moved in concert with one another across the canvas.

Dunphy: "Round 13 and I wonder if it will be unlucky for either of these two great fighters . . ."

Louis and Conn moved to center ring, Billy flicking out punches. Joe was short with his blows but continued moving forward. Dunphy watched Louis and thought he was trying for that one opening, that one move that would allow him to catch Conn.

Billy knew he was leading on the judge's scorecards. He wanted the title, but he wanted the knockout too. Billy dug a left hook into Joe's body and, following the pattern of the combinations he had confounded the champion with all night, switched his attack to Louis's head and landed another left.

Dunphy: "They go to close quarters. Conn, after hooking a left to the body brings up a left to the jaw . . ."

The early exchanges saw Conn continue to outpunch Louis, Billy landing five solid blows to two by Louis. A ringing right hand cut Louis's ear. Now bleeding from the ear and nose, Louis swatted Sweet William with a hard right. Billy's head snapped back violently.

"I knew he was ahead on points," Louis remembered, "and I kept saying to myself, 'Make him fight your fight.' Something told me my chance would come, and it did."

Sensing blood in the water, the Bomber blasted two lefts to the head and a right to the body and Billy wilted a bit. "Conn was hurt," the AP reported. Chris Mead wrote that Billy's head was "bouncing like a yo-yo."

Dunphy: "Louis staggers with a right uppercut and Conn wisely holds on. Louis hurts Conn again with a right and left to the body . . ."

Louis's left jab brought blood from Billy's nose. Conn was hurting, but Sweet William not only stood his ground; he belted the Bomber with another violent outpouring of punches. The two best fighters in the world stood toe to toe. The Kid flailed away, firing both fists at the champion. Billy's punches were coming so fast the AP was unable to keep count, reporting that Conn "fired at least 20 punches at the head and body."

Dunphy: "A left hook to the jaw by Conn, a right to the jaw, two more rights as he outswings the champion . . ."

Joe Williams watched Billy's bold assault with amazement; Conn, he wrote, "went haywire in the 13th."

"A 20-punch combination," William Detloff says with some amazement. "Conn stood in there and punched."

Louis's supporters inside the Polo Grounds were in a panic. Conn's fans watched the former light heavyweight champ attacking the heavyweight king and went wild with each punch landed by the Kid. *Slam . . . Bam . . . Hot damn!* The Kid's crowd might have watched Billy's blurring gloves and remembered the words of the great Irish poet Yeats: "Hands, do what you're bid."

Casting caution to the wind, Conn went all out for glory. Now operating on a knife's edge, the Kid was extending a Homeric effort; if he succeeded, sportswriters would speak of his stunning victory in epic prose which would echo in eternity. There would be odes written in the Old World as well as in the New, paeans to Conn fighting with the passionate intensity of his Irish ancestors.

"In the 12th round I staggered Louis, it made me feel good," Conn remembered. "I knew I had the title if I wanted to box for it. But I thought how great it would be to beat the unbeatable Louis at his own game."

Louis could hear Conn's corner men screaming above the riotous crowd, "Keep him boxing!" Louis knew better. "Billy had other ideas," he said.

"I went into the 13th," Conn recalled, "with the idea of knocking Joe cold."

There were no grins now; the action in the ring had grown grim and dangerous. In the heat of battle Fierro heard Conn cussing Louis. *"You miserable . . ."*

"Billy always talked to his opponents in the ring," Fierro said. "Nobody could curse like Conn."

"He's gone mad," Tim Conn thinks when he watches his father cussing Louis and taking the fight to the Bomber in the 13th. "He's gone crazy!"

The Pittsburgh Kid had reverted to his street fighting days, and he and the Brown Bomber were going *mano a mano*. They put every ounce of power into their punches, both fighters gunning for the big finish. The furious exchange brought trainer Mannie Seamon to his feet in the champion's corner.

Out of the melee a Louis hook found its mark and reopened the cut over Conn's right eye. Billy was bleeding again, and Joe moved in. Feder thought the Bomber "came to life."

Dunphy: "Conn jabs a left and . . ."

Lightning crashed. Timing the punch, the Bomber caught the Kid with a short, sharp right cross. It was the assassin lurking in the shadows, and it had stepped forward. Mead called it the "one solid punch Louis needed, and it slowed Conn just enough." Joe's blast froze Billy. His knees buckled, and he bent forward from the force of the blow. Conn biographer Andrew O'Toole wrote that for the first time all night, "a look of bewilderment" filled Conn's once-confident eyes.

Perhaps the Kid's surprise stemmed from being unable to believe he had been caught by Louis. Billy had been teasing, taunting, and tantalizing the Bomber all night, landing his left and using it as a precursor to a follow-up right hand in a rapid combination.

"I remember cocking my left hand, about the middle of the round, for the final punch of the fight," Conn said. "And that's all I remember."

"Son of a gun," said Louis. "He started that long left hook I'd been waiting for. I zapped a right to his head."

Nat Fleischer noted that the Bomber "sensed the situation at a glance, took immediate advantage of it, [and] laced home a powerful right to the jaw to start the ball rolling."

Joe Williams wrote that Louis's cause "was helped by the heedless, hot-headed, swashbuckling, young Irisher."

Louis, using less flowery prose, said simply, "Conn got too cocky."

Williams credited the Bomber with quickly sensing "the vital promise of the situation" and having enough stuff left at this late stage of the fight to catch the Kid. It was a fortuitous situation, Williams said, but one that Louis "handled like a champion."

Mike Tyson calls Louis an "incredible fighter" who was much craftier than people thought. "He was so pragmatic," Tyson said.

Freddie Guinyard thought Joe a consummate ring tactician who noticed every move an opponent made. "Every step backward, front, or side Joe watched," Guinyard told Joe Louis Barrow Jr. and writer Barbara Munder for their book *Joe Louis: 50 Years an American Hero*. Conn made a move he had been making all night and Louis saw his opening. Instead of stepping back as he had been doing, the Bomber stepped forward.

"Gotcha now," Louis thought.

Guinyard noted that both Blackburn and Louis had noticed Conn's flaw in earlier rounds. But it wasn't until Round 13 that Joe could capitalize on it. When he did, the force of his punch was such that Louis believed Conn "turned numb" from the hard right to the head.

"He was waiting for me," said Conn, who was shattered by the blow he hadn't seen coming. "They tell me Joe hit me with a right hand."

Louis stated in his autobiography that he had been studying Conn all night and was waiting for Billy to wind up with his left. Joe figured this was his only hope of winning. Blackburn had told Louis in his corner prior to the 13th, "You're losing on points. You gotta knock him out!" Louis retorted, "I can't catch him!"

Even with his title slipping away, the champion didn't panic. He waited for his chance, waited for Conn to throw his left and leave himself open to the Bomber's counter right. It was a small window of opportunity, but it was the only prayer available to Louis as the witching hour approached.

Cus D'Amato, who trained Tyson and fellow future heavyweight champ Floyd Patterson, said Louis had the experience and determination to persevere through problems. "He wouldn't give up," D'Amato said. "He wouldn't get frustrated."

Williams likewise admired Louis's grace under pressure, a trait Hemingway famously prized above others. "This was one time when even the icy Louis might easily have been betrayed into high excitement and hysterical hustle," Williams wrote. "He was behind, he was losing his title, he had been staggered and hurt a few minutes before, a smaller foe who had publicly belittled him, laughed at him and taunted him in the ring, was in the process of humiliating him before one of the largest crowds to ever see a fight in the big town."

It took incredible nerve and mental restraint on the part of Louis, said Williams, to "remain sure and steady under such circumstances."

Months earlier Conn had gambled and gotten caught by Lee Savold; history was repeating itself, except that he was now facing Joe Louis. The Bomber knew Billy sometimes lost his cool in the ring; he had seen it firsthand in Conn's sparring sessions. His championship in jeopardy, the Bomber was banking on the Kid to do something rash.

"I was hoping he'd lose his head pretty quickly," Louis said, "because I knew I was losing the title."

Even now, the courageous Conn came back slugging, doubling down on his belief he could engage Louis in toe-to-toe exchanges and outpunch him with quick combinations.

"The Glamour Boy tried to fight back," Feder wrote, "and for a moment held Louis off."

Dunphy: "Conn … is staggered by a right cross thrown by Joe Louis. Conn is hurt! Louis comes back with a right and a left to the body and Conn hooks a left to the jaw. Conn every so often is staggered but he comes fighting back … He's got remarkable recuperative powers …"

Billy's thick neck acted as a shock absorber, keeping Conn upright when others would have long since fallen. But Louis would not be deterred from his destiny; in Feder's words, Joe "smelled the kill." He landed another right to the head and Sweet William staggered again. Turning his body to leverage his punching power, the Bomber straightened Billy up with a vicious uppercut.

Dunphy: "A right cross to the jaw by Louis. Louis takes Conn's head back with a right uppercut . . ."

The force of Louis's uppercut made Conn's slicked-down hair fly up and caused the crowd to scream "Oh!" Uppercuts were a prime weapon in the Bomber's arsenal. It is the shortest of punches, and when Louis delivered it, he did so by assuming the proper stance. Facing Conn, Joe bent to his right, shifted his weight from right to left, and brought his right arm up in an underhand arc to Billy's chin. The slight twist that Louis gave his right hip, simulating the move he executed in throwing a hook, added what the Bomber called "plenty of force" to the blow.

The gutsy Conn was in serious trouble. Joe knew it and nailed Billy with three more heavy shots. Feder thought the force of each of the Bomber's blows was such that it "might have broken a plank in two."

"Move, Billy, move!" Johnny Ray and Freddie Fierro screamed. Conn's corner men were in a panic, but their instructions were beyond Billy at this point. Conn couldn't move; the Bomber's blows were paralyzing; they took away the Kid's mobility.

Realizing his elusive quarry was finally stationary, Louis beat a steady drumbeat on Sweet William's head and body. The champion smartly alternated his attack and brought both hands to Billy's ribs to drain his remaining resources. The sound and fury moved United Press staff correspondent Jack Cudahy to call Louis's onslaught a "barrage of hooks and uppercuts that battered [Conn] around the ring and dressed him for the 'kill.'"

The Kid wobbled. "He'd have never hit me if I didn't make a mistake and try to knock him out," Conn told Heller. "Of all the times to be a wise guy, I had to pick it against him to be a wise guy."

Said Louis, "He made his mistake. He wanted to try and slug it out."

Billy absorbed the blows—"I had a strong neck," he said—but as Feder noted, Conn was "badly shaken."

Dunphy: "A left jab to the jaw and a right cross scored by Joe Louis and Conn is hurt! Louis rips a right to the jaw. Conn is staggering but he won't go down . . ."

Buoyed by his fighting heart, Billy was trying to find his way through the darkness. Louis, seeing Conn hurt, detonated dynamite rights and lefts.

"I went into my routine—rights and lefts, rights and lefts," he recalled. Suddenly it was 1938 again, and the Bomber was back in the springtime of his career. Fierro saw a look come over Louis's face; Freddie had seen that look before, the Bomber frowning and biting his lip as he prepared to drive his opponent into the canvas. Louis's punches were frighteningly powerful, his accuracy unerring.

"He hit me about twenty-five real good shots," said Conn. "Every damn one of them was on my chin."

"He didn't miss a punch," wrote Williams, noting that once Louis got Conn in trouble, he cut Billy down methodically and mercilessly.

"Most any other fighter, finding himself in such desperate position and gotten an unexpected reprieve would have tried to smother the stricken Conn with a wild hurricane of frantic punches," Williams added. "Not Louis. Weary and worn as he was, he fixed Conn with those cold eyes of his and went to work on him with a systematic merciless finality."

The Bomber belted Billy with a left to the body, a right uppercut, and a left hook. Louis sometimes used his left hook as a countering punch; in this instance against Conn, he used it as a finishing blow. Louis knew that the shorter the punch, the greater the effect. He turned his body to the right, shifting his weight to his right leg and throwing his arm in an arc to Conn's head. The Bomber's intent was to punch through his target and not at it, his knuckles up at the impact of the punch.

Dunphy: "Louis jabbing a left and uppercutting his right to Conn's head . . . Conn reeling around the ring. . . ."

The Kid was dazed, just barely hanging on, but still he came forward. James P. Dawson of the *New York Times* watched Louis unload on Conn and thought it a "furious attack." Pushing off his back leg and feeding his frustration and fury into every punch, the Bomber was crashing down on Conn brutal blows. Feder thought it a "fearful bombardment."

Fearful enough to make Sweet William shudder from the blunt force trauma. Writer Gay Talese studied the fight film years later and was moved to write that when Louis hammered Conn in Round 13, "Billy's bones seemed to shake."

"When he had my dad hurt," Tim Conn states, "every punch was accurate and strong."

Said D'Amato, "No one finished [the fight] once [Louis] hurt them."

Williams wrote that even in Louis's "comparatively slovenly performance against the speedball from Pittsburgh, one of his rare gifts stood out in undiminished brightness." It was Louis's gift for the kill, what Williams described as "the cool, composed, deadly manner in which he goes after a victim in distress." Williams opined that only Dempsey had this "macabre gift to a comparable degree."

Dunphy: "Louis hooks a left . . ."

The Bomber then connected with a screaming right hand; "a right hand that had haymaker written all over it," Feder wrote. Cudahy called it "a thundering straight right that caught [Conn] on the head." Dunphy thought the blow "vicious." Others saw it as an axe-like punch that finally brought Billy down. Conn's head shook with the destructive force of the blow, his legs trembled. Louis's punch was so hard Sweet William was spun part way around.

"That," Conn recalled, "was the end of the line."

Louis was readying another right when Conn pitched forward— "dropped like a shot horse," Cudahy said—and began a slow descent to the blood-spotted canvas. Billy recalled his body feeling paralyzed. Bent at the waist, Conn fell limply, like a marionette whose strings had been cut.

Ringside flashbulbs popped wildly as Conn landed on his right side near Louis's corner, Billy's head bouncing violently on the ring floor. Sweet William's bruised, cut face came to rest in the rosin.

Dunphy: "Conn is down from a right cross to the jaw!"

On the porch of 5435 Fifth Avenue in Pittsburgh, the colleens of the Conn clan shrieked in horror in reaction to Dunphy's call. Billy's sister Mary Jane buried her grief-stricken face in her hands; two other members of the Conn family and friends followed suit.

A photographer from the *Pittsburgh Press* caught the awful moment with his camera. On the floor of the Conn family home the pieces of a phonograph record, shattered by young Davey minutes before in his excitement over Billy's beating the champ, lay scattered. The title of one of the discs was *It Makes No Difference Now.*

Louis, head bowed in typical fashion, turned and headed toward a neutral corner. In what can be called perfect symmetry, the Bomber had thrown the final 13 punches of the 13th round.

As Joe walked away, his shoulders rose and fell in a visible exhale, a sure sign of relief. Williams stared at the champion in repose and wondered if fans ever stopped to consider that Louis had taken the measure of fighters of every style and size. "The orthodox, such as Schmeling and Braddock, free swingers like Max Baer, canvas-creepers like Godoy and Farr, track men like Pastor, giants like Carnera and Buddy Baer, and finally, elusive shadows like Conn."

Trading blows with Joe Louis proved to be a bridge too far, even for Billy Conn. Inside the Polo Grounds, the Kid's fans were shocked at the sight of brave Billy on the floor.

"Had my father not buckled in the 12th round and Billy not thought he could knock him out in the 13th, he would have won the title," Joe Louis Barrow Jr. states.

In the neutral corner, the bone-tired Louis struck his familiar pose, his arms draped on either side of the ring post. Referee Eddie Joseph moved toward the fallen Conn and picked up the count from George Bannon.

Joseph: "Three . . . Four!"

In Louis's corner an animated Seamon, a towel slung over his right shoulder, excitedly motioned his left arm in conjunction with the referee's count.

Joseph: "Five . . . Six . . ."

As Conn lay on the canvas, it would not have been surprising if some of Billy's followers could hear, in the recesses of their minds, the haunting lyrics of "Danny Boy," the saddest of all Irish ballads:

*The summer's gone and all the flowers are dying . . .*

Joseph: "Seven . . . Eight!"

Dunphy screamed into his microphone, "He's taking the count!" Had Yeats surveyed such a scene, he might have thought of Conn in relation to his own writings: "the wick of youth being burned, and the oil spent."

Largely motionless until Joseph reached eight, Billy suddenly stirred. He glared at Louis, who leaned forward from the neutral corner, ready to commence with the combat. Billy was ready too and pulled himself to a sitting position.

Joseph: "Nine!"

Dunphy watched Conn struggling to get up on one knee. "Brave," the broadcaster thought. Conn rose and his gloves were close to clearing the canvas. The round was nearing its end, only a scant few seconds remained. If Billy could beat the count, he would have a full minute's respite to recover.

"I saw him trying to get up," Louis said.

The sports world held its breath.

In the time between "Nine" and "Ten" Conn rose, but were his gloves cleared of the canvas?

Joseph: "Ten!"

"No go," wrote Feder. "It was all over."

Dunphy: "The bout is stopped!"

The referee spread wide his arms, indicating the fight was finished. The end for Billy Conn came at 2:58 of Round 13. The Kid was just two seconds shy of surviving the round.

Says Tim Conn, "Dad abandoned his tactics, lost his head, and it cost him the fight. Credit to Louis, he caught him, but my dad almost beat the count."

In her room at the Waldorf, Mary Louise heard her Aunt Helen scream from the next room. Helen had been listening to the fight on the radio, and now she ran into the bathroom where Mary Louise was waiting out the fight. The aunt pulled her niece close as she burst into tears.

"[Conn] was brave," Dunphy recalled. "He just couldn't make it."

Fans of the Pittsburgh Kid listening to the broadcast fell silent. In Forbes Field, the Pirates and Giants returned to the playing field. Perhaps drained emotionally by the stirring action of the past hour, they failed to score any additional runs and played to a 2–2 tie that was finally called after 11 innings.

Billy stood upright and his cut face creased into a cocky grin. Louis left the neutral corner and walked toward Conn. For a moment it appeared the two warriors would meet and exchange post-fight comments. But Joseph was still patting Billy on the back, so Louis bowed his head again and detoured to his corner where Blackburn and Seamon were climbing through the ropes to greet him.

Ray and Fierro rushed toward their beaten warrior, removed his mouthpiece, and splashed him with cool water from a sponge. Still in a dazed state, Conn asked his corner men, "Why'd they stop the fight?"

Ray told Billy he'd been knocked out. Conn was overcome by emotion. As he was led back to his corner the Kid began to tear up. Fierro steadied him. "Champs don't cry," he said softly.

The Kid's followers, together with fans of great theater, lamented that the fight ended just short of the bell. Some thought Conn had beaten the count, that his gloves cleared the canvas prior to Joseph reaching 10. It was another layer of intrigue added to a fight that was already creating as many questions as it answered.

Dunphy: "The winner and still champion, Joe Louis! But what a fight Billy Conn gave!"

Bill Corum had covered many great ring wars. By his own admission, he had never witnessed anything like what had just taken place.

Corum: "There'll never be another one like that! No better and no greater fight did anyone ever see. Louis came back from the brink of defeat after Conn had made as great a fight as you could possibly imagine."

At that moment, Harry Balogh stepped to center ring and grabbed the silvery microphone. "At two minutes, 58 seconds of the 13th round, the winner by a knockout and still the world's heavyweight champion, Joe Louis!"

Balogh grabbed the right arm of the champion and raised it high in the air. The weary, hurting Louis made a small wave to the crowd. The Bomber's face bore testament to the fierce battle that had been fought. Joe's nose was bleeding, he had a small mouse beneath his right eye, both eyes were swelling, and his ear was cut.

Keeping to the teachings of his co-managers, Louis maintained the mask that hid his feelings. Dunphy thought Joe as impassive in victory as he had been in battle. Louis stood in center ring surrounded by photographers and flashing cameras. Seamon hugged the champion and then went looking for Conn. He found Billy on the opposite side of the ring and patted him on the back. Dunphy saw Conn shaking his head; Sweet William still seemed bewildered.

Just as Joe showed the effects of a tough fight, Billy bore the marks of battle as well. As Conn left the ring and returned to his dressing room, fans seeing him up close took note of the open cuts on the bridge of his nose, above and below his right eye, and bruises on both sides of his face.

Louis was setting a record with every championship victory, but this one hadn't come easy. "That was one hard win," he thought. The Bomber had triumphed, but the Kid had given him a scare. "That sucker almost had it," Joe said.

Leaving the ring, Louis caught sight of Roxborough smoking a cigar. "How many of those you swallow tonight?" the Bomber deadpanned.

The big ballpark was buzzing over the fight's finish. Hype Igoe, tapping away on his typewriter keys, gushed over Billy the Kid's gamble. "Gorgeous audacity!" Igoe wrote in his *New York Journal-American* story. "Cruel overconfidence!"

Writer Meyer Ackerman took the referee to task for what he thought was Joseph's overt partiality to Louis. Ackerman even suggested that Joseph played a part in Billy's defeat.

"Conn," he wrote, "was annoyed by Referee Eddie Joseph, who came to the corner and remonstrated to Conn to 'step on it.' A world's heavyweight championship at stake and the New York State Athletic Commission had to designate an official who showed he was partial to Louis from the first round to the finish."

Ackerman charged that during each round Joseph "cast suspicious glances at Conn's corner for the appearance of Vaseline smears while Louis was left alone to do what he liked. It was another indication that Joe Louis does not get the worst of it, regardless of who referees in this state, although he needs no help."

Joseph, unaware of the criticism leveled at him, changed clothes in a room in the Polo Grounds and headed to his home atop Bement Avenue in Staten Island.

The postmortem saw Louis and Conn reach their respective dressing rooms surrounded by reporters, photographers, and cameramen. Flashbulbs lit up the scene and newsreel cameras whirred as the combatants answered questions.

"Just another 13-inning game," said the baseball-loving Louis. "I didn't know I had him until I actually knocked him out.

"When he started punching me around, I figured he'd start to gamble. And he did. In the 13th he threw a right and left hook that way, so I straightened him up with my hook and caught him with the right."

Louis said the Kid's quickness posed problems for him.

"I couldn't get started against that fast Conn," Joe said. "He was a mighty hard boy to get to. I had to gamble to get over with my left and that almost cost me the fight."

Louis said he "really got sore" after Conn hurt him in the 12th round. He knew that when he headed out for the 13th he was "far behind and had to knock the boy out."

The Bomber credited the Kid with a tremendous fight, saying Billy did a great job of keeping his head for the first 12 rounds. Joe told reporters he expected Conn to start slugging after getting hit hard.

"I was waiting for him to lose his head," said Louis. "He's a real smart fighter and you got to admit he's faster than I am."

The champion recalled the challenger telling him, "Joe, you're in for a tough fight tonight."

Standing next to the seated Louis inside the packed room, Blackburn revealed to reporters that Louis hurt his hand in Round Seven when "Joe pushed Billy against the ropes."

The champ acknowledged he had been in more danger of losing his title than in any of his prior defenses. "Billy was just too fast; I couldn't catch him."

Associated Press sportswriter Orlo Robertson noted that while Louis sat in comparative quiet, a throng whooped it up in Conn's quarters over the Kid's gallant stand. Robertson thought Billy appeared "joyous over the fact that he not only stood up for nearly 13 rounds but that he hurt the Bomber."

Had reporters been in Conn's quarters minutes before, they would have seen quite a different scene. Billy initially burst into tears, sobbing in the shower as he lamented losing his cool. Igoe recalled Conn "cried like a baby," Billy knowing he had allowed the heavyweight title to slip through his fingers.

"I have only myself to blame," Conn told Igoe. "I lost my head and my title, too. I know I can lick him. I didn't do it tonight; I was counted out. You've got to give all credit to Louis. They pay off on knockouts and he scored the one I was trying to ring up."

By the time reporters were allowed in, Billy's bonhomie was back. He sat upright on a rubbing table, stripped to the waist and covered by a white towel.

"I lost my head and a million bucks," he quipped.

Asked about the knockout Conn said, "I don't remember any particular wallop in that 13th. All I know is there were a helluva lot of them."

Was he aware that he was ahead after 12 rounds?

"I didn't care," Conn said. "All I wanted to do was fight. I did that, didn't I?

"And," Billy added, "I hurt him."

Conn stated that he wasn't hurt until Louis let loose with his barrage in Round 13.

"I don't know how many punches he threw," Billy said. "There were plenty of them. But don't forget, I didn't quit. I went out fighting."

Asked if he heard the referee's count, Conn nodded.

"Sure I did. I got up, didn't I?"

Questioned why he went for the knockout, Billy smiled. "What's the use of being Irish if you can't be thick?"

Several writers changed Conn's words to read, "What's the use of being Irish if you can't be dumb?"

"I know Uncle Mike's gonna give me another chance and I know I can win," Conn told reporters. Thinking of Maggie and Mary Louise, Billy said, "I guess I had too much to win for tonight, and I tried to knock him out."

The Kid flashed his famous grin.

"Otherwise," the ever-cocky Conn said, "I'd a won easy."

# GREATEST HEAVYWEIGHT CHAMPIONSHIP EVER?

As Billy Conn met the press, promoter Mike Jacobs burst into the dressing room. Grabbing Conn's cut face in his hands, Uncle Mike kissed both cheeks.

"I want to meet that guy again," the Kid said.

"You'll get it, Billy," Jacobs said, guaranteeing a rematch on the spot. "Don't worry."

Twenty minutes later the Kid left the Polo Grounds and began walking the seven miles to the Waldorf where Mary Louise was waiting. Conn walked through Harlem, drawing applause from fans, and waving to them in appreciation. When Billy reached their room at the Waldorf, Mary Louise saw the look on his face; he was happy but sad. Happy to see her; sad he had lost.

"My dad told her, 'I'm sorry I lost. I did the best I could,'" Tim Conn said.

"She told him, 'It's okay, Billy.'"

Mary Louise would say later that Billy didn't brood about the outcome. It wasn't in his nature. Nor was it in the nature of the Conn clan and the people of Pittsburgh to accept defeat. "Billy won," Aunt Helen insisted. "He won, but he lost."

News of the spectacular fight and its stunning climax made headlines across the country. The front page of the *New York Times* the following morning trumpeted the tremendous finish:

## LOUIS, NEAR DEFEAT,
## STOPS CONN IN 13TH AND
## RETAINS TITLE

Bomber Suddenly Turns Tide, Hammering Foe to Floor with Furious Attack

Sid Feder led his AP story with the following:

"Joe Louis held on to his world heavyweight championship tonight—but he never came closer to losing it. For 12 full rounds, Billy Conn, the 'fresh kid' from Pittsburgh who wasn't supposed to have a 'prayer,' the good little man who was laughed at as a challenger, gave the Brown Bomber more than he sent. Then Joe found the range and with a fearful bombardment that lasted less than a minute and a half, he chopped Conn down in the 13th."

As millions read the stories chronicling the fight, Billy and Mary Louise left the Waldorf and drove home to Pittsburgh. Several days later the young couple returned to the road, seeking a Catholic priest who would marry them. They headed to Brockway, Pennsylvania, before turning their car east. Billy and Mary Louise eloped and were married July 1 in Philadelphia; the following April they welcomed Tim, the first of their eventual four children. Billy used his earnings from the Louis fight to pay cash for a handsome brick home in the affluent Squirrel Hill District; he and Mary Louise would live there the rest of their lives.

Maggie died not long after the Louis bout and Billy, honoring his mother's wish, purchased for her the closest available plot to Harry Greb in Squirrel Hill's Calvary Cemetery.

Conn's fight against Louis made him a national celebrity. Hollywood came calling and Billy headed west that July to play the title role in a semiautobiographical film, *The Pittsburgh Kid* for Republic Pictures. Meeting with reporters awaiting his arrival, the Kid quipped, "I shoulda knocked Joe Louis's block off."

Billy then hurried off to a press luncheon at the stylish Los Angeles Biltmore Hotel. A highlight of *The Pittsburgh Kid* was the nearly two-minute clip of a sparring session between Conn and Henry Armstrong: two all-time greats sharing the same ring for the only time.

Jacobs's promise to Conn that he would get a rematch with Louis was sincere. It wouldn't be immediate; a fight with Lou Nova, a colorful heavyweight who proclaimed to have a "cosmic punch" was set for September 29 back in the Polo Grounds. Ranked number eight by *The Ring* magazine, the 28-year-old Nova hailed from Alameda, California, and was nicknamed the "Alameda Adonis" for his good looks.

Nova's talk of his "Cosmic punch" and yoga left Louis wondering. "What the hell is a cosmic punch and what the hell is yoga?" Pressed by reporters, Louis said he didn't care about the cosmic punch; the Bomber didn't go in for "mysterious stuff."

Nova's "cosmic" punch and the big money rematch with Conn were sizable incentives for Louis. And there was something else. "There's never been a heavyweight champion in the army before," Louis told reporters. "That's me."

Just prior to the bout, the champion received a surprise phone call.

"Hello, corporal," said Conn.

"Hello, you movie actor," replied Louis.

"I want to be sure you take good care of Nova," said Conn.

"You bet I'll attend to that, movie man."

Louis made good on his promise, stopping Nova late in Round Six with a right hand that AP sportswriter Gaye Talbot called "the sort of picture punch that a fight fan might wait a lifetime to see." The blow caught Nova flush on his jaw; the big Californian dropped, Talbot wrote, "as though he had collided with a boxcar."

Climbing to his feet as referee Arthur Donovan shouted "9" in his count, Nova was met with what Talbot said were "20 or 30 cruel shots to his head and body." Nova reeled around the ring. When Donovan rescued Nova there was one second left in Round Six. Lou's manager Ray Carlen criticized the referee for stopping the bout so close to the end of the round, but Nova didn't complain. It took a full two minutes after the fight was stopped for his legs to stop wobbling and the dazed look to leave his face.

"Joe's the hardest hitter I ever fought," Nova said.

Louis took time off for the holidays and like millions of Americans was stunned by Japan's attack on Pearl Harbor on December 7, 1941—"a date which will live in infamy," FDR famously declared in his Declaration of War speech.

The sneak attack infuriated millions of Americans, Louis included.

"I was furious," he recalled. "This is my country. Don't come around sneaking up and attacking it."

Louis responded to America's involvement in World War II by issuing one of his most famous quotes. "We'll win," he said, "because we're on God's side."

Louis's statement brought a standing ovation from his audience and quickly became part of the American lexicon. FDR sent the Bomber a telegram complimenting his choice of words. Joe's statement provided the inspiration for a recruiting poster and a poem by Carl Byoir, "Joe Louis Named the War," which was widely circulated in the *Saturday Evening Post*.

The Bomber put his words into action. He had registered for the peacetime draft and was classified 1-A by a Chicago draft board. Because Louis was the sole supporter of his mother, wife, and numerous family members, he might have qualified for a deferment. But he wanted to serve, and was cautious to avoid the kind of controversy that followed Jack Dempsey for not serving in World War I.

When Jacobs approached Louis with the idea of putting his title at stake with the winnings going to the Navy Relief Fund, Joe quickly agreed. He corrected those who said he was fighting for nothing. "Ain't fighting for nothing," the Bomber countered. "I'm fighting for my country."

Louis donating his winnings to the Navy Relief Fund stirred the patriotic fervor of the national media. Jimmy Powers of the *New York Daily News* wrote, "You don't see a shipyard owner risking his entire business. If the government wants a battleship, the government doesn't ask him to donate it. The government pays him a fat profit. . . . The more I think of it, the greater guy I see in this Joe Louis."

The Bomber returned to the ring on January 9, 1942, for a rematch with Buddy Baer. Madison Square Garden was so filled with American flags it looked to Louis like the Fourth of July. As Blackburn taped Louis's hands he told him, "Chappie, I can't make it with you in the corner tonight."

Knowing Blackburn was suffering from rheumatism and arthritis, Louis looked him in the eyes and made a promise. "Chappie, if you get up those stairs with me, I'll have Baer out before you can relax." Blackburn issued a tired smile. "Ok."

The Bomber kept his word, backing up Baer 22 seconds into Round One with a right hand. The champion cut Buddy's left eye and hammered the huge challenger around the ring. Louis floored the 250-pound Baer three times before Buddy was counted out at 2:56 of the first round following a series of dynamite rights. The spectacle prompted Jack Guenther of the United Press to pen a memorable line: "Buddy Baer came in at 250 and went out at 2:56."

Baer never fought again. "The only way I could have beaten Louis that night," he said, "was with a baseball bat."

Louis's purse for the fight was $65,200. Following deductions for training expenses, Joe donated the remaining $47,500 to Navy Relief. Baer and Jacobs also contributed to the cause, bringing the total donation to more than $88,000. The next day Louis enlisted in the Army and reported for duty at Camp Upton on Long Island. The champ was offered an officer's rank but turned it down, preferring instead to be a private first class. Eventually he would earn the rank of sergeant.

Three days following Louis's win over Baer, Conn climbed into the ring for the first time since his fight with the Bomber and earned a decision over Henry Cooper in Toledo. Sixteen days later Billy beat Jay D. Turner on points in St. Louis. Three weeks after that the Kid was back in New York, staring across the Madison Square Garden ring at middleweight tough guy Tony Zale, also known as the "Man of Steel."

The Conn-Zale fight is largely lost to history, but it was an intriguing matchup between two ring legends. Their 12-round non-title fight was held on February 13, Dunphy and Corum calling the action on the Gillette Sports Cavalcade Broadcast while 15,033 fans filed into the Garden.

Conn outweighed Zale 175¾ to 164¼ and reportedly won as many as 10 of the 12 rounds. Several rounds were close enough that they could have gone to Zale. Louis was in attendance and told Tony, "I thought you beat him."

Louis had his sights set on a fight much bigger than anything taking place in a ring. On March 27 Joe turned giant killer again, knocking out Abe Simon in six rounds in their rematch at Madison Square Garden. It was the first professional fight Louis fought without Chappie in his corner, Blackburn being hospitalized in Chicago. The Bomber scored late knockdowns in Rounds Two and Five, the bell saving Simon each time. In Round Six Louis recorded another knockdown and referee Eddie Joseph counted out Simon, who protested without success that he had arisen at 9.

Once again Joe donated his purse to the Armed Services, this time sending $36,146 to Army Relief. Simon and Jacobs contributed as well for a total donation of $55,000. During his radio broadcast of the bout, Dunphy linked Louis's victory to America's determined war effort.

"We won't stop punching, just as Joe Louis does," Dunphy told listeners, "until we win."

The champ was having domestic and personal issues. Marva had served divorce papers on Joe the previous April, and Chappie was hospitalized with pneumonia. Louis was also in debt, owing the IRS $217,000 in back taxes. He owed Jacobs $60,000; Uncle Mike was also owed $35,000 by Conn. Looking to get repaid before Louis and Conn had to forego their rematch to enter the armed services, Jacobs proposed another charity bout for Louis, this time against Conn in Yankee Stadium in October 1942.

A record radio broadcast deal and brisk advance ticket sales all but guaranteed a million-dollar gate. When Secretary of War Henry Stimson learned that the debts Louis and Conn owed to Jacobs would be deducted from their purses, he called off the fight. Despite the estimated $750,000 the rematch was expected to provide Army Relief, Stimson explained that the proposed bout wasn't fair to millions of American soldiers who didn't have the opportunity to work off personal debt while fighting for their country.

Conn was having difficulties in his personal life as well. He remained at odds with his father-in-law Jimmy Smith. Greenfield Jimmy refused to speak to his new son-in-law until the christening party for Tim. The truce between the two most important men in Mary Louise's life was brokered by Steelers owner Art Rooney, a friend to Billy and Jimmy.

At the party, Smith began needling Billy. Conn was sitting on top of the stove when Jimmy began harassing him. Rooney, a party guest and witness to the scene, said Jimmy always acted as if he was the boss, forever giving orders, telling people what to do. On this occasion Jimmy tried telling Billy that if he was going be the father of his grandson, he had better start attending church more regularly.

"And by the way," Jimmy added, "champion or no champion, I can beat the hell out of you anyway."

"Hey Jimmy, just leave me alone," Conn retorted.

Smith's needle got a little sharper. "You're afraid of me, aren't you?"

Rooney shook his head. Greenfield Jimmy, he thought, had just said too much.

"I'm afraid of no man living," a now angry Conn snapped, and he leapt forward from his stovetop seat.

"I can still see Billy come off that stove," Rooney said years later.

"That was all my father needed," Tim Conn says.

Conn aimed a left hand at his father-in-law's chin. Smith, no stranger to fighting, ducked and Conn connected instead with the top of Jimmy's hard head.

It was a million-dollar blow, and there's irony in the fact that a punch that might have changed heavyweight history was landed outside the ring. The blow broke Billy's hand, the busted bones costing him any chance at a blockbuster rematch with Louis in the foreseeable future.

Angry and frustrated that he had broken his left hand, Billy smashed a window with his right hand, leaving him cut and bleeding.

Conn's face was likewise scraped from his scrap with Smith, prompting the *New York Times* to print a photo of the injured boxer and describe him looking "as if he had tangled with a half-dozen alley cats."

The dust-up would cause Louis to kid Conn through the years. "Is your old father-in-law still beating the hell out of you?"

Louis-Conn II in 1942 became the greatest rematch never fought. Like Conn, Louis's fights were not confined to the ring. He fought for desegregation during his Army years, quietly demanding that crowds at his exhibition bouts be integrated and placing calls to influential power brokers in Washington, DC, to alert them to overt racism aimed at Black soldiers. Louis's activities had a positive effect; his stand against racism directed at him and his friend Sugar Ray Robinson at Camp Siebert in Alabama led to military buses being integrated.

"My father was a quiet fighter for race relations," Joe Louis Barrow Jr. says. "He entertained three million troops during the war. Black soldiers were in the back rows, and my father said he wasn't going to give the three-round exhibitions unless Black soldiers weren't put in the back rows."

Louis was part of one of the more influential war propaganda movies, Frank Capra's 1943 film *The Negro Soldier*. The 40-minute documentary used highlights of the second Louis-Schmeling fight as an allegory for the Allies' fight against the Axis. "An American fist won a victory," the narrator says in Capra's film. "This time it's a fight not between man and man, but between nation and nation. A fight for the real championship of the world, to determine which way of life shall survive."

On August 30, 1943, Louis began a 100-day boxing and physical fitness tour. Serving with the Army's Special Services Division, Joe fought in 96 exhibitions and ventured 70,000 miles. The champion experienced close calls outside the ring. Louis survived an emergency landing while aboard a damaged bomber as well as V-12 rocket attacks in London. On one occasion when Joe was in Italy, he was pictured pulling the lanyard of an artillery piece. The next day the same piece malfunctioned and exploded, killing several soldiers.

Conn enlisted in the Army and joined Bob Hope and other celebrities on a morale tour. Billy boxed exhibition bouts with division champions in the European Theater. He also boxed with brother Jackie, and New York writer Jimmy Cannon recalled their bouts being brutal battles. The Conn brothers cursed each other and fought viciously in the ring.

During the war years Corporal Conn and Sergeant Louis became close friends. They posed together several times in their uniforms for photos, and visited one another in training. Joe and Billy appeared together in uniform on the cover of the July 1942 issue of *The Ring*.

Japan's surrender in September 1945 brought an end to World War II. Louis received his honorable discharge from the Army in October and two weeks later agreed to the long-awaited rematch with Conn. The bout was scheduled for June 19, 1946, in Yankee Stadium. It would be five years and a day following their epic encounter.

Louis-Conn II proved historic. For the first time, a world heavyweight championship fight would be broadcast live on the groundbreaking new medium that was television, NBC carrying the bout to viewers. That the fight was free on TV didn't deter an audience of 45,266 paying $1,925,504 to watch the action in person.

Louis returned to train at Pompton Lakes, which served as Conn's site for their first fight. Joe liked Mannie Seamon, but he missed Chappie. Louis looked bad in training and writers reported as much. At the same time, word reached the champion that Conn was "training up a storm."

"I hope he doesn't leave the fight in the gym," Joe responded.

Sportswriter Harry Keck believed that might have been what happened. "Maybe," he wrote, "we'll find out one of these days just what happened to Billy Conn before his second fight with Joe Louis.

"You never saw a better conditioned or more confident challenger in a training camp than Billy or a more unimpressive-looking heavyweight champion than Louis. But the day of the fight Billy suddenly went limp.

He doesn't remember going to the weigh-in, has only a vague recollection of the fight. He was walking like a man in a dream."

At the weigh-in, Louis studied Conn closely. Joe estimated that Billy had gained 15 pounds since their first fight; Louis's weight of 207, meanwhile, was just five pounds above his normal fighting weight. The Brown Bomber realized this wasn't the same Pittsburgh Kid who had taken him into deep waters five years earlier; the extra weight Billy was carrying meant he couldn't be as quick as he was five years earlier.

"He wouldn't be a prima ballerina this time around," Louis recalled. "I knew I had him."

Eddie Joseph would again serve as referee. But Joseph's presence was one of the few similarities between the '41 classic and its '46 sequel. Advancing age and ring rust from the war years robbed Louis and Conn of their transcendent talent, and much of the magic, drama, and excitement of their first fight was missing from the rematch.

The crowd was so large that Louis and Conn had trouble getting inside Yankee Stadium. The celebrity-studded audience included Frank Sinatra, who sat ringside next to Mrs. Bob Hope. At the bell for Round One, Conn resumed his habit of talking to opponents. "Take it easy, Joe. We've got 15 rounds to go."

The remark made the Bomber break out laughing. The two sparred throughout the opening round and it was clear to Louis that Conn wasn't fast at all; Joe felt he was faster than Billy. Louis saw the early rounds as Conn jumping around and dancing; he waited for Billy to come to him as he had in 1941. Billy hadn't fought an official fight since facing Zale in February 1942, and the ring rust was more evident on him than it was on Louis.

Louis-Conn II was largely dull. Conn boxed and moved, and Louis stayed after him in dogged pursuit, but the pitched battles that marked their first meeting were few and far between.

"[The rematch] was nothing," Conn told Peter Heller. "It was a stinker."

By Round Three Louis knew he'd have to go after Conn to initiate the action. The Bomber moved forward, economic in his actions but keeping the pressure on. Using what speed he still had, Billy sought to stay out of range. Conn would circle to Louis's right, backpedaling the entire time. The slow pace of the fight reflected the declining skills of the aging legends. Prior to Round Eight Louis told Seamon he was going to step up the pace to see if Conn could still take a punch.

Joe shot a right hand to the head that opened a cut under Billy's left eye. Another hard right buckled Billy's knees. A right uppercut and left hook followed, and Conn fell backward to the canvas. Just as he did in their first fight, Billy struggled to his feet. But for the second time in his career, Joseph counted him out.

Louis later cited the uppercut as one of the decisive punches in his rematch with Conn. "I set him up with several left jabs in the early rounds," he remembered, "and after gaining an opening by using first a right cross and then a right uppercut, I let go a thunderous left hook that staggered him and sent him tumbling to the floor for the count."

Said Conn, "I was out for four years, couldn't fight no more. [Inactivity] takes the edge away. You know what to do but you're not there anymore. That was a bad fight. I was just out too long."

Tim Conn, however, wonders if there was something amiss.

"The second Louis fight, there was something funny about that," he states. "My dad was at Toots Shor's [Restaurant] before the fight and it was like someone slipped him something; he looked terrible."

Keck wrote there had been "many rumors" that Billy was drugged by persons "interested in the betting angle."

Says Tim, "There was a lot of money coming in from all over the country on my dad and it was covered immediately."

Billy spoke later about seeing a newspaper headline the morning after the fight declaring a "Terrible Showing by Conn." Disappointed by his performance, he retired from the ring. Like many ring retirements it didn't stick. Three months later Billy was campaigning for a third fight with the Bomber; Conn wanted the bout so badly he promised to donate his entire purse to charity. Conn didn't fight again until November 1948 when he stopped Mike Dowd and Jackie Lyons within 10 days of each other.

Three months after his rematch with Conn, Louis returned to Yankee Stadium and claimed his second straight stoppage, knocking out Tami Mauriello in the first round. In December 1947 Louis was floored twice in Madison Square Garden by his former sparring partner Jersey Joe Walcott but received a controversial 15-round split decision victory.

The public demanded a rematch and on June 25, 1948, Louis and Walcott met in Yankee Stadium. Walcott dropped Louis yet again and looked to have the fight under control when he went into his celebrated "cakewalk." It was a mistake getting too cute with the Bomber; a hard right stunned Walcott in Round 11 and a barrage of blows finished Jersey Joe.

Louis had one more ring encounter of note that year. On December 10, Joe and Billy faced each other one final time, a six-round exhibition bout in the International Amphitheater in Chicago. A small crowd looked on as Louis delivered what the Associated Press called "a neat but none too impressive boxing lesson."

The *Pittsburgh Courier* reported that Louis battered Conn and "displayed a merciful heart by letting up when Conn appeared to be ready for the laundry. Louis would have knocked him out with those big 14-ounce 'pillows' he was wearing for gloves, but instead held back until the bees stopped buzzing in Billy's brain."

A poll of the eight newspapermen at the exhibition revealed a 6–1–1 decision in favor of Louis. Conn never again stepped into a ring as a fighter, though he spoke of coming out of retirement to fight Ezzard Charles. Louis didn't intend to fight anymore either, the Bomber announcing his retirement in March 1949 to end a record-setting reign of nearly 12 years and 25 title defenses. Financial problems forced him to return to the ring. Balding, old, and slow, Joe fought into 1951 before retiring for good.

When Frank Deford penned his popular piece, "The Boxer and the Blonde" for the June 1985 issue of *Sports Illustrated*, he opined that the first Louis-Conn fight "might have been the best in the history of the ring. Certainly, it was the most dramatic, all-time, any way you look at it."

Mike Tyson calls Louis-Conn I one of his favorite fights. If he's depressed, Tyson puts on the film of Louis-Conn I. "It makes my day."

That Louis versus Conn still fascinates is due to the numerous layers of the story itself. Two tremendous talents, two men who were arguably the greatest heavyweight and light heavyweight champions of all time, engaged in a back-and-forth battle for what was then the most glamorous title in sports.

Add in the dramatic clash of styles; the contrasting personalities of the stoic, soft-spoken champion from Detroit and the smiling, bragging challenger from Pittsburgh; the Brown Bomber versus the Kid; and it's clear Louis-Conn I ranks among boxing's greatest bouts.

The fight's climax, which saw Billy brashly casting his fate to the wind and striving boldly for a glorious finish that would thunder through time, reads like Greek legends of old. That Conn was KO'd in his quest for immortality is Shakespearian in its tragedy.

"If I listened to the fellas in the corner, I would have been all right," Conn told Curt Gowdy. "I think if I stayed away, I would have won it. I knew I was ahead. The corner told me, 'You only have a couple of more rounds. Just stay away from him. Joe's still dangerous.'"

Tyson, having studied the fight numerous times said, "Billy Conn made a big mistake by trying to put pressure on Joe Louis. In Louis's prime he made people pay for their mistakes."

Asked by Gowdy to rank Billy as an opponent Louis said, "Conn gave me my toughest fight."

The belief that Billy beat the count of Eddie Joseph was held by some in the Polo Grounds that night. Hype Igoe, one of the writers who predicted a Conn victory, watched closely as the Kid climbed off the canvas.

"He got up to his feet," Igoe wrote in the September 1941 issue of *The Ring*, "though still bending over with his glove tips touching the floor. Under the rules he still was down and Louis was not entitled to strike again. Just as the referee, Eddie Joseph, roared 'ten' into Billy's ears, Conn lifted the tip of his gloves from the canvas and was erect! It was that close."

Popular history states that Conn lost because he altered his fight plan in the fateful 13th. Billy, Joe, and Johnny Ray all spoke of it as a rash decision in the immediate aftermath, and the writers covering the fight believed the same. Igoe thought the challenger's tactics a reflection of the Kid's "gambling spirit" that the writer saw firsthand in the lead-up to the fight. Igoe watched Conn and his friends play a Pittsburgh card game called "skin" at training camp in Pompton Lakes.

"He is a gambler, this Conn," Igoe wrote. "Billy was betting a hundred here and a hundred there on the next turn of a card!"

Wrote Meyer Ackerman in *The Ring*, "Conn was a victim of too much courage in his fight with Joe Louis . . . Conn, with his Irish do-or-die fiery disposition, was determined to flatten Louis."

Linking Conn's loss to his Irish heritage was a theme put forth by several observers.

"If he hadn't been Irish, he'd be boss this morning," wrote Caswell Adams in the *Herald Tribune*. "But being Irish, he wasn't content to coast and dance in the last three rounds."

Conn's manager, Johnny Ray, told reporters that if Billy "had a Jewish head instead of an Irish one, he'd be champ."

Igoe wrote that Johnny begged Billy to be careful, that the Kid was winning and not to take any foolish gamble.

"That didn't suit Conn's nature," Igoe wrote. "He is a fighting Irishman."

Says William Detloff, "It's so perfect that Billy Conn's Irish. It fit the existing narrative."

Nat Fleischer steered clear of bringing Billy's heritage into the discussion but was among those who believed Billy "lost his head and came out slugging in an effort to score a knockout."

Louis believed the same, saying for years afterward that if Billy had kept his cool, "he might have been the champion."

Fleischer's colleague at *The Ring*, George Tickell, considered Conn greater in defeat than Louis in victory due to the Kid's willingness to gamble when he could have played it safe.

"Billy Conn," Tickell wrote, "while employing all the resources of science and speed, threw discretion to the winds at a crucial moment when victory appeared to be well within his grasp, undertook to slug it with the foeman of heavier gunning metal, and was knocked out himself!"

Tickell thought the knockout "a sensation because of the narrow margin by which the champion escaped defeat, and a thrill-revelation in the light of extraordinary speed and ring craft displayed by the loser."

When writer Roy McHugh visited the Conn household to do a story on the 50th anniversary of the fight, he reported that Tim Conn questioned his father about his change in tactics in Round 13 as they watched the fight film together.

"You're flatfooted! You're standing still! Why did you stop moving, Dad? Why did you change your style?"

Responded Billy, "When you hurt a guy, you try to take him out. That's your business. That's what you're supposed to do."

Some consider the story of Conn's shift in strategy more myth than reality. The June 22, 1981 edition of the *New York Times* carried an article written by esteemed sports columnist Red Smith and headlined "The Myth of Louis-Conn."

"One of the indestructible myths of sports," wrote Smith, who was in press row at the Polo Grounds the night of the fight, "tells us that Billy Conn would have won the heavyweight championship of the world in his first bout with Joe Louis if he had not recklessly abandoned his hit-and-run tactics, tried to slug it out with Joe, and been knocked kicking."

Smith called it "a dandy myth, lacking nothing but truth." There was no visible change in Conn's tactics, Smith wrote. Billy had been "living on the brink of disaster from the opening bell, and he just got caught, as did most of Louis's adversaries."

Boxing writer Monte Cox says the myth was widely repeated because it was the reason Conn gave the press for his defeat following the bout.

"If one watches the fight," Cox writes, "all one sees is Billy boxing the thirteenth as he had the previous rounds that he was winning, by circling and backing away. Conn started the round circling to his left. Louis came out invigorated, perhaps from a rush of adrenaline. Showing no effects of the previous round Louis fought more aggressively due to the urging of [Blackburn] . . . Conn, for his part, continued to circle left, he was not being aggressive, and he was not 'going for a knockout.'"

The question persists: Had Billy stayed away from Joe in the closing rounds, would he have pulled one of the greatest upsets in sports history? Conn's corner men pleaded with him to box his way to the finish, believing his lead being sufficient to win.

Yet a review of the official scorecards reveals that the Kid could not have cruised to the title. Three rounds remained, and had Conn tried to "coast in" as Johnny Ray implored him to do, he might have lost on points or by stoppage to a fired-up Louis who was urged by Blackburn to "knock that son of a bitch out!"

One more layer of the Louis-Conn legend focuses on what could have happened had Billy beaten the count. Only two seconds remained in the round, not nearly enough time for Louis to relaunch his attack.

"Had Billy arose at exactly 'nine' and held," wrote Igoe, "the bell would have saved him, and the minute's rest might have made it possible for him to have continued outpointing the slower big man."

Conn would have come out for Round 14 still leading on two of the three official scorecards. Billy stated that he would have returned to his hit-and-move strategy. Yet Harry Markson, the former boxing director emeritus for Madison Square Garden, opined that had Conn reached Rounds 14 and 15, "the beating he absorbed made it certain Louis would have won the last two [rounds]."

Winning the final two rounds would have given Louis a majority decision—8–7 on Eddie Joseph's card; 9–6 on Bill Healy's; and 7–7–1 on Marty Monroe's card. In the latter, a draw decision in a championship fight favors the titleholder.

Conn saw it differently. "If the bell would have rang to save my ass and they got me in the corner then I would have wised up, he'd have never hit me anymore. I'd have just kept going. He couldn't hit me, then I'd start to fight like hell in the last round. I would have beat him."

Says Tim Conn, "My dad said, 'If I had gotten into the 14th and 15th I would've moved.'"

Louis didn't doubt Billy would have gone back to boxing at long range but didn't believe that given Conn's condition he could have survived the final rounds.

"I had [two] rounds to go and was coming on after the 12th round," Louis said. "He took a good beating in the 13th round and the 14th round would have been, from his standpoint, a slow-motion thing, because I don't think he could have picked up the speed he had in the other rounds."

The final mystery to Louis versus Conn focuses on whether Billy would have defeated Joe in a rematch had it been fought in 1942 as originally planned. Igoe believed Conn would beat Louis in a return bout.

"I still say that a clever man will defeat [Louis]," Igoe wrote then. "Corbett, Johnson, Tunney ... defeated the great punching champions of their day. Isn't it easy then to understand why I've harped on Conn's possible chance to win the title from one of the greatest punchers? After all, there is more to fisticuffs than a mere knockdown-and-drag-out finale. Fate has a strange way of bringing back the clever men to thrash the heavy hitters. Boxing history will repeat itself."

Fleischer acknowledged that the champion was made to look surprisingly slow by his challenger. "Conn fought so fast," Fleischer wrote, "that Louis seemed like a snail in comparison."

Yet Fleischer balked at the possibility of Sweet William winning the rematch.

"I shall go on record now with the statement that the result would be the same as in the first bout, except that the end would come sooner,"

Fleischer wrote in 1941. "Billy's temperament and his weight are against him. He showed in the recent fight that he can sock pretty hard when his punches land squarely, but his hard-hitting is only spasmodic. They come in dribs and drabs as against terrific clouts to the mid-section that land with regularity when Joe tosses them."

Louis and Blackburn were known for using their time between bouts to adjust strategy. The results were that Max Schmeling, Bob Pastor, Buddy Baer, Arturo Godoy, Abe Simon, Natie Brown, and Lee Ramage all suffered savage knockouts in return bouts with the Bomber. Of these, only Pastor survived longer than in his first fight with Louis, but was still knocked out, Pastor being stopped in Round 11 after dropping a 10-round decision in the first meeting.

Schmeling, Buddy Baer, Godoy, Simon, Brown, and Ramage lasted a cumulative average of nearly seven fewer rounds than they did in their initial encounter with a man many still believe to be the best heavyweight in boxing history.

"With 12 years as champion and 25 title defenses, Joe Louis stands alone," stated Tyson. Joe Louis Barrow Jr. reveals that at the funeral for his father, Muhammad Ali told him his father was the greatest heavyweight ever.

Conn likewise may have been the best light heavyweight champion; certainly, Louis believed Billy to be number one.

"My opinion of Billy as a champion is that he was the best light heavyweight I've ever seen," Louis said in the 1970s, placing Conn above Ezzard Charles, Archie Moore, et al. "His moves were perfect; he didn't make too many mistakes in the ring."

A rematch with Louis in 1942 would have had many fans believing that the lessons Conn learned from his fight with Louis would make for a different ending. Billy's loss to Louis was his first ever in a championship fight and at the time he was 4-1 in title bouts and 11-2 against world champions.

"My dad was in great shape [in '42]," says Tim Conn. "He would have fought differently than in the first fight."

Proponents of Louis point to his 7-1 record at the time against fellow world champions and his 6-0 mark in rematches. By the time he retired as world champion in 1949, Louis improved those numbers to 10-1 and 8-0, respectively. His final record stands at 68-3, with 54 knockouts. Two of his three defeats came in his forced comeback, tax problems with the Internal Revenue Service driving his return to the ring when he was far past his prime and no longer interested in fighting.

Louis eventually faced eight former or future world heavyweight champions, a total unmatched by anyone prior to the modern era of multiple champions in each division. Conn also fought the best of the best; one-third of his pro fights coming against champions. According to the International Boxing Hall of Fame, Conn's record stands at 64-12-1. He was inducted into the Boxing Hall of Fame in 1965 and the International Boxing Hall of Fame in 1990.

Billy would have one more fight, though it doesn't appear in his official record. In 1990, the 72-year-old former champ and Mary Louise were seated at the lunch counter close to the cash register of their local delicatessen. Billy's friend owned the deli, and on that day a young man walked in off the wintry street and demanded the owner hand over the cash from the register. When the owner resisted, the would-be robber hit him. Protecting both his friend and Mary Louise, Conn grabbed the man's coat with his huge right hand and hammered him with his left, sending the thief sprawling to the floor.

"You always go with your best punch—straight left," Conn told TV station WTAE.

"My instinct was to get help," Mary Louise said to reporters. "Billy's instinct was to fight."

Unable to extricate himself from Conn's strong grip, the thief panicked and pulled free of his coat. Billy handed it to the deli owner, who located the man's identification and address; he was soon arrested by police.

"I think I interrupted his plans," Billy said.

Neither the Pittsburgh Kid nor the Brown Bomber ever had a fight like their legendary bout in June 1941. Through the years, Louis and

Conn watched the film together several times; Billy would sit through the end of Round 12 and then stand to leave.

"Call me if the ending changes," he would tell Louis.

A few minutes later, Joe would find him. "Sorry, Billy, the ending didn't change."

Louis would state that Conn was the heavyweight champion of the world—for 12 rounds. Two weeks after their first fight Billy and Joe saw one another and Conn talked about the tough break he had in the unlucky 13th.

"I had your ass beat," he told Louis. "I could've won and been the champion of the world for six months, I could've gone around and told all the fellas, 'Look, I'm the champion of the world.'"

"You had it for 12 rounds and couldn't keep it," Louis replied. "How the hell were you going to keep it for six months?"

Both men laughed. Once locked in a desperate struggle, the former combatants became close friends, comfortable in each other's company.

"Joe's one of the best fellas I ever met," Conn remarked.

Said Louis, "As friends, we're two of the closest among fighters."

Tim shared his father's feelings about Louis. "I met him a couple of times. He was nice; very quiet. He came to our house once. He and my dad became really good friends. Joe was nice to everybody. He never criticized anybody, never said a bad word about anybody."

When Joe Louis Barrow Jr. was writing his book about his father, he visited Billy at the Conn home in Squirrel Hill. Billy gave him a guided tour and asked Barrow repeatedly, "Do you like my house?"

"Yes, I like your house. Why do you keep asking me?"

"Because your dad bought it for me."

It was a reference to the purse money Billy earned from his first fight with Joe.

"So," Barrow replied with a smile, "it's *my* house!"

Joe Jr. and Billy laughed at the remark and the two became friends, just as his father had been a friend of Billy. "They were collegial," Barrow recalls. "It was the type of relationship they had."

Tim remembers how his father and Joe would pal around together at casinos.

"Joe would have a pocket full of chips worth $100 each and a pocket full of chips worth $5 each," he says. "A guy would go up to Louis and ask if he could have a chip and Joe would give him a $100 chip.

"My dad would ask, 'Why did you give him a $100 chip?'"

"Joe would say, 'I'd only lose it at the tables anyway.'"

In retirement, Billy stayed in boxing for a time, serving as a referee; he was the third man in the ring for the hotly disputed 1966 world lightweight fight between Sugar Ramos and Carlos Ortiz. Conn's decision to stop the fight due to Ramos's cut eye fueled a riot that saw fans flinging bottles and rocks. Billy had to fight his way to safety.

In retirement Conn largely lived off the earnings from his ring career, but he also made investments—oil wells, an apartment building. "They'll never hold a benefit for me," he said proudly. He was also paid by a car dealership and for three years managed the Stardust Casino in Las Vegas. Billy spent hours every week fulfilling autograph requests and signing memorabilia that arrived in his mail; he also appeared in several documentaries and small films.

Sadly, time was not kind to Joe and Billy, nor to their managers. Jack Blackburn died at age 59. He had battled pneumonia for two months and was hospitalized. On April 24, 1942, he was undergoing a physical when he suffered a fatal heart attack.

"I guess I thought I'd be heavyweight champion forever and Chappie would always be with me," Louis said. "Chappie had been another father, a teacher, and a friend. When you think about it, I lost three people, not one."

Johnny Ray's hard life caught up with him as well, his bouts with the bottle taking their toll.

"I met him once, outside of Forbes Field, and he seemed pretty far gone," Tim Conn remembers. "He was down and out. The second Louis fight Johnny was drunk the whole time, he didn't help at all. He was in the corner, but he didn't help."

Like Blackburn, Ray died relatively young, two months shy of his 65th birthday.

As he aged, Billy largely withdrew from public life. "When he was older, he would sit around the house more," Tim Conn recalls. "Budd Schulberg wanted my dad to be in the movie *On the Waterfront*. There were other fighters in that movie [Tony Galento, Tami Mauriello, Abe Simon]. My dad liked [Marlon] Brando. But dad didn't want to do the movie. I asked him, 'Why didn't you do it? That would've been a great thing!'

"I would ask him, 'Why don't you have more ambition? Why don't you get out of the house more?'"

A doctor later told Tim that a part of the brain—the anterior cingulate cortex and dorsolateral prefrontal cortex—impacts motivation, and that part of the brain is affected by the thousands of punches fighters absorb in their careers. It leads to pugilistic dementia, a condition caused by concussive blows to the brain and one that affects an estimated 15 to 20 percent of amateur and professional fighters.

"Dad would wake up in the middle of the night and he would be nervous," Tim says. "He'd say, 'Where are we? Who's paying for this room?' He would panic if my mother wasn't around."

Louis exhibited dementia symptoms as well in his later years and developed paranoid schizophrenia that was linked to cocaine abuse and may also have been genetic, Joe's father having been institutionalized for mental illness. Unfortunately for both Joe and Billy, they had finally found an opponent tougher than each other.

Louis was 66 years old when he died in Desert Springs Hospital in Las Vegas on April 12, 1981. His former ring rival, Max Schmeling, paid Louis's funeral expenses. A national hero for his patriotic actions during World War II and a Black man embraced by White America like no member of his race had ever been, Joe Louis was laid to rest, fittingly, in Arlington National Cemetery.

"He is a credit to his race," New York sportswriter Jimmy Cannon wrote of Louis, "the human race."

Joe Barrow Jr. recalls how Billy's eyes would tear up in his later years whenever he talked about his dad.

Billy really loved my father," Barrow says, and it was a feeling shared by many Louis opponents, Schmeling in particular. "Every opponent of my father was an opponent for 15 rounds but a friend for life."

Billy Conn died of pneumonia in a Veterans Affairs hospital in Pittsburgh, passing away in his sleep at age 75 on May 29, 1993. He is buried in Calvary Cemetery, his grave close to that of his mother and Greb. Billy's beloved Mary Louise lived to age 94, the boxer and the blonde being reunited upon her passing in April 2017.

Decades earlier, when the Brown Bomber and Pittsburgh Kid were in the springtime of their youth, their fight fascinated millions living on the brink of a second world war. For one memorable night, Louis and Conn provided a world weary of war with a treasured gift—one of the last moments of normalcy.

Louis versus Conn remains as captivating today as it was in that long ago summer of 1941, ambition colliding with fate in spectacular fashion. Tim Conn recalls meeting Dunphy decades after the fight and talking with the Hall of Fame announcer about that June night.

"He said, 'First big fight I did and what a fight! After the 12th round Louis was really beat.' He told me the best round he ever saw was the 13th."

McHugh says everyone remembers Louis-Conn '41 because Billy transformed the fight "into a morality play—or to be more accurate, a cautionary tale. . . . He remains an object lesson in the danger of over-reaching. . . . It was hubris that brought him to grief."

Joyce Carol Oates wrote that for a fan to go from viewing an ordinary fight to viewing Louis-Conn I was like "listening or half-listening to a guitar being idly plucked to hearing Bach's 'Well-Tempered Clavier' being perfectly played."

McHugh believes Conn's coming down off his toes to slug with Louis in the 13th "a burst of doomed recklessness more suggestive of Wagner than of Bach."

Detloff calls Louis versus Conn "a wonderful story." Douglas Cavanaugh says high drama helps Louis-Conn rank as one of the greatest fights ever. Dunphy called Louis versus Conn "a masterpiece of a fight." Decades after the final bell had tolled in the Polo Grounds late on June 18, 1941, the aging announcer's eyes still sparkled at the memory of that magical New York night. The world was younger when Dunphy settled into his ringside seat inside the Polo Grounds, when the Brown Bomber and Pittsburgh Kid engaged in grim battle on a brightly illuminated white canvas.

The sights and sounds of a fight Dunphy called "the greatest heavyweight championship of all time" endure to this day:

"They're fighting again ... Conn dancing around and Louis is after him ... Louis with a left hook to the body, Billy fighting back with a right to the jaw. The battle has turned again!"

# ACKNOWLEDGMENTS

Any work of this size is never accomplished alone. I thank my wife, Michelle, my children Patty and Katie, and all the members of my family for their love and support. I am blessed to be a part of their lives.

Niels Aaboe of Lyons Press supported this project from the start, and his hard work helped bring to these pages the first full-length telling of one of the greatest championship fights in boxing's long history. I'm extremely grateful to Meredith Dias and all those at Lyons Press who played a part in taking this book from an idea to the finished product.

This book could not have been completed without the invaluable insight provided by Tim Conn, Billy's oldest son, and Joe Louis Barrow Jr. Both men provided candid, behind-the-scenes looks at their famous fathers and their most famous fight.

Tim graciously agreed to write the foreword for this book and was extremely helpful in supplying background information in the many discussions and email exchanges shared throughout the writing, research, and editing phases.

Joe Louis Barrow Jr. was very helpful in sharing insight into his father and into Billy Conn as well, and how he became friends with Billy and the Conn family and spent time with them in their Pittsburgh home.

The personal recollections of Tim and Joe helped paint a complete picture of their fathers, who rank as arguably the greatest light heavyweight and heavyweight champions, respectively, of all time.

I thank boxing historians William Detloff and Douglas Cavanaugh for taking time to share their tremendous insight with me. They are respected ring experts and authors, and their extensive knowledge helped place Joe Louis, Billy Conn, and their classic 1941 championship fight in historical perspective.

As a Pittsburgh boxing historian, Cavanaugh provided additional insight into the life and times of Billy Conn, the "Pittsburgh Kid," and the state of boxing in the Steel City during Billy's rise to prominence in the 1930s and 1940s.

To all of the above, and to many more, I offer my humble thanks and appreciation.

# SOURCES

Astor, Gerald. *"And a Credit to His Race": The Hard Life and Times of Joseph Louis Barrow, a.k.a. Joe Louis.* Saturday Review Press, E.P. Dutton & Company, Inc., 1974.

A Sip of Sports. "Stories You Should Know: Louis vs. Conn." Asipofsports.com, January 11, 2018.

Associated Press. "Joe Louis-Billy Conn Title Bout Cancelled." September 25, 1942.

———. "Ex-Fighter Billy Conn Dies at 75: He Nearly Defeated Joe Louis for the Heavyweight Championship in 1941, but Decided to Slug It Out." *Los Angeles Times*, May 30, 1993.

———. "Billy Conn, 75, an Ex-Champion Famed for His Fights with Louis." *New York Times*, March 31, 2016.

Barrow, Joe Louis Jr. Interview with the author, June 2021.

Barrow, Joe Louis Jr., with Barbara Munder. *Joe Louis: Fifty Years an American Hero.* McGraw-Hill, 1988.

BoxRec.com: Boxing's Official Record Keeper. Boxing Record for Billy Conn.

———. Boxing Record for Joe Louis.

Cavanaugh, Douglas. Interview with the author, April 2021.

———. *Pittsburgh Boxing: A Pictorial History.* Independently Published, 2020.

Conn, Billy. "How I'll Beat Joe Louis, As Told to Haskell Cohen." *SPOT: The Entertaining Picture Magazine*, June 1941.

Conn, Tim. Interviews with the author, June 2020–June 2021.

Corum, Bill. *Off and Running: The Autobiography of Bill Corum.* Henry Holt and Company, 1959.

Cox, Monte. "Louis Close Call Against Conn." Cox's Boxing Corner, https://coxscorner.tripod.com/louis_conn.html, June 2006.

Daniel, Daniel M. "Louis-Conn Fight Gets Expert Preview: Daniel Gives Conn a Chance." *Ring*, July 1941.

———. "Louis in Army? No, He's in 3A." *Ring*, September 1941.

Dawson, James P. "Louis-Conn Fight Gets Expert Preview: Dawson Doubts Billy's Punch." *Ring*, September 1941.

———. "Louis Stops Conn in the 13th Round." *New York Times*, June 19, 1941.

Deford, Frank. "The Boxer and the Blonde: Billy Conn Won the Girl but Lost the Fight." *Sports Illustrated*, June 17, 1985.

Dempsey, Jack. "How I Size Up the Conn-Louis Fight." *Liberty*, June 14, 1941.

Detloff, William. *Ezzard Charles: A Boxing Life.* McFarland & Company, 2015.

———. Interview with the author, March 2021.

Dunphy, Don. *Don Dunphy at Ringside.* Henry Holt & Company, 1988.

Erenberg, Lewis. *The Greatest Fight of Our Generation: Louis vs. Schmeling.* Oxford University Press, 2007.

Feder, Sid. "Joe Louis Finds Range in 13th for Knockout." Associated Press, June 19, 1941.

———. "Little Things Build Joe Louis Legend." *Ring*, August 1946.

Fleischer, Nat. "Nat Fleischer Says: Readers Disagree with the Judges and Scribes, Say Movies Show Louis Leading Billy Conn." *Ring*, September 1941.

———. Louis-Conn Fight Story. *Ring*, August 1946.

Heller, Peter. *"In This Corner . . . !": 42 World Champions Tell Their Stories.* Da Capo Press, 1973.

Igoe, Hype. "Conn's Big Gamble." *Ring*, September 1941.

International Boxing Hall of Fame. Billy Conn Biography. Joe Louis Biography. IBHOF.com.

Kennedy, Paul. *Billy Conn: The Pittsburgh Kid.* AuthorHouse, 2007.

Liebling, A. J. *The Sweet Science.* North Point Press, 2004.

———. *A Neutral Corner: Boxing Essays.* North Point Press, 2016.

*Life.* "Better Boxer Billy Conn Tilts Joe Louis' Crown." June 30, 1941.

Louis, Joe. *My Life.* Harcourt, 1978.

Louis, Joe, with Edward J. Mallory. *How to Box.* Philadelphia: David McKary, 1948.

Margolick, David. *Beyond Glory: Joe Louis vs. Max Schmeling, and a World on the Brink.* Knopf, 2005.

McHugh, Roy. *When Pittsburgh Was a Fight Town.* Independently Published, 2019.

Mead, Chris. *Joe Louis: Black Champion in White America.* Dover Publications, 2010.

———. *Champion Joe Louis: A Biography.* Robson Books, Ltd., 1986.

Mee, Bob. "On This Day, Joe Louis Met Billy Conn in One of History's Most Dramatic Heavyweight Title Clashes." Boxingnewsonline.net, June 18, 2021.

Miller, Margery. "In This Cor-r-r-ner . . . !" *Liberty*, June 1946.

Monninger, Joseph. *Two Ton: One Fight, One Night—Tony Galento v. Joe Louis.* Steerforth, 2006.

Myler, Patrick. *Fight of the Century: Joe Louis vs. Max Schmeling.* Arcade, 2012.

Oates, Joyce Carol. *On Boxing.* Doubleday, 1987.

Odd, Gilbert. *Boxing: The Great Champions.* Hamlyn, 1974.

O'Toole, Andrew. *Sweet William: The Life of Billy Conn.* University of Illinois Press, 2007.

Perno.com. "The Billy Conn Myth."

Ray, Johnny. "My Boy Billy." *Collier's*, May 24, 1941.

Roberts, Randy. *Joe Louis: Hard Times Man.* Yale University Press, 2010.

Schaefer, Steve. "Boxing Hall of Fame Names First Inductees." United Press International, April 7, 1990.

Silva, Anderson. "Examining Joe Louis: The Blackburn Crouch and Rear Hand Parries." Andersonsilvablog.blogspot.com, July 21, 2012.

Smith, Red. "The Myth of Louis-Conn." *New York Times*, June 22, 1981.

Streetz, Ian. "Alternative Boxing Stances: The Blackburn Crouch." Boxing-Tutorials.com, March 25, 2020.

Sugar, Bert Randolph. *Boxing's Greatest Fighters.* Robert Hale Ltd., 2006.

———. *The Great Fights. A Pictorial History of Boxing's Greatest Bouts.* Gallery Books, 1981.

———. *The 100 Greatest Boxers of All Time.* Bonanza Books, 1984.

Talese, Gay. *The Silent Season of a Hero: The Sports Writing of Gay Talese.* Walker & Company, 2010.

Tickell, George. "Conn Greater in Defeat Than Louis in Victory." *Ring*, September 1941.

*Time.* "Champion Joe Louis: Black Moses." September 29, 1941.

Thornburg, Adam. "The Blackburn Crouch." The Combative Corner, combativecorner. wordpress.com, December 30, 2015.

Tyson, Mike. Interview with the author, November 1996.

Vaccaro, Mike. *1941: The Greatest Year in Sports: Two Baseball Legends, Two Boxing Champs, and the Unstoppable Thoroughbred Who Made History in the Shadow of War.* Doubleday, 2007.

# INDEX